SUICIDE
A Social and Historical Study

DEATH OF LUCRECE: CRANACH

SUICIDE
A Social and Historical Study

By

HENRY ROMILLY FEDDEN

ILLUSTRATED

☆

Man doth not yield himself to the angels, nor unto death utterly, save only through the weakness of his feeble will.　GLANVILL

On ne peut juger de la beauté de la vie que par celle de la mort.　LAUTREAMONT

ARNO PRESS

A New York Times Company
New York • 1980

Reprint Edition 1980 by Arno Press, Inc.
First published London, 1938
Reissued 1972 by Benjamin Blom, Inc.

LC 80-1697
ISBN 0-405-08498-6
Manufactured in the United States of America

TO
JOHN

CONTENTS

ILLUSTRATIONS

CHAPTER I

INTRODUCTION

THE only thing one cannot do about suicide is moralize. The end and intention condition every action and general judgments are here irrelevant. St. Augustine finds the act " utterly damnable "; but Diogenes Laertes counselled it to the wise and the brave. Cato chose this exit. Evidently one must tread warily. It is, however, both possible and important to discover the elusive boundaries of suicide, to detect where it masquerades under strange shapes, and where it appears as martyrdom, or bobs up as self-sacrifice. The universality of the phenomenon is certain, but its categories and types are diverse and hardly classified. The Indian widow officially dying on her husband's pyre is not to be linked with the lonely individual strung up in his garret, nor may Cato fairly be compared with Miss Moyes who first popularized the Monument as a place of suicide and started a London epidemic. What, too, of the poet Young, living as it were within pleasant touch of death, his study darkened, and a skull upon his lamp-lit table? And Donne, who, clothed in a white sheet upon an urn, sat for his own mortuary monument and kept the finished work by his bed until he died? And the leicophiliasts? These do not harmonize with the reluctant magnate whom Wall Street fluctuations push out of the world. Again, soldiers resolutely marching to a certain death are from one aspect suicidal. But the same cannot be said of the lemmings, the Gadarene swine of science, who march in their thousands to drown themselves off the Norwegian coast; since they apparently have no just idea of the outcome of their migration. Zeno, that great Stoic, took his life from sheer ennui at having cut his finger, and St. Jerome and the Venerable Bede reverently place even Christ among the suicides.

It is interesting that until the nineteenth century there should have been no attempt to account for the recurrence of this phenomenon, to study its causes, and to give it laws. Discussion of suicide there was in plenty, but usually of an irrelevant sort. The subject was treated from a religious or moral point of view, and only the highly debatable question of its "rightness" or "wrongness" was taken into consideration. As a result few of the early writers on suicide are now of much interest. Moral judgments, being hopelessly relative to time and place, pass so soon out of date. Among the Massegetae it was customary and decent behaviour to eat one's friends as they grew old; similar action would be impossible in London. From centuries of useless polemic we can to-day gain none of the figures and very little of the data on suicide which we should like. The isolated incidents and stories handed down one must dig out of a mass of prejudice and rusty argument. Here and there an exception stands out, but then it is not so much for the scope of the matter that one will praise it as for the mind of the man who wrote it or for his style. Such exceptions are St. Augustine on one side and Hume on the other; with Donne's *Biathanatos* lying somewhere between the two. All these works, however, concern themselves only with the rightness or wrongness of the act; their problem is to fit it into the particular moral or religious framework which they happen to fancy. They are not interested in getting a close-up of the thing in itself.

At all times and in all places there has been suicide. A certain number of individuals have continuously found this act the most efficient and satisfactory response to circum-

stances which they did not choose to put up with, or to
which, in their poverty, they could find no other reply.
Everywhere there appears not only a diversity of type and
motive, but also of the social interpretation that follows the
act. It is with the latter that this book is chiefly concerned.
It sets out the history of people's attitudes to suicide. In so
doing it throws light on suicide itself and introduces some
sort of order into its curious variety.

One whole province must regretfully be left untouched.
Though wild-fowlers assert that the canvas-backed duck,
that most delectable bird, takes its own life, and though,
in the British Isles, terriers pine away on the deaths of their
masters, the question of animal suicide is doubtful. We
must remember that extinction is a concept which animals
do not have, and that death which is the result of the cessa-
tion of a voluntary action (for instance feeding) is not necessarily volitional. Like the five dogs of Daphnis, the originator
of pastoral poetry, which starved upon his tomb, animal
suicides seem always to occur in a conveniently legendary
past. Among the classic stories, however, even Boswell's
scorpion must give pride of place to Aristotle's horse. The
latter having refused to mount his dam was induced to do so
by the expedient of veiling her. On discovering his mistake
he jumped intentionally from a cliff and was killed by the
fall, thus showing an antique moral discrimination unknown
to his descendants.[1] On the other hand, monkeys, notably

[1] Athenaeus in the *Deipnosophists*, a fascinating collection of
anecdote, scandal, and gastronomic wisdom of the third century
A.D., retails another animal suicide springing from an even nicer and
more easily outraged moral sense. " A bird called the porphyrion
[probably *Fulica porphyrio*, of the same family as the Common
Coot], when it is kept in a house, watches those women who have
husbands very closely; and has such instantaneous perception of anyone who commits adultery, that, when it perceives it, it gives notice
of it to the master of the house, taking its own life by hanging
itself."

devoid of principle, have cut their throats with razors; yet this, due to the imitation of men shaving, seems simply to have been an unfortunate death. The llama's self-destruction, the death of Donne's pelicans, and the conflagrations of the storks, are equally strange stories, but, like the abortive suicide of the Phoenix accomplished every three thousand years, they escape certainty.

In a purely personal way the study of suicide will bring writer and reader a certain reassurance. Sir Thomas Browne says that "The long habit of living indisposeth us for dying." This statement is disproved by figures, and we find self-destruction becomes more tempting with age. This is a legitimate consolation; for one rightly is afraid that as one grows older and passes the 'literary' period of suicide in the early twenties, when to most people it seems possible to detach themselves with grace and even *éclat* from the business of living, one will come to cling more piteously and tenaciously to a life one may either fear or dislike. Facts, if they do nothing else, dispel this apprehension that life will become more and more indispensable. The universality of suicide and its increase with age give one the assurance that the door remains always open; a certain claustrophobia is relieved and one sees gratefully that one may perhaps continue to be able to refuse to 'play', if refusal seems the wisest course. This belief in the possibility of suicide though it may be flattering—since circumstances intervene and theory does not easily become practice—is certainly helpful. It lends a certain dignity, an illusion of free will, to one's progress. It is the life-belt the Stoics clutched. "As I choose the ship in which I will sail, and the house I will inhabit, so I will choose the death by which I will leave life. . . . The lot of man is happy because no one continues wretched but by his own fault." The Roman consolation is available for us.

And yet even as one embarks on a study of social attitudes

towards suicide, a sense of proportion and fairness forces one to bear in mind the relative unimportance of death viewed as a single event in any one life, whether that death is suicide, a scaffold, bed or battlefield. The time occupied by death is usually little, and one must be grateful for this; the last twenty-four hours of a man's life, how he makes his end, are in average circumstances not likely to be much more significant or important than any other similar period of time. The day on which you die is probably less important than that on which you are married, read Plato, climb a mountain, see Florence or Vienna. As schoolboys we pity and regret the character that dies on the scaffold, and our forbears crossed themselves by the grave of a suicide. And yet these facts represent a small fragment in the course of long lives. How these lives were lived over years of time, how fully, and how from moment to moment, is the real question. There is something very niggard, very middle-class, very non-conformist, in judging a life by its exodus. Johnson's reply to Boswell answers perfectly the false accent laid by society on death and the hasty estimation of a man merely by his ending: "No, sir, let it alone! It matters not how a man dies, but how he lives. The act of dying is not of importance; it lasts so short a time." The usual Johnsonian exaggeration overlooks the fact that we are very conscious of death all our lives. But there is an essential grain of truth in his dictum, for it is not our death itself but our previous knowledge of its inevitable arrival that is important.

Whether or not the general importance of suicide has been exaggerated in summarizing the history or value of a life, it is certain that its horror, its macabre and unpleasant side, have been distorted and given unnatural prominence. A popular and primitive taboo revulsion, aided to-day by a popular and sensational press, have helped to bring this about. Suicide has become unsavoury in a way

that would have been incomprehensible to the Romans;
one's sole approach is now via the gas ovens of the Sunday
Press, and it has acquired a flavour of vice and furtiveness
that is unnatural. Its better elements have been obscured. A
certain humanism and dignity in the step as practised by
the ancients, and by no means absent to-day, is lost to view:
often suicide is not the unwilling act of a harassed sufferer
but an individual's voluntary and precise assertion of his
own freedom. Even in romantic suicide these positive
features are not absent. The suicide pact, and the death of
the man for whom the world is inadequate, can both be
praised in their own way. Lessing longed that one spring
nature might be red and not an everlasting green: the feeling
of the frightful repetitiveness of experience and the conviction that natural and scientific laws present no adequate possibilities for the particular life a man happens to want, are
not unworthy reasons for suicide.

Villiers de l'Isle Adam's *Axel* epitomizes in an extreme
nineteenth-century form, the type of aspiration and idealism
which can make even romantic suicide a dignified and positive action. Axel, after a varied odyssey, finds the woman
for whom he has been long searching. Suddenly he has
everything and the world is at his feet. He is alone with a
love which he has not yet possessed, and dawn approaches.
Together they envisage the life that lies before them; there
is nothing they cannot see, nothing they cannot obtain.
Their life and love stretch out in an infinite perspective; in
imagination they visit all the countries, and enjoy all the
beauty, of the world.

" Come, let's leave at once," she cries; " throw on your coat.
Outside, the carriage horses are already pawing the morning dew.
They'll take us past scented orange groves, and out on the roads
people will soon be about. We shall pass villages and towns. . . .
Beyond, there will be more towns waking in the sunlight, the

whole world will be waking. We can at last give reality to all our dreams."

As she speaks dawn breaks. She lifts the curtain at the window.

"Leave it alone," Axel says. "What do you want with the sun? Our dreams are too rare to be realized in the daylight."

At first she does not understand him.

"But look," she cries, "there is the world! Let's live!"

"No," Axel answers. "Our existence is complete; our cup is now full. We've already exhausted the future. No clock can count the hours of this night—and what will the realities of to-morrow be worth compared to these visions that we've seen? Why try to turn into current coin—as all the rest do—our drachma of gold, stamped with the authority of dreams? At this moment we hold the obol of the Styx in our triumphant hands!"

"Do you think such desires as ours will put up with the earth from day to day? Don't you see that the earth, this drop of congealed filth, has become the illusion? Don't you see that in our hearts we've done away with the love of life? It's in *reality* that we've exchanged our souls. We owe it to ourselves not to accept this substitute—life. . . . Let's leave the banquet, forever satisfied with this our moment. The poor fools, who can only measure reality by sensation, can have the pleasure of picking up the crumbs."

So the woman is at last persuaded and takes the cup of poison: "Since only the infinite tells the truth, we will go, forgetful of human speech, into our own infinity." They have both turned away from life, which they know is unequal to their demands. As they lie dead, the sun breaks in upon them; from outside the rustle of a country wind, the murmur of a waking plain, and the long buzz of life, hum and play across their bodies, and are unable to disturb their silence.

CHAPTER II

SERVANT AND WIDOW

BAYET, in his admirable book *Le Suicide et la Morale*, produced a formula which goes far to explain why, at certain times, suicide has been bitterly attacked and at others as firmly defended. He exposes the hand of both those who absolutely defend, or condemn, suicide on moral grounds. Give me, he says, the type of judgment prevailing among people at any given time and place, and I will tell you whether they consider suicide criminal or not. Since it is with just this question of the attitude to suicide that the present book occupies itself, it will be wise to give a short account of Bayer's theory. It appears to fit in with the facts and we shall use it frequently for reference and illustration.

There are, and have been since the intellectual type was first differentiated, two sorts of morality. The first and primitive sort (*morale simple*, Bayet calls it) is the morality of the mass of the common people; it is founded on religion and superstition and has a definite link with taboos and tribal custom. The second sort (*morale nuancée*) is the moral of aristocracies and of the educated and intellectual minority; it has its roots in reason and does not judge an act in itself but on its results and social repercussions. The *morale simple*, if it condemns an act, does so out and out; certain things are in its eyes intrinsically wrong, tainted, immoral (primitive ideas of magic of course come in here). The *morale nuancée*, ideally speaking, considers each case on its own merits and after deliberation passes judgment. Each of these moral forces has been uppermost at different periods; and each, when victorious, tries to dictate the general tone and attitude of society. Naturally, the moral " in opposition " is never altogether destroyed, and even if temporarily silenced merely awaits its opportunity to bob up again.

Applying this idea of twin-morality to history, we find that it explains very adequately the fluctuations in the status of suicide. As rationalism and education decline so the penalties against suicide increase; and vice versa. Thus the Classical and Renaissance tolerance of suicide follows the defeat of the *morale simple* of early times and of the Dark Ages. Within any given period, and on a more delicate scale, the theory also works out nicely. For instance, the temporary revival of learning and civilization under Charlemagne resulted directly in a certain modification and lenience in the Church's anti-suicide legislation. Thus Bayet shows that the contemporary type of moral everywhere dictates the attitude towards personal suicide.

Before embarking on the general history of personal suicide it is, however, necessary to isolate an altogether different type of self-destruction to which we may give the name of sacrificial or institutional suicide. Unlike personal suicide which has always been frowned on by the community, except in certain exceptional societies, institutional suicide is in itself the creation of the community and meets with recognition and approval. The crux of the opposition between these two modes of suicide lies in this, that whereas the personal suicide is a rebel, the institutional suicide dies, not as an individual at all, but in some social capacity (the classical example of institutional suicide being the self-destruction of the widow involved in *suttee*). Such suicides have also been called *altruistic* since they can only be common in groups where the sense of self and personal individuality is poorly developed. Thus, as personal suicide may be said

B

to result from hyperindividuation, so institutional suicide
results from a lack of consciousness of individuality.

Institutional suicide, then, is the self-destruction which
society may demand of an individual in his social capacity.
Such a demand usually arises in societies where the life of
the individual is valued not for itself, but as a function of
the community, where in fact his individuality is subordinated to a collective good. It is a type of suicide, therefore,
which we shall expect to find most prevalent in the highly
developed social organization of primitive communities. As
the fully grown man detaches himself from his parents, so
the fuller consciousness of individuality results in an ever
greater detachment of the individual from the community
Thus forms of institutional suicide tend to decrease with the
progress of decentralization in society.

From Western Europe most set forms of institutional
suicide have long since disappeared. In one case after
another it was discovered that the sacrifice demanded of the
individual served no good purpose and had been originally
instituted through superstition or a misinterpretation of
facts. Our general attitude towards sacrificial suicide to-day
is, however, still one of approval where the act can be shown
to have a practical basis and a reasonable necessity. Thus
the convention that a captain must not desert his ship is a
set form of institutional suicide and represents the type of
this suicide which may be expected to persist indefinitely.
In the same way the action of anyone who deliberately
sacrifices his life for another, even though the action has a
purely personal character, meets with approval. Such a
suicide can be classed as institutional since it conforms so
exactly to the ideal values and the ideal outlook of society.

The line of demarcation between institutional and personal suicide is not always easy to draw, particularly as
recognized forms of institutional suicide are always being
modified to suit changing ideas. To-day the duty of the

civilian to take up arms for his country, and the utility of
the institutional suicide demanded from the conscript, begin
to be questioned. A series of wars to end war makes certain
people suspect that this form of institutional suicide may be
no more reasonable than that involved in the Indian *suttee*.
It may equally well derive authority from a false chain of
argument.

In primitive societies where institutional suicides usually
adopt set ritualistic forms, such doubts must be rare. The
question is more cut and dried. A survey of the subject
shows that institutional and ritualistic suicides have existed
from the earliest times and have been practised in nearly
every part of the world. They divide fairly easily into
certain types or categories. Commonest among these is the
custom which compels a widow to take her life on the death
of her husband, if he is a person of rank. This type of
institutional suicide appears in varying forms in many
countries. Among certain Central Africans and Melanesians
the wife was customarily buried alive with her husband;
among the Natchez of North America and the Maoris she
met death by strangulation. Elsewhere she was burnt
on her husband's pyre, and it is with this custom, as it
appears in the *suttee* of the Hindoos, that we are most
familiar. For centuries the Hindoo widow immolated herself with her husband, and as late as 1803 two hundred
and seventy wives willingly met death in this way within
thirty miles of Calcutta. In 1821 there were still over two
thousand deaths of this sort in all India. The voluntary
nature of these suicides is attested by the difficulty which
the British have found in putting a stop to the custom since
it was declared illegal in 1829.[1]

[1] The following appeared in the *Daily Telegraph* for August
31st, 1937:
" Three men are on trial at Gwalior for aiding and abetting
the practice of suttee. A widow of fifty announced her intention

Herodotus, speaking of the Crestonaeans of Thrace, says that no sooner does a man die than "a sharp contest" follows among his wives as to which has the best right to share her husband's grave. Prescott, in his *History of the Conquest of Peru*, writing of events two thousand years later, goes out of his way to emphasize a similar eagerness among the Incas. When a great man died a number of his attendants and favourite concubines were immolated with him, and, says Prescott, " the women have been known, in more than one instance, to lay violent hands on themselves when restrained from testifying their fidelity by this act of conjugal martyrdom."

Similar to the suicide of the widow was the sacrifice of the servants and followers of a great lord or king, who were often compelled by custom (and urged by their feelings) to share their master's death. Caesar, when he tells how certain picked warriors, or soldurii, were unwilling to survive their chieftain, is merely instancing a form of institutional suicide found in the most divers countries. A traveller reaching Pekin as late as the fourteenth century saw four female slaves and six guards buried at the funeral of the Chinese Emperor. Herodotus tells how, in Scythia, a dead king

---

of immolating herself on her dead husband's pyre. The result was that a crowd of 15,000 gathered to follow the bier.

" The police made efforts to persuade the woman from her intention, but without success. The crowd also refused to help the police, who were unable to reach the pyre.

" Brandishing a sword, the woman jumped into the flames and was burnt to death while the crowd delivered incantations."

Such obstinate survivals of *suttee* are peculiarly odd, since it appears that the practice once died out spontaneously, and for a long time persisted in a purely symbolical form. The wife simply lay down on her husband's pyre, preparatory to rising again for a second marriage. Only after the sixth century did the increased power of the Brahmins, who hoped to get the dead wife's property, reintroduce *suttee* and spread the custom again throughout India.

was buried with his cupbearer, cook, groom, lacquey and messenger. A year after his death fifty of his servants and fifty of his horses were strangled, stuffed, and set upon scaffolds round his tomb, every dead man riding a dead horse and ready still to serve and fight for his dead master. Officially, at any rate, the death of these servants and warriors who followed their lord into the next world was voluntary. For instance, the king of the Sotiani among the Celts had six hundred picked companions who vowed to live and die with him. "In return for which," the historian says,

> they also share his power, and wear the same dress, and eat the same food; and they die when he dies as a matter of absolute necessity, if the king dies of any disease, or if he dies in war, or in any other manner. And no one can ever say that any of them has shown any fear of death, *or has in the least sought to evade it when the king is dead.*[1]

In Africa the burial of the King of Benin was habitually the occasion for a strange scene, whose voluntary character is attested. The King's favourite lords and servants leaping into the tomb, used actually to vie with each other for the honour of being buried alive with his body. The sequel to their enthusiasm shows the ritualistic and social nature of these suicides.

> After the dispute was settled and the tomb had closed over the dead and the living, sentinels were set to watch it day and night. Next day the sepulchre would be opened and someone would call down to the entombed men to know what they were doing and whether any of them had gone to serve the king. The answer was commonly, " No, not yet." The third day the same question would be put, and a voice would reply that so and so had gone to join his majesty. The first to die was deemed the happiest. In four or five days, when no answer came up to the question and all were silent in the grave, the heir to the throne was informed, and he signalized his accession by kindling a fire on the tomb, roasting flesh at it, and distributing the meat to the people.[2]

[1] Athenaeus, quoting Nicolaus of Damascus.
[2] Frazer, *The Dying God.*

In Japan such devotional suicides of a semi-ritualistic and institutional nature have always been common. As late as 1912 the suicide of the Count and Countess Nogi astounded Western Europe, but assured them a household immortality in Japan. As the Emperor Meiji's funeral *cortège* left the palace, the Count, who had been the hero of the Russo-Japanese war, and his wife committed " junshi ", or devotional suicide. They hoped by their death to accompany the divine Emperor heavenward.

The origin of both these institutionalized types of suicide —widows and followers—is probably to be found not only in the idea that they were expected to provide in their several ways for the wants of their master in the next world, but that, like the weapons and utensils buried with them, their presence would make unnecessary the return of an unsatisfied ghost to fetch them. The burial-places of the Pharaohs show this idea in its most complete development. Although the progress of Egyptian civilization replaced the body of wife or servant by image and representation (and there was thus no actual suicide involved), the tombs reveal that each great man was buried with a complete outfit calculated to set him up comfortably wherever he might be. Not only were the obvious necessities included, such as weapons, wife, and the means of grinding corn, but the man was supplied with scents, combs, luxuries, and now and then a suite of furniture.

Another class of institutional suicide involved the death of an individual either sacrificed to, or representative of, a god. The perfect example of such an individual is provided by the young man who, among the Aztecs, impersonated the god Tezcatlipoca, and for a year received the homage and reverence of the people. At the end of this term, but choosing his own moment, the man-god delivered himself up proudly and voluntarily to his stipulated death.[1] To

[1] Cavan, *Suicide*.

this category also belong Frazer's priest, slain on the wooded shore of Lake Nemi; and types such as the representatives of Attis, who, in primitive times, died yearly in imitation of the god and by their deaths hoped to effect his resurrection and with it the return of spring. Such institutional suicides—to honour the gods or promote the yearly cycle of crops—have occurred in places as far removed as Scandinavia and the Philippines, nearly always with the underlying idea that the death of the victim was a voluntary one. In India similarly destined victims, rescued by the military, escaped whenever possible and gladly returned to a lingering death; in Uganda eye-witnesses of institutional sacrifices have related that the victims rarely complained and submitted to their fate under the impression that they were doing a great service to their tribe and laying down their lives for an ideal. The idea of a *voluntary* sacrifice seems indeed to have been so essential that when animals came to replace human victims, flatteries and tendernesses were sometimes whispered in their ears as they were led to the altars so that they might be supposed to be willing participants in their own death. Closely connected with these institutional sacrifices were the compulsory, yet voluntary, deaths of primitive tribal kings whose tenure of office for a certain number of years was ritualistically terminated by their deaths. Among the countless examples of such suicides we need only mention one. The King of Calicut on the Malibar coast, known by the highly sacred title of *Samorin*, reigned only twelve years. At the expiration of this period, as an eighteenth-century traveller relates, he was accustomed to give a vast feast to his numerous nobility and gentry. After the feast he saluted his guests and went up on to a scaffold prepared specially for the occasion, and there, in view of the whole assembly, very decently cut his own throat.[1]

[1] Alexander Hamilton, *A New Account of the East Indies*, quoted in Frazer, *The Dying God*.

Somewhere into this sacrificial category must also be fitted the Jaïna sect of Southern India, who threw themselves under the wheels of the Juggernaut, and the devotees of the Japanese divinity Amida, who, amidst applause, made hecatombs for their divinity, throwing themselves into the sea or burying themselves alive. Similarly, to this type of institutional suicide must belong those *anciens habitans des Isles Canaries*, of whom Jean Dumas speaks. At certain festivals, having celebrated the rites of the god in their temple on the summit of a mountain, many of them tripped down the verdurous slopes with song and dance, and so, without hesitation, over the precipice edge which was to lead them to eternal happiness. Among the Northern peoples the fabled death of Odin resulted in approved and almost institutional suicides. The God-hero, on the approach of death, had assembled his warriors and, taking a spear, had wounded himself in nine symbolic places, saying that he thus went to join the Gods at their immortal feasting, where he would receive with honour all those who similarly died with their weapons in their hands.[1] As a result many of the hyperborean peoples, when faced with sickness, age, or the possibility of captivity, were accustomed to take their own lives, hoping in this way to ensure themselves a place in Valhalla. At the same time they were probably influenced by the primitive idea that the body will appear in the next world in the same state as it leaves this, and they preferred to make their entry into heaven with honourable wounds rather than decrepit and diseased.[2]

[1] A second tradition supposes Odin to have ended his earthly existence by hanging.

[2] There is a type of religious and institutional suicide distantly allied to some of the above examples, which exhibits a charming illogicality. It used to be the custom in Malabar for those taken ill to pray for recovery, vowing themselves to their idol in return for the grace that should cure them. Once hale and whole, the grateful

More philosophic and reflective is the type of institutional suicide connected with Brahmin asceticism. Broadly speaking, suicide among them seems always to have been praiseworthy when it was brought about, not by dislike of this world, but by a desire for the next. It was essential that it should involve no perturbation of spirit, and that it should be merely the ultimate application of those self-negatory principles which lead to Nirvana. The Institutes of Menu say: "As a tree is loosened from the river bank when the current carries it off, as a bird leaves the branches of a tree, so he who leaves his body . . . by his own volition, is delivered from a monster." And again: "The Brahmin who leaves his body by one of the devices [holding the breath, starvation, etc.] which the saints and great ones have practised, is admitted with honour into the realm of Brahma." Strabo says that at one time many of the Brahmins believed that sickness and disease were shameful and that the only honourable way to die was by fire. Thus, at the approach of disease or old age a Brahmin would erect a funeral pyre, preparatory to suicide. Then, says Strabo, " he anoints himself, sits down on the pyre, orders it to be lighted, and burns without a motion."

Buddhists in China used to show the same preference for fire in the institutional suicides which were performed in the mountains of Tien-tai, where three or four monks every year used to sacrifice their lives. They hoped to attain for themselves Nirvana, and for their community protection from evil influences, blessings, and a reputation for sanctity. Wide publicity was given to the suicidal solemnity, and on a fixed day the institutional suicide, in view of a large concourse of people, entered a furnace. There he

patients fattened themselves for a year or two and then, upon one of their recurrent festivals, committed suicide by cutting off their own heads before the idol which had saved their lives. (Frazer, *The Dying God*.)

took his place on a wooden seat and the door was slammed to. The furnace was lighted, and after the ceremony the ashes of the suicide were collected, preserved, and washed with the reverence accorded to the relics of a saint.

Institutional suicides of a more practical flavour, whether with reference to the next world or to this, have always existed coincidently with such religious practices. Dumas says that the Gauls, before throwing themselves on the pyres of their chiefs or relatives, would make away all their goods and property, with the stipulation that these should be returned at a proper rate of interest when the recipients themselves should at last reach heaven. In Sparta the demands of a military state created what was practically another form of institutional suicide in the unwritten law that no Spartan might turn his back on an enemy. So strong was the feeling in favour of this law that the sole survivor of Thermopylae, having escaped an institutional suicide, was driven to a purely personal one. Another form of institutional suicide with a practical basis arose in countries where there was a danger of food shortage, such as Siberia and Greenland. In such places the suicide of the old and the sick, whether voluntary or forcibly imposed by the community, was closely connected with euthanasia. On the coral atolls of the South Seas, where the food problem was particularly acute, the necessity for such measures was got over by abortion and infanticide.[1]

[1] Stevenson tells us that in his time in certain of the Ellice Islands only two, and sometimes only one, child was allowed to each couple.

CHAPTER III

THE SUICIDE HORROR AND THE SAVAGE

I

PERSONAL suicide, whether in the classical or modern world, bears no relationship whatsoever to institutional suicide. Personal suicide is a conscious revolt, a protest against either life or society; it is the most extreme act of individualism of which a man is capable. Unlike the institutional, the personal suicide is usually persecuted by society, or only grudgingly recognized even in times of tolerance. His history is not an account of attitudes and customs, but of individual actions and unique situations; often complex; not to be untangled; and lost to memory when the life itself is taken. General laws here are useless, and statistics are no more than numbers. The only true history is a tale carried on from day to day of lives that end in this way. Life itself is the only true log of such death. The bullet strikes down, the parasite gnaws home; there one can collect facts and make statements. But who will detect where and when, over how many years and through what woman, belief, or trick of the fancy, a man nurses his own ending?

Neither is it the obvious factors, the surface changes that new civilization brings, which alter the sum of these individual suicides. Though you may argue that Cato to-day can carry his integrity to the new world, or Romeo and Juliet remove from Mantua, Cato and such lovers will still die, unless they think in a different mould. Growing as each civilization flowers and then fading with the return to

27

barbarity, suicide is unaltered by the superficial. Simple hardships do not cause these deaths. The struggling tiller of the constricted spade-work centuries, with nothing to lose, never turns against himself. Only when he has stopped frantically scratching the soil and can take a moment's breath, only when he looks at his curious hands and listens to the monotonous tapping of his heart, does something break through into his consciousness. He takes gun, poison, water, fire; and so goes on his way.

Though statistics in their proper place must come in for what they are worth, the most effective way one can visualize and consider this turning back to death is, as it were, in a mirror. The one thing which we can follow, the one thing which is not altogether bound up in the particular, is the general attitude of society towards the individual suicide. By tracing this from the vaguest times until the present day, we shall watch the ebb and flow of opinion which, in its movement over this subject, will throw into the light innumerable single cases far removed in time and type, giving them a reality of background. By turning on these dead men the praise or blame to which they were once subjected —a social measure which we can gauge fairly exactly—we may reanimate the time and circumstances, pick out here and there from oblivion just the valuable and authentic fragment.

Personal suicide is in its broadest definition any action or abstention from action which causes death and which was undertaken with the knowledge that death would *probably* ensue. The degree of probability is of course most important, and different people will consider that quite different degrees are high enough to make an action suicidal. Usually the greater the critic's own intrepidity the higher will be the rate of probability necessary to make an action appear suicidal. In this definition the adjective *personal* automatically eliminates the man who gives his life for another, or the soldier who faces death on the battlefield. Fundamentally, these are not personal suicides; and men in such cases act as social units. Their death is a sacrifice for the general good. If one wished, though the scope of this book is not large enough, one could extend our definition to take in self-mutilation, castration, and all sorts of metaphorical suicide, such as renunciation of ambition; also it would take in the things to which people refer in phrases like " social suicide " and " political suicide ", when these are consciously undertaken. One knows of people who continually do the wrong thing, as if with intention, and continue to live as though dead.

The word *suicide* is itself of fairly recent origin. Though obviously derived from Latin, it corresponds to no single Latin word, for the Romans themselves always used periphrases to express the thought. Phrases such as *sibi mortem consciscere*—to procure his own death; *vim sibi inferre*—to cause violence to himself; or *sua manu cadere*—to fall by his own hand, are the commonest expressions. In England the early name for suicide seems to have been *self-homicide*, which brought the action into line with the current legal attitude. The word *suicide* first appears about the middle of the seventeenth century. In Edward Philipps's *New World of Words*, published in 1662, we find the following :

> One barbarous word I shall produce, which is *suicide*, a word which I had rather should be derived from *sus*, a sow, than from the pronoun *sui*, unless there be some mystery in it; as if it were a swinish part for a man to kill himself.

In France the word probably came into use rather later. Richelet's dictionary of 1680 does not mention the word (though it gives *parricide*), and the general idea seems to be that its first appearance is in the *Dictionnaire de Trevoux* in 1752.[1]

[1] Horace Walpole in 1763 has not adopted the new word; possibly it was not fashionable. He writes to the Earl of Hertford : " November passes with two or three self-murders and a new play."

We see that the English seventeenth-century writer has violent ideas about self-destruction. Before beginning to follow the fluctuations of public opinion, its incidental changes, and the long history of suicide, we must peg down at its origin this writer's violent prejudice. We must trace back to its first sources the suicide-antagonism, which different men and differing societies intensify or relax. This antagonism appears everywhere as an essential background, that civilization and ideas must modify before a reasoned attitude to suicide can be established.

The more obvious causes for such a suicide-antagonism, the directions in which one immediately turns for an explanation of the prejudice, are invariably only of secondary and contributory importance. They never themselves account for the basic horror. Let us first go back to the Jews. Suicide among these people prior to their final dispersion is extremely rare. The Old Testament presents, in all, nine cases spread over a period of some thousands of years, and for this reason one might be tempted to think that we had inherited an enduring prejudice from a Hebraistic attitude and teaching. Such, however, is not the case. There is no specific anti-suicide teaching in the Old Testament, and, what is more positive evidence, Saul's suicide is recorded without a hint of criticism. Later, Josephus says that " the bodies of those who commit suicide remain unburied until after sunset, although soldiers killed in battle may be buried before ". This mild usage seems hardly serious enough to be a punishment. Josephus himself proves that among the common soldiery suicide was regarded as an appropriate sort of behaviour on certain occasions. After the defeat of his army by the Romans in Judea, Josephus wished to surrender to Vespasian; his troops, however, would not hear of it and flocked round him, urging him to kill himself and allow them to follow his example in a mass suicide. Josephus himself seems to have had a technical dislike of self-destruction, as he insisted on their substituting for simple suicide a drawing of lots by which each man was to kill his opposite. In this way a large number of his troops died. Luckily the historian himself was able to arrive at some sort of *modus vivendi* with his partner and thus both were spared.

Neither, as we shall see later in a detailed examination of the classical period, do we find the origins of the suicide-horror among the educated Greeks and Romans. Such an irrational attitude would run directly contrary to the usual conception of the classic spirit; traces of it certainly do appear in this period, but they are to be found in a sort of popular morality, subterranean, hardly expressed in literature or society, and dating back to something Dionysiac, primitive, and of an earlier date.

Similarly, and in spite of the ideas generally held, it is useless to look to Christianity for the origin of the suicide-antagonism and horror. The New Testament nowhere condemns suicide; and, as is shown elsewhere in the suicide history of the Christian and medieval periods, the Church offers no opposition to suicide before the third century. It is only after that date, when the Church has to shoulder the old popular moralities which come to the fore on the disintegration of civilized standards, and the break-up of the Roman Empire, that its attitude to suicide undergoes a gradual change.

No, it is in something far more primitive than classical Rome or the Christian Church that one must look to find the basis of the horror of suicide. Literature will not help us very much, for literary productions being always more or less the outcome of a certain degree of civilization will usually not be in touch with the primitive and irrational section of society which fosters the suicide horror, nor will literature exist at all in the early stages of social development when the suicide horror is born. It is rather to works on magic

and primitive religion, to the accounts of African tribes and
Australian aborigines that one must look. There, in the
rudimentary era of magic and superstition, the horror of
suicide is formed, and it is through our inherited unconscious
that it is handed on to us with other strange ideas whose
original meaning has been equally obscured by time and
transformation.

In the primitive taboo lies the origin of the suicide horror.
Now the taboo itself originated in the belief generally held
among primitive peoples in a " power " (mana, etc.) which
permeates everything.

> Among primitive peoples "power" is its own cause it exists
> before and independently of gods and spirits. It is merely "power",
> and whether it is good or evil depends upon how it comes into
> contact with man. Man must beware of it and act cautiously in
> regard to it, for if it can help, it can also harm. Anything which
> is filled with power must therefore be treated with certain meas-
> ures of precaution; only certain specially qualified persons can
> come near it, others must avoid it.[1]

It is in fact taboo, and taboo represents the negative side
of magic; it is magic that is not directed to obtaining specific
ends but rather to warding off possible evil.

Now this " power " was quite naturally believed to be
particularly inherent in certain acts and situations, such as
birth, marriage, and death, and it was about these points that
taboos accumulated. They involved almost always a ritualistic system of lustration—which, though varied in form,
had always the same end, the magic purification of those who
had come into contact with the " power ". Their unclean-
ness was viewed as a sort of infection that could be got rid
of by washing, sacrifices, or some more complicated ritual.
Until this infection was at an end the taboo effectually
isolated the tainted individual from general society. The

[1] Nilsson, *A History of Greek Religion.*

dead were always unclean or taboo, and in Greece a bowl of water was placed outside a dead man's house so that the mourners might purify themselves before departure. Even more dangerous and unclean, however, were homicides and their victims; in fact, all those who had undergone a dangerous and sudden death. Both warriors and the slain were included in this taboo. Innumerable examples from all parts of the world testify that these feelings were widely and generally held.

One can distinguish two separate features in the fear of the unnaturally dead, and the murderer. First is the primitive and fundamental fear of the ghost which seems to be at the bottom of the whole thing. Not only will the man who has been snatched from life bear rancour and a desire for revenge, but the very fact that his soul has been taken by force and hurried away will mean that it retains a portion of matter; it is soiled and unclean, and will come back to haunt the earth. Lack of a proper burial was often considered to have the same effect, and it will be remembered how Odysseus punctiliously returned to Circe's Island to make a pyre for the dead Elpenor, even though the latter was " no great fighter, and loose minded ". Secondly, there is the element of blood-guilt; though perhaps primarily connected with the ghost fear, this idea obviously acquired other social and almost moral significances. The idea of the " rightness " or " wrongness " of shedding certain blood (the tribe's or the family's) comes into play.

Three or four examples from the Indies and Europe will serve to illustrate the taboos which surrounded unnatural death. In the island of Timor in the East Indies the blood-stained chief, returning after battle, had to undergo a most exacting purification. "A special hut is prepared for him, in which he has to reside for two months, undergoing bodily and spiritual purification. During this time he may not go to his wife or feed himself; the food must

c

be put into his mouth by another person."[1] Such precautions are dictated by the tribe's simple fear of the ghosts of the slain to whom sacrifices are meanwhile offered in appeasement. Among the Puna Indians the purification was even more complex.

> Attended by an old man, the warrior who had to expiate the crime of blood-guilt retired to the groves along the river bottom at some distance from the villages or wandered about the adjoining hills. During the period of sixteen days he was not allowed to touch his head with his fingers or his hair would turn white. If he touched his face it would become wrinkled. He kept a stick to scratch his head with, and at the end of every four days this stick was buried at the root and on the west side of a cat's claw tree and a new stick was made of greasewood, arrow bush, or any other convenient shrub. He then bathed in the river, no matter how cold the temperature. The feast of victory which his friends were observing in the meantime at the village lasted eight days. At the end of that time, or when his period of retirement was half completed, the warrior might go to his home to get a fetish made from the hair of the Apache whom he had killed. The hair was wrapped in eagle down and tied with a cotton string and kept in a long medicine basket. He drank no water for the first two days, and fasted for the first four.[2]

The essentially superstitious nature of such purifications and their direction against the ghosts of the dead is proved elsewhere by certain tribal usages, in which the element of purification is subordinated to positive measures taken to frighten off the ghosts themselves. Such is the case in New Guinea, where a whole village will turn out to try and terrify the ghost of a murdered man with shouts, threats, and the beating of drums. The Greeks also believed that the newly dead haunted their murderers, who, for this reason, became taboo. In Greece a murderer was not allowed to return to the district where his victim had been slain without a ritual-

---

[1] Frazer, *Taboo or the Perils of the Soul.*
[2] F. Russell, *The Puna Indians.* Bureau of American Ethnology.

istic purification. Only the sacrifice of a pig could lift the taboo and re-admit him to community life and the temple.

Plato, in his Laws, speaking of the involuntary killing of a free man, shows how, in his time, the close connection of penalties and punishments with superstition and taboo had not been lost sight of. " There is," he says,

> an ancient tale, told of old, to which we must not fail to pay regards. The tale is this—" that the man slain by violence, who has lived a free and proud spirit, is wroth with his slayer when newly slain, and being filled also with dread and horror on account of his own violent end, when he sees his murderer going about in the very haunts which he himself had frequented, he is horror-stricken; and being disquieted himself, he takes conscience as his ally, and with all his might disquiets his slayer—both the man himself and his doings. Wherefore it is right for the slayer to retire before his victim for a full year, in all its seasons, and to vacate all the spots he owned in all parts of his native land " . . .

If such precautions were taken to calm the ghosts of the murdered and to counteract the uncleanliness of the murderer, how disturbing to primitive minds must the suicide ghost have been. Not only had blood been spilt, but the blood of the family; for suicide is family blood-guilt *par excellence*.[1] Whereas, the ghost of a murdered man bore malice only against his executioner, the ghost of the suicide was believed to harm society in general, and the latter was held to be indiscriminately and collectively responsible for his death.

The suicide, it was thought, must have been grievously wronged or troubled; thus his spirit would be particularly revengeful. Among the savages suicide is indeed often committed as an act of direct vengeance; the suicide trusts that in a disembodied state he can more successfully work

[1] The Goajuro Indians of Columbia carry this idea yet further. If a man even accidentally cuts or wounds himself he is considered to have spilt family blood, and his maternal relations are entitled to demand blood-money as compensation.

evil on those who have harmed him. In Homeric times suicide came to be considered an effective act of vengeance for a double reason. Not only would the ghost haunt, but the act was in itself a supreme sacrifice, in return for which the gods would be almost bound to take such steps as the dead man had desired. Ajax, before falling on his sword, called to the furies to avenge his death upon the Greeks; later the defeat of the Spartans at Leuctra was attributed to the suicide of Skedasos, who long before had taken his life in vengeance for the violation of his daughters by Spartan soldiery.

The primary preoccupation of early society with the ghosts of suicides and of the violently dead is still reflected in popular superstition all over Europe. The ghost story, the appearance of the murdered man, the house of the suicide, prove that the unfortunate spirit does, in the belief of the people, even to-day, take vengeance on society. At Beaumont in Picardy, legend has it that the ghosts of certain *jeunes filles* who drowned themselves to escape the violence of the Knights Templars, still take appropriate vengeance. The long dead chevaliers are to be seen flying across the countryside pursued by the spectres of the infuriated girls. Even the dead, it seems, are not immune from molestation by the spirits of suicides. (It is worth while noticing that those " honourably " dead, that is, those whose suicide or violent end occurred in the service of the state or the state's ideals— those in fact whose death was sacrificial—do not usually haunt. Heroes and soldiers have no ghosts.)

Though we now tolerate our spectres, in early times strict measures were taken against those who thus " walked ". The only way that society could protect itself was to destroy or annihilate the corpse, so that the risen ghost would be incapable of harm. Thus, at Porto Nuovo in New Guinea the public executioner was allowed to keep the jawbones of those he had killed and hang them on the walls of his hut.

This rudimentary precaution made it impossible for the ghosts of his victims to come and disturb him by their cries, groans, and imprecations. Similarly the aborigines of Australia used to cut off the thumbs of the enemies whom they murdered in order that their ghosts might be unable to fling a spear at them. The gunman without his trigger-finger would presumably be equally ineffective.

Such precautions taken against violent deaths, were doubly necessary against suicides whose rancour had a wider scope and did not confine itself to a single murderer. Thus in Athens at one time it was customary to lop off the hand of a suicide; if possible that with which he had taken his own life. A one-handed ghost was hardly formidable. In the island of Cos, if a man hung himself, not only was his body sent safely beyond the borders of the country, but with it went both the tree and the rope with which he had accomplished his purpose. All connection with the man's death was thus carefully severed. This may be well compared with the medieval custom observed at Metz, where suicides were put in a barrel and floated down the Moselle and so out of the territory which they would naturally wish to haunt, and away from those on whom they would want to be revenged. Another common expedient for getting rid of the ghost of a suicide was to burn the body, so that his spirit should find it impossible to " walk ". Among the Wajagga of East Africa the fear of the suicide's ghost finds expression not in mutilation or banishment, but in an attempt at mollification. When a man has taken his own life by hanging, a goat is substituted for his body and hung from the same noose. It is subsequently cut down and killed as a sort of placatory sacrifice to the ghost of the dead man, which it is hoped will thus be restrained from haunting the community.

It is among the Baganda, however, that the procedure with regard to suicides gives us the most direct clues as to the origin of later practice in medieval Europe. The

Baganda women, having no knowledge of the real cause of pregnancy, believed that they could be impregnated by the particularly active and frustrated ghosts of suicides who wished to return to life. For this reason, whenever they passed the spot where a suicide had been burned, they threw a little grass or a few sticks on the place, thinking in this way to circumvent the ghost. Exactly similar precautions were used, and for similar reasons, when passing the grave of a child who had been born feet first. The ghosts of suicides and children were thus both considered to be specially active. Now, what is of particular interest, as showing the reasons for later European procedure, is the treatment of these unfortunate children. Every child born feet first was considered unclean, and strangled. Then, in order to confine its restive spirit, it was securely *buried at a cross-roads*. Here is the link that directly explains our later English custom of burial at a cross-roads.[1] Even our habit of transfixing the suicide's heart with a stake, can be traced back to a simple anti-ghost measure. In order to restrain the vampire from "walking" and doing its harm, a stake had to be driven through its heart, thus pinning within the body the evil and errant spirit; the transfixing of the suicide is analogous.

Thus the whole basis of the historical suicide-horror can be traced back to a primitive taboo and the fear of the ghost. The prejudices of Saint Louis, of Hamlet's grave-diggers, and of Victorian society, fall into line with the best aboriginal ideas, and are not out of place to-day in mud-huts, kraals, and jungles.

It remains, however, to trace the transference of these simple ghost fears and taboo horrors into the realm of ethics and religion. How and when did these fears and horrors put on respectability? It will be remembered that tabooed

---

[1] Such a spot may have been chosen so that the suicide's ghost should not be able to find its way home.

persons were thought to be in some way ",unclean ". Now this notion referred to something purely physical. No idea of moral uncleanliness was involved, for even the successful warrior whose victims were a source of honour to himself and the community, came under the ban of the " unclean ".

To get rid of this physical uncleanliness and to come out of taboo, a certain magic had to be observed and certain altogether practical purifications had to be performed, such as elaborate washings, shaving of the hair, abstaining from foods and so on. In time, however, these purifications lost their original and practical meaning and took on a symbolic significance. Thus the idea arose that they cleansed the subject from moral guilt rather than from a simple taint. The growth of religious ideas gave a particular twist to the situation and these purifications were viewed as efforts to make atonement to some god for a wrong done. Thus the original act which had involved the taboo became a moral and religious sin. The elaborate precautions taken to lay the ghost of the suicide seemed in time to be either expiatory sacrifices to the gods for a sin committed (the Wajagga's goat, for instance), or direct punishments brought by society against the corpse of the suicide (cf. the Athenian custom). In this way by an altogether erroneous interpretation of the facts, suicide itself became criminal, an offence against gods and men.

There was, however, another coincidence which accelerated this process. It so happened that hanging, and in a lesser degree drowning (both favourite forms of suicide), were directly connected with certain religious and mythical rites. Even to-day a particular opprobrium attaches to these types of suicide. The reason for this opprobrium can be traced back to classical times, where it first appears from a remote and unplumbed past. The rites of Artemis, Attis, Bacchus, and Odin in the North, all probably involved at some time or other the hanging of a voluntary priest or involuntary victim as sacrifice, and in this way hanging came to be considered as a semi-sacred death. With the progress of time and the growth of moral ideas these victims to the gods were replaced either by symbolic dolls or by swinging festivals, in which the celebrants on swings symbolized the suspended sacrifice. The social conscience now looked back with shame and disgust on the human sacrifices of the past, and, by a familiar paradox of primitive thought, what had been sacred, became accursed. The ritualistic death by suspension, the praised social and sacrificial suicide, disappeared and was replaced by a horror of hanging, and particularly of suicide by hanging. (This transference of feeling corresponds to a general law which might run something like this: when any type of sacrificial suicide loses its social sanction, it becomes invested with a suicide horror which tends to be strong in direct ratio to the strength of the earlier sanction.)

A glance at the use of suspended puppets, swinging, and swinging festivals, will show how widespread was the belief in the religious nature of these acts, and thus, originally, in the religious nature of the hanging they represent. The custom of swinging as a magic or religious rite intended to bring about a certain end is general among primitive peoples. In the Indies priests rock themselves to and fro to obtain inspiration, others swing at harvest time, and yet others swing to ensure good hunting. In Esthonia the custom is connected with the summer solstice, and to-day in Calabria at Christmas-time swinging is still practised, and its devotional aspect is recognized.

Athens in classical times celebrated a swinging festival in which, more clearly than elsewhere, the religious origin of the custom is to be seen. Bacchus, when he brought the gift of wine to man, entrusted his secret to a certain Icarus, whom he sent out into the world to spread the precious knowledge.

So Icarus loaded a wagon with wine-skins and set out on his travels, the dog Maera running beside him. He came to Attica, and there fell in with shepherds tending their sheep, to whom he gave of the wine. They drank greedily, but when some of them fell down dead drunk, their companions thought the stranger had poisoned them with intent to steal the sheep; so they knocked him on the head. The faithful dog ran home and guided his master's daughter Erigone to the body. At sight of it she was smitten with despair and hanged herself on a tree beside her dead father, but not until she had prayed that, unless the Athenians should avenge her sire's murder, their daughters might die the same death as she. Her curse was fulfilled, for soon many Athenian damsels hanged themselves for no obvious reason. An oracle informed the Athenians of the true cause of this epidemic and instituted the swinging festival to appease Erigone; and at the vintage they offered the first of the grapes to her and her father.[1]

We see here the link of swinging rites not only with religion but with suicide; a double connection that is later repeated in Rome. There, when a man had committed suicide by hanging, a doll was hung up in a tree on the day that the parentalia of the dead man were celebrated.

Such puppet and swinging rites, though deriving from religion, can be connected in two ways with the general suicide horror. First, the idea of swinging—either the puppet in the wind, or a living celebrant—may well have an extended significance as a practical move to frighten the ghost. It bears great similarity to the Malayan practice, where a witch-doctor will swing to and fro to chase away disease or evil spirits. Secondly, the familiar idea of purification probably entered into the custom, for air, like fire, was regarded as an efficacious agent against things " unclean ".

The particular horror attached to suicide by drowning, and its religious nature, was mentioned above. This horror was brought about by the same sort of forces that made hanging so reprehensible. Firstly, rivers were almost always sacred to some local deity, and suicide by drowning was an

[1] Frazer, *The Dying God.*

act of impiety that contaminated the water. Further, it
appears that death by drowning was once sacred. The primitive Roman cult of the Tiber included the sacrifice of human
beings who were flung into the waters. Later these, like the
suspended victims, were substituted for a symbolic sacrifice,
a bundle of osiers; and thus in time the peculiar horror of
suicide by drowning developed.

There are two other reasons for the growth of the suicide
horror, which, though less fundamental than the taboo and
religious causes, nevertheless were operative before the traceable history of suicide begins. In the first place, suicide
shows a contempt for society. It is rude. As Kant says, it is
an insult to humanity in oneself. This most individualistic
of all actions disturbs society profoundly. Seeing a man who
appears not to care for the things which it prizes, society is
compelled to question all it has thought desirable. The
things which makes its own life worth living, the suicide
boldly jettisons. Society is troubled, and its natural and
nervous reaction is to condemn the suicide. Thus it bolsters
up again its own values.

The last force which turns opinion against the suicide is
the economic one. Though a Marxian interpretation of the
social attitude to suicide would be amusing, the economic
element has in actuality usually played second fiddle to religious and superstitious factors. Even in primitive societies,
however, the economic factor is easily discoverable. A
grown male suicide deprives the tribe of a useful warrior; a
woman's suicide means the death of a potential mother.
Within the primitive family-unit similar arguments work
even more strongly. From an early age every able-bodied
son is a productive unit in the family economy. His suicide
causes dislocation and reduces the production of wealth.
The loss of the father is even more serious.

The strongly economic attitude of parents in primitive
society is illustrated in an extreme case by certain islanders

(and also in antiquity by the customs of Asia Minor and Cyprus). These islanders as a matter of course let their unmarried daughters out on hire, and mothers "wait impatiently for the time when their young daughters will be able to help the household by their earnings ".

In England in the nineteenth century the capitalist system produced a state of affairs in which the industrial labouring family could only keep its head above water by utilizing its every unit from the age of six and eight up. In such a family, as in the average farming household, and even in the economy of the medieval artisan, an individual suicide put an added economic burden on all those who remained. Later, in tracing the history of suicide, it will become clear how slavery, feudalism, and the practice of confiscating the property of suicides, in their turn all lead to an accentuation of an economic prejudice against suicide. It must be noticed, however, that this economic prejudice, as well as the affront offered to society by the fact of suicide, create an antagonism to the act that is reasonable, tempered, and usually definable; an attitude, in other words, that differs sharply from the blind, unreasoning, vindictive, hate and horror, which are based on the old taboos and ghost fears.

II

Institutional suicide, as we have seen, flourishes among primitives; yet personal suicide among certain savages seems to be unknown. When questioned on the subject the aborigines of Australia and the natives of the Caroline Islands apparently laughed at the very idea of a man killing himself; the notion was to them preposterous. Generally, however, personal suicide does occur among primitive peoples in varying degrees of frequency. It differs, however, very considerably from suicide as it has developed in the Western world, self-destruction is not often caused by the nostalgia, melancholy, pain, fear, love and poverty that we meet in civilization. Most commonly, primitive suicides result from anger, jealousy and (particularly) desire for revenge. These suicides, from their very nature, are anti-social. Usually they meet with the disapproval that one would expect. For instance, among the Pelew islanders suicides are not buried, and the natives of Borneo, half-anticipating Dante, believe that those who commit suicide by drowning spend their existence in the next world up to their waists in water. Condemnation of personal suicide, however, is not universal, and different tribes take differing attitudes. One meets everything from complacency to absolute condemnation.

The relative rareness of the usual European suicide motives can be partly accounted for by the closeness of primitive tribal organization which leaves little room for the unappreciated individual or the bewildered and isolated misfit. The supply of essential wants—sex, food, and so on —is regulated by the community; and in the same way it supplies and regulates ideas and mental patterns. When a psychological misfit of some sort does lead to suicide, the subject, thinking in the terms of his tribe, usually believes that he is possessed and that his personality has been affected by malign influences. Such misfits apparently are not uncommon in parts of the Niger valley, where usually the suicide, unable to fight against the melancholia which has come to " possess " him, simply and literally " holds his breath " until he dies.

The most common type of primitive suicide—the revenge suicide, with an element of uncontrolled anger often visible—is best illustrated by a reference to child psychology. The child who has been misused or punished wishes to die, and thereby to be revenged on its parents. It says, "If I were dead, *then* you'd be sorry." The primitive goes a step further. He puts the threat into practice. Such suicides, though they grow less common in succeeding stages of civilization, by no means disappear. Chatterton, damning an unappreciative public before he died, reflects an element of such a revenge suicide.

That even to-day the revenge motive can be carefully and naïvely elaborated in a primitive way is shown by the story of a French nineteenth-century lover whose mistress had betrayed him. Before killing himself he called his servant and gave orders that after his death a candle should be made of his fat and carried, lighted, to his mistress. To accompany it he wrote a note, saying that as he had burned for her in life, so he did in his death. Proof of his passion she would find in the light by which she read his letter—a flame fed by his miserable body.

Among primitives the cause of suicide is often slighter than among such "civilized" people, and members of the Iji tribe will sometimes destroy themselves at the slightest provocation, abuse, or chaff. Such primitive suicides expect to get their revenge in one of two ways. Either they believe that their ghosts will haunt and plague their enemies, or, more rarely, they hope to bring into operation the tribal law of retaliation whereby their enemies will also be compelled to commit suicide. The nature of the revenge expected varies from tribe to tribe and country to country. In Northern Siberia the suicide relies on his ghost to revenge his death; in Southern India he leaves the task to tribal custom, for in the Peninsular the law of retaliation prevails in all its rigour. If a quarrel takes place and a man tears out his own eye or kills himself, his adversary must do the same, either to himself or to one of his relations. The women carry the barbarity still further. For a slight affront put on them, a sharp word said to them, they will go and smash their head against the door of the woman who has offended them, and the latter is obliged immediately to do the same. If a woman poisons herself by drinking the juice of a poisonous herb, the other woman who drove her to this violent death must poison herself likewise; else her house will be burned, her cattle carried off, and injuries of all kinds done her until satsifaction is given.[1]

Naturally in many tribes complex influences modify the simple anger-revenge suicide. Thus among the Todas, one finds the actual method of suicide dictated by religious belief. In their Kwoten god-myth suicide occurs by strangling; thus a Toda, when furiously angry and threatening to commit suicide, will say, " My neck tying, I will die." And this, in fact, is the type of suicide that is chosen.

For our purpose we may class most of the personal suicides of the Orient until the last hundred years with primitive suicides; for these Eastern civilizations, though highly organized, exhibit the same static qualities as primitive civilizations. Among Orientals, however, something very curious happened. Apart from the usual types of institutional suicide, such as death of widows and attendants, or military suicide, there was an absolute institutionalization of the typically primitive anger-revenge suicide. This prevalent type of personal suicide was, in fact, made social and thus officially sanctioned; at the same time the complex nature of Eastern civilization broadened and complicated the causes which in primitive tribes produce the simple anger-revenge suicide. In China, for instance, the particular position of the father, and ideas of metempsychosis, brought new elements into play. In Japan the whole thing was given a decidedly political and national twist, so that a man would commit suicide out of dislike for a policy rather than a person, or because he had failed in some public mission.

None the less, the institutionalized survival of primitive motives everywhere remained the basic element of typical Oriental suicide. Between the five hundred Chinese philoso-

[1] Father Martin, *Lettres edifiantes et curieuses*, 1781, quoted in Frazer's *The Dying God*. Such suicides are semi-institutionalized.

phers who threw themselves into the sea in the reign of
the Emperor Chi-Tiang-Ti, being unwilling to survive
the burning of their books, and the last political suicide
of this century, there is usually a persistent similarity of
motive.

The semi-institutional nature of all *hara-kiri* is particularly plain. But certain types of *hara-kiri* were inevitably
more social and less personal than others. Thus the *hara-kiri*
committed by criminals and defeated opponents with the
gracious permission of authority was a procedure as absolutely institutionalized as Hindu *suttee*. This concession to
the condemned resembles in some ways the *mortis arbitrium*
of the Romans which we shall meet later. Marco Polo
describes the Chinese procedure in detail.

> When a man [he says] in the great province of Mabar has
> committed a crime and has been condemned to death, he tells the
> king that he wishes to kill himself for the honour, and in the love
> of, such and such an idol. The king accepts, and then all the
> relatives and friends of the man who is to kill himself place him
> upon a seat and, having provided him with at least twelve knives,
> carry him around the town, crying: " This brave man is going to
> kill himself for the love of such and such an idol." Having thus
> paraded him, they arrive at the place where the execution is to
> take place, and he who is to die takes a knife and cries aloud : " I
> kill myself for the honour of such and such an idol." And with
> one knife he stabs himself in the arm, and with another knife he
> stabs himself in the other arm, and with yet another he stabs him-
> self in the stomach, and so dies. And his relatives then burn his
> body with acclamation.

Thus even the execution of *hara-kiri* always was, as it
still is, a solemn ceremonial. Usually staged in the presence
of witnesses, it involves a set ritual, though not always one
similar to that which Marco Polo saw. More commonly a
dagger, held in the left hand, is plunged into the belly on
the same side below the navel. The cut is then carried across
to the right, where the blade is turned and finally drawn

upwards. The operation must be carried out with absolute impassivity.[1]

It must be emphasized that the foregoing remarks do not attempt to cover the whole ground. They refer simply to what seems most characteristic of Oriental suicide, and they are chiefly relevant to a period prior to the infiltration of Western influences. To-day the situation conforms much more to that of Europe. Both the causes of suicide and the attitude of society towards it have changed and are still changing. East and West begin to approximate even here. In Japan *seppuku*, *hara-kiri*, and the old forms of suicide, are disappearing. It is no longer possible to say as Montesquieu did in the eighteenth century that the Japanese "rip open their bellies for the least fancy". To-day nine out of ten Japanese suicides drown or hang themselves. In nineteenth-century China, opium—certainly not in the approved tradition—became the commonest instrument of suicide. None the less, several thousands of cases showed the old anger-jealousy-revenge motives still paramount, though other causes, such as the marriage relationship, were also of considerable importance. An examination of five Chinese towns in 1898 led to the belief that there were half a million suicides per annum for the whole country, or 1 person in 800. Such estimates are unreliable, but the fact remains that a society was formed to keep four boats circulating around the Foochow bridge to save intending suicides from drowning.

[1] In 1868 twenty Japanese knights involved in the murder of a French officer were condemned to execute *hari-kari* before the French ambassador. The latter, however, found it impossible to appreciate to the full this token of Nipponese friendship. When eleven of the victims had done their duty he could bear the sight no longer and the remainder were reprieved and banished.

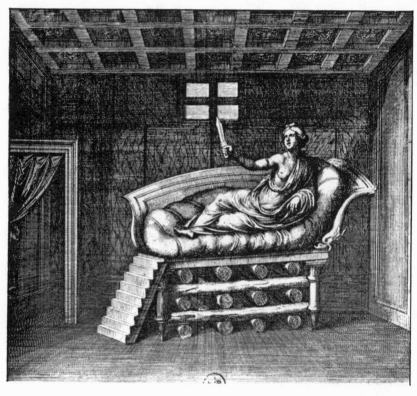

DIDO   *(18th century engraving)*

"UPON THE FYRE OF SACRIFYS SHE STERTE
AND WITH HIS SWORD SHE ROOF HER TO THE HERTE"

(Legend of Good Women)

CHAPTER IV

THE LIBERTY TO DIE

I. CLASSIC TYPES

WITH the classical age we pass from the primitive and anonymous to the specific, from the type to the particular. For the first time we can view our phenomenon over a wide and civilized area, and note a fairly coherent response from a large society. Suicide now begins to be the object not only for instinctive reactions but for thought and discussion. Redeemed from odium it is incorporated into reigning philosophies and practised by social paragons.

Broadly speaking, throughout the whole period the primitive and religious forces that create the suicide horror are steadily weakening, or at any rate becoming less vocal. The growth of civilization and the exchange of ideas, though they could not destroy these forces, succeeded in keeping them underground; that is, they confined them to the lower classes. One of the feats of the ancient world is the admirable way in which it moulded religion to suit its social needs; nowhere has the differentiation of religion for the rich and for the poor, for educated and uneducated, been more successfully achieved. While the old polydeistic religion, with the blood horror and the ghost fears that it implied, went on undisturbed below, the upper class adapted its gallery of gods to its philosophic theories and sophisticated outlook. Paganism was taken symbolically and its atavistic paraphernalia, including the suicide fears, were disregarded.

49

Contemporary with this religious differentiation there was everywhere a loosening and widening of the social unit, and everywhere a growing scope for individual uncertainties and difficulties. From the small city state with its precise recognizable issues, and with its definite authority and specific moral, we move into the almost limitless space of the Roman Empire. There the complication of factors cuts up the easy picture; international philosophies upset local certainties, Rome disturbs the Scythian *morale*, and barbarians come to wear the purple. The imperial mandate and the hexameters of international culture, break up a thousand little microcosms. It is just this loosening of local ties, this weaning from a close parental control, moral or religious, that makes for the increase of suicide. The more the individual has to think for himself, the more he seems prone to commit suicide.

We shall, therefore, both for religious and social reasons, see the practice of suicide growing throughout the age. Only one deterrent, the economic one, increases in strength, coming to a final maturity when the slave system gives way to feudalism in the subsequent period. Apart from the suicide of desperate escape, the socially unimportant expedient of the cornered beast, of which Nero's end is an example, four main types of suicide can be distinguished far more common than the rest. First there is the suicide committed for the sake of honour : in this class we find both the woman who wishes to preserve her chastity, and the Roman who will not fall into the hands of his foes and insists on dying a free man—Lucrece and Brutus. An amusing extension of this idea of dying a free man at all costs is provided by Corellius Rufus, a Roman nobleman. He put off committing suicide throughout the reign of Domitian, saying that he did not wish to die under a tyrant. Once this powerful Emperor was dead he took his own life with an easy mind, and as a free Roman. The second type of suicide is that

committed to avoid the pains and ignominy attendant on
disease and old age. This, in practice, often approached
closely to the honour suicide; for often the motivating idea
behind such deaths was that man, the noble animal of
humanism, ought not to allow himself to be reduced to
doddering and imbecile old age, or to be subjected to a
diseased body : such a state of affairs was not consonant
with his honour and dignity. In practice, suicides to avoid
the effects of disease and old age were a late development
and they only become common with the spread of certain
philosophic ideas under the Empire.

The third common type of suicide is that particularly
mentioned by Plato : " for human love, for dead wife, for
dead son, many a man has gone willingly to the house of
Hades, drawn by the hope that in the world beyond they
might see and be with those they loved ". It is the bereave-
ment type : Paulina attempting to follow Seneca, and Portia
taking her life out of sorrow for the death of Brutus. In
this category the rareness of " love " suicides and of the
suicide pact is remarkable, and it is only to be explained
by the status and meaning of love in classical times. There
are six suicides in Plutarch's *Five Tragical Histories of
Love*, but only one of these is a " love " suicide in our sense
of the word. The commoner type is Melissus throwing himself from Neptune's tower in sorrow for the death of his son
Actaeon, or Skedasos dying in Sparta to avenge his
daughters. Extreme physical passion was, of course, as
strong as (possibly stronger than) it is to-day, but leaving
out the question of homosexuality, the range of emotions,
forces and interests, marshalled under the direction of "love"
was infinitely smaller. The conception of the Virgin Mary,
the ideas of the troubadours, nineteenth-century romanticism, and perhaps even Queen Elizabeth, have all helped to
extend infinitely the dominion of love. The modern does
not find it difficult (though one foresees such a difficulty

arising again in the near future) to situate most of his transcendental values, his aspirations, and ideals, in a single
woman, or in consecutive women. A simple attraction to
the female has been made the vehicle for intensely important
and valuable emotions. Naturally when he is " let down "
by a woman, she takes so much of his personality that life
seems no longer worth living. Many values with which the
woman has intrinsically nothing to do are lost by her departure. Thus it is not surprising that suicide should often
be the outcome of an unhappy love affair to-day.

To the Greek and Roman, however, a woman was a
woman, neither the mother of God, nor the Virgin Queen,
and they would have understood with difficulty the sentiments of the nineteenth century, which Browning expressed
in the phrase " Love is best ". For the ancients there were
so many other things to take into consideration; they
had not put all their transcendental eggs into one fragile
basket.

The question also arises how far the Romans, at any rate,
felt the need for transcendental values, and consequently of
a vessel to receive them. When the Roman, or the Greek,
was deceived in love, he might be unhappy, piqued, hurt or
angry, but he rarely suffered that feeling of utter loss and
desolation which his modern counterpart knows. Similarly
when one of these people married, he might complain that
neither his wife's figure nor her temper were as good as he
had been led to believe, but he rarely experienced those
bitter and terrible deceptions which characterize Christian
marriage. Expecting only a certain modicum, there was no
room for the disappointments of the soul. The writings of
the classics here bear us out; even the passion of Catullus is
essentially practical and subject only to rational disappointments and reasonable excitation. Lesbia plays, in fact, an
intense but limited role. That love suicides did occur from
time to time is indisputable (witness the tragic end of Castor

and Pollux; Hero who drowned herself in the Hellespont, imitating her lover even in the place of her death; Pyramus and Thisbé; and Sappho who threw herself in unrequited love from the suicides' rock at Neritos)[1], but such suicides were rarities, not regular occurrences. They must be distinguished from the typical affection-suicide of which the classic period is as full as any other. The reasons which made Portia commit suicide on the death of Brutus are equally effective to-day. They have not so much to do with love, either in the mystical or the sensual senses of which we have been speaking, as with loyalty, trust, a long habit of affection, and the impossibility of making a drastic and intolerable change in one's way of life at a fairly advanced age.

The fourth type of suicide might almost be classed as ritualistic and sacrificial, since it is the voluntary death of a man who thinks that his own departure will advance his state, cause, party, or family. In practice, however, it is not sacrificial, since the agent does not usually act in an official capacity and may as well be opposing as supporting the *status quo*. This type is essentially classic in character and accounts for some of the noblest and most spectacular deaths of the period.

With the exception of compulsory suicides which we shall consider apart under the classical laws of suicide, most self-destruction in Greek and Roman times can be fitted in under one or the other of these four headings. What is particularly

---

[1] The origins of the popularity of this rock are not altogether simple. The rock had religious associations. It was crowned originally by a Temple of Apollo where an annual human sacrifice was celebrated. The victim was a condemned criminal who was thrown over the cliff into the sea. The humanity of later ages attached a number of birds to the unfortunate man, whose frantically beating wings helped to break his fall. Boats were stationed below and rowed out to rescue the victim if he had survived. (Raymond Mortimer, MS.; and Delisle de Sales.)

interesting is that two types common to-day—suicide from economic change, and suicide from depression—are extremely rare, too rare in fact to form categories of their own. Menippus, a cynic and pupil of Diogenes, who committed suicide in the first century B.C. on the loss of his fortune is exceptional. Poverty, it seems, only becomes an adequate cause for suicide in a highly developed commercial or capitalistic civilization, where all values are apt to be chained to a money basis, and loss or lack of money means loss of respect, prestige, and a hundred other things. In the small city state riches were rare at the best of times, and Sparta, whose lead currency was elsewhere intentionally valueless, is an extreme example of the disrespect and distrust which could be associated with wealth. With consuls like the farmer Agricola, and Emperors like Marcus Antoninus who, in spite of the tradition of imperial luxury, lived with the greatest frugality, poverty was not likely to be considered an unbearable burden and the poor were not necessarily social outcasts. Even the amassing of large fortunes, such as that of Herodes Atticus, who could afford to present theatres to Athens and Corinth, a racecourse to Delphi, an aqueduct to Olympia, baths to Thermopylae, and a gift to every Athenian citizen, did not altogether alter these ideas. A man's family, functions, and character, could usually discount an empty purse.

Suicide from long depression and melancholia is equally rare. Such depression, though usually physical in root, is fed and fostered by the Christian, and subsequently the romantic, attitude. Life, the vale of tears, caused both by original and acquired sin, the unfortunate prelude to an exclusive paradise, is in direct contrast to the classic idea of the infinite possibilities and unfortunate brevity of a mortal's span. From Homer until the coming of the stoics we get no idea of the burden of life; on the contrary its shortness and desirability are insisted upon. Life and light are op-

posed to the darkness of Hades and to those unfortunate
and undignified wraiths who wander there. The dead share
no paradise; they long only to pass the styx and regain a
pulsing earth. All the portraits of Antinous, the beautiful
favourite of Hadrian, are melancholy, and perhaps his otherwise inexplicable suicide in the Nile (which Dio Cassius
oddly suggests was a voluntary sacrifice to bring Hadrian
good luck) may be attributed to this streak in his character.
If so, he stands outside his time and we must list him
among the depressed moderns. Hadrian, overwhelmed by
his death, deified his memory, raised an altar to him at
Athens, and founded the city of Antinoöpolis to perpetuate
his memory.

It is interesting that the earliest Greek suicide of which
we have mention—the hanging of Jokasta on the dis-
covery that she has been living with her own son and her
husband's murderer—is regarded by Homer as a perfectly
natural action to which no blame or horror attaches. It appears as the only dignified way out of an intolerable situation. An exit not only dignified, but honourable. No other
sacrifice could have absolutely proved her good faith; the
taking of her own life is the only real atonement possible.
Jokasta is, in fact, the first Greek suicide for honour. As we
move on into history proper such suicides multiply. Pan-
titas, one of the two Spartans who survived Thermopylae,
found in suicide the only possible redemption of his reputation and the only adequate answer to those who taunted
him with cowardice. A far nobler honour suicide, however,
was that of Charondas, the wise law-giver of Catana, one
of the Greek colonies in Sicily. He had laid it down for the
preservation and peace of the community that anyone
entering the public assembly armed should be punished with
death. One day, having been outside the limits of the city
engaged in cleaning up a band of robbers, he hurriedly returned to make a formal report to the citizens and inad-

vertently entered the assembly without laying aside his weapons. Taxed with breaking his own laws, death seemed to him the only vindication of his position, and he took his life then and there before the assembled people.

Concurrently the idea gained ground that it was not consonant with one's dignity and the way a man should die, to fall alive into the hands of one's enemies. Thus, later in the same century, Thucydides tells us that the oligarchs of Corcyra trapped in the temple of Hera and condemned to die, " destroyed one another in the enclosure of the temple where thy were, except a few who hanged themselves on trees or put an end to their lives in any way they could ". Isocrates, the Athenian orator, starved himself to death, at the age of ninety, rather than yield to Philip of Macedon; and a century later Demosthenes took the same way out, to avoid falling into the hands of Antipater, whose ambassador required of the Athenians that they should give up their orators. This, like the ring containing poison which Hannibal always kept for the extremity which at last overtook him in Bithynia, was his only means of personally retaining that liberty on behalf of which he had so long tried to rally the Athenians.

Though suicide as a whole was not as common under the Republic as later under the Empire, in Italy the honour suicide crops up at an early date. The suicide of Lucrece in the sixth century B.C. is a famous and isolated instance. But at least seventy years before her death a regular epidemic of honour suicides had broken out among the Roman soldiery. Many of the latter, forced by Tarquinius Priscus to work at cutting drains and sewers, considered the work servile, beneath their dignity and unconsonant with a soldier's honour; they finally put an end to the situation by pitching themselves off the Capitoline Rock, a spot usually reserved for throwing down criminals. With the beginning of the internecine struggles for mastery

that preceded the Empire, honour suicides become more frequent. After his defeat one of the Gracchi requests his slave
to kill him; Brutus, unable to persuade Cleitus and Volum-
nius to do the same office for him, runs on his own sword.[1]
In Pontus, Mithridates involved in the unsavoury expansion
of the Roman Empire, and tricked, cheated and beaten by
Pompey, takes his own life and that of his family by poison,
intent to die a free man rather than adorn another Republican triumph.

Pompey was also involved in the heroic end of the
Tribune Vulteius and his cohort. Lucan relates how these
men, supporters of Caesar, were cruising down the Illyrian
coast in a small vessel, when they suddenly ran into Pompey's fleet. Escape was impossible and the tribune decided
to fight rather than yield. All day the solitary vessel defended itself with extraordinary courage, and one attack after
another was repulsed. Finally, however, thinned in numbers
and wearied by hours of fighting, they saw the situation
grow hopeless. It was then that Vulteius called on his
soldiers to die by a death of their own choosing, rather than
fall alive into the enemy's hands. " Dear comrades," he said,
" I have already renounced the light : death touches me and
its fury is upon me. No one can know how blissful it is to
die until he attains to his last hour. Vulgar men alone, from
whom the gods hide themselves, consent to carry a life that
is a burden." Moved by his words and finding his advice
wise and honourable, the remnant of his cohort took their
own lives upon the decks, and none fell into the hands of
Pompey. One is inevitably reminded of the story of the
Revenge, and of Sir Richard Grenville's wish to blow up the
boat and sink with all hands. " Having by estimation eight
hundred shot of great artillery " through his vessel, he

---

[1] It is interesting to discover that Brutus, as a young man, wrote a
philosophical work proving that it was wrong to take one's own life.
The essay was occasioned by the suicide of his uncle.

commanded the master-gunner, whom he knew to be a most resolute man, to split and sink the ship, that thereby nothing might remain of glory or victory to the Spaniards, . . . and persuaded the company . . . [that] they should not now shorten the honour of their nation by prolonging their own lives for a few hours or a few days.[1]

With the coming of the Empire honour suicides get fewer. Boadicea, on her defeat by Suetonius, took poison to avoid falling into Roman hands, and Cocceius Nerva strikes the old Republican note in the reign of Tiberius. Starving himself to death as a protest against the morals and extravagance of the time, he was determined to die at least with his own integrity unsullied. Not long after, Statius, pardoned by Nero, committed suicide rather than incur the shame of being " spared " by the man who had murdered Agrippa and Britannicus.[2] But such examples are not common, and when they occur have usually a flavour that connects them with the ideas of contemporary philosophy and are therefore treated in another place.

More or less parallel to the honour suicide both in Greece and in Italy, but showing on the contrary a decrease rather than an increase with the passage of time and the complication of events is what we have called the Patriotic suicide. A thousand years before Christ, Codrus, the last of the Athenian kings, sets the pattern. Athens was at war with the Heraclidae and victory had been foretold by an oracle to the

[1] Sir Walter Raleigh.

[2] Strictly speaking, even the pathetic Sporus might be included among the suicides for honour. This young man, owing to his resemblance to Sabina, was publicly married to Nero in Greece. Tigellinus gave the " bride " away and prayers were offered up for legitimate issue. After Nero's death Dio Cassius says that Vitellius " proposed that Sporus should be brought on the stage in the rôle of a maiden being ravished, but he would not endure the shame and committed suicide beforehand."

side whose king fell in battle. Codrus, therefore, sacrificing his own interests to those of his country, entered the enemy camp in disguise, picked a quarrel with a soldier, and allowed himself to be killed. His suicide, as prophesied, brought victory to Athens. Rather similar were the deaths of the beautiful Cratinus and his friend Apollodorus, who offered themselves as sacrifices to wipe out a blood-guilt that lay upon the city. More famous still and more lasting in its results was the example of Lycurgus, almost a contemporary of Codrus. As legislator of Sparta he left Lacaedaemon to consult the Delphic oracle about the new code which he had just drawn up. Before his departure he imposed an oath on the people that they would preserve his laws at any rate "until his return". Having reached Delphi he sent back in writing the favourable response of the oracle to the effect that "the laws were excellent, and would render the people great and happy who should observe them". He then proceeded to starve himself to death, so that the Spartans might never be absolved from their oath and obligation. The laws whose sanction he thus indefinitely prolonged, were operative for seven hundred years, and much of the greatness of Sparta resulted from their ascetic, martial and uncompromising, character. The next great patriotic suicide whom we meet is Themistokles. This brilliant and tragic man, banished from Athens, offered his services and talents to the Persians, who were without a competent general. When the latter turned their attentions to the conquest of Athens, whose fleets under Cimon had been causing them trouble, they called on Themistokles to make good his promises. Given the leadership of the Persian armies, he was commanded to subdue his own country. The thought of conquering Athens, however, was insupportable, and as no alternative remained he committed suicide by drinking bull's blood, as the story goes. Thus he renounced honour, wealth, and probable victory. By his death he averted from Attica the danger of a conquest that, without his knowledge and military genius, could not be undertaken with any chance of success.

A century later in Rome there opens the epic of the Decii. Rome at this time was engaged in her desperate struggle with the neighbouring Latins, upon whose successful outcome hung not only the future of the city, but the existence of a civilization. Decius Mus, at that time consul, led out the army against the Latins, and in the thick of the battle, as an example to his soldiers, dashed into the ranks of the enemy and sacrificed his life. Forty-one years later, fighting against the Gauls at the Battle of Sentinum, his son, the younger Decius, repeated his father's sacrifice, and, as Livy phrases it, " devoted himself to death ".

This epic of suicide participated in a quick and concrete reward. The final defeat of both Latins and Gauls left Rome the assured mistress of central Italy.

Regulus provides the other prominent example of patriotic suicide under the Republic. Consul and commander in the first Punic war, he was defeated, captured, and taken to Carthage. After two years of unpleasant and humiliating exile he was dispatched to Rome to effect terms and try to persuade the Senate to an exchange of prisoners. Before his departure he had been bound by oath to return to Africa if unsuccessful. Considering on his arrival in Italy that the offers he brought were disadvantageous to his countrymen, he did everything in his power to dissuade them from accepting the Carthaginian terms. His efforts were successful, the proposals were turned down, and Regulus went back to Carthage and certain death. A barrel lined with spikes was prepared for him, and in this he met his end—the most stoic and perhaps the finest of the Roman suicides.

Earlier than the end of Regulus or the Decii had occurred the fabled suicide of Marcus Curtius. The story was traditional in Rome. In the fourth century B.C. a vast smoking gulf is said to have opened in the Forum as the result of an earthquake. The town was in consternation. Consulted on the matter, the oracles said that only the gift of Rome's most precious possession would close up the rift. Marcus Curtius, saying that there was nothing more precious than a brave citizen, leapt into the gulf. Its subsequent closure was attributed to his sacrifice.

With the coming of the Empire, and the loosening of the social unit, and of the personal and idealistic ties which bound a man to the state, the forces making for patriotic suicide lessen in strength. The suicide of the Emperor Otho in A.D. 69 stands out as a noble exception. Having suffered one defeat and sacrificed many lives in his efforts to keep Vitellius out of Italy, he suddenly decided to give up the contest, although his chances of ultimate victory were still very fair and his troops fanatically loyal and willing. His reason, as he told his protesting soldiers, was that he would not expose such brave and courageous men to further dangers or waste the youth of Rome in civil war. For the good of his country he thought it better to terminate the war, even if this end could only be achieved by his own death. Plutarch records his magnificent speech:

> Looking round with a countenance composed and cheerful, he said, " This day, my fellow soldiers, I deem more blessed than that on which ye first made me Emperor, since I see you so devoted to me and am judged worthy of so high an honour at your hands. But do not rob me of a greater blessedness—that of dying nobly in behalf of fellow citizens so many and so good. If I was worthy to be Roman Emperor I ought to give my life freely for my country. I know that the victory of our adversaries is neither decisive nor assured. . . . Still it is not to defend Italy against Hannibal, or Pyrrhus, or the Cimbri, that our war is waged, but both parties are waging war against Romans, and we sin against our country, whether we conquer or are conquered. Believe me when I insist that I can die more honourably than I can reign. For I do not see how my victory can be of so

great advantage to the Romans as my offering up my life to secure peace and concord and to prevent Italy from beholding such a day again."

Having compelled the senators and his generals to leave him and retire to Rome, and having destroyed all the correspondence which could inculpate his followers, he retired to his tent.

As evening approached he slaked his thirst with a draught of cold water. Then two daggers were brought him; he tried the points of both and placed one beneath his pillow. . . . He passed a quiet night, and indeed, as is affirmed, he even slept somewhat. At dawn he fell on the steel.[1]

So moved were the common soldiers at the news of his death that many killed themselves, not only beside his funeral pyre, but at Bedriacum, Placentia, and distant camps.[2]

Suicides which come under the class of affection are not so easy to trace down as they usually are of a personal character, and do not involve the limelight of publicity or the comments of historians. However, this type too has a respectable classical history that goes right back to almost prehistoric times. When Theseus had set out for Crete to slay the Minotaur, he had arranged with his father, Aigeus, that the sailors on his returning ship were to hoist a white flag in token of success when Sunium hove in sight; if on the contrary they sailed back to Attica with their usual brownish-black canvas, it was to be a sign that Theseus, lost in the labyrinth, had succumbed to the bull. Theseus and the sailors, in the excitement of a victorious return, forgot the prearranged signal, and Aigeus, in sorrow at his son's imagined death, flung himself from the cliffs where he was waiting into the Aegean, the sea that since has kept his name. Homer tells that only the staying hand of Antilochus kept Achilles from

[1] Livy.

[2] Something rather similar had happened in Spain. On the assassination of Sertorius, the brilliant Marian, in 72 B.C., many of his soldiers sacrificed their own lives to the memory of their leader.

suicide, when, before Troy, he wished to cut his throat in despair at the death of his love, Patroclus. Affection, too, caused Dido's death, who, rather than marry again, stabbed herself on her husband's funeral pyre, having sworn eternal fidelity to the memory of her dead husband Sichaeus.[1] Under the republic and in that tight social cadre, one would have thought that personal affection had hardly room enough to become so all-absorbing or to express its sorrow by the extreme gesture of suicide. And yet one discovers, in the Republic's last days, that a partisan of one of the two factions which so bitterly disputed the chariot races sacrificed his life on the funeral pyre of a favourite coachman. A more plausible sorrow, caused, it is said, by the temporary absence of their husbands and lovers, produced a severe epidemic of suicide among the women of Miletus. Even this, however, seems an act of unworthy impatience when contrasted with the calm and devoted action of " noble Portia ". Life without Brutus seemed to her worthless, and on receipt of the news of Brutus's death at Philippi she swallowed red-hot coals. Similarly the widow of Sejanus refused to outlive the murder of her children, and Cornelia committed suicide after the defeat and death of her husband, Crassus.

The dramatic end of Arria, however, has eclipsed that of the other Roman women who died for their husbands. Detected in a liberal and unsuccessful conspiracy against Claudius, her husband, Caecina Paetus, was condemned to death. He felt that suicide was his only dignified move, but a natural fear made him hesitate. Thereupon, Arria, to show him the way to liberty, seized his dagger and stabbed herself; dying, she handed the weapon to him with the famous words, " *Paete, non dolet* "—" Paetus, it doesn't hurt ". Her daughter, also called Arria, tried later to imitate the mother's example, when her husband was condemned by Nero. She was, however, dissuaded.

[1] Vergil's Dido-Æneas legend appears to be pure invention.

Suicide, to avoid the degradations and the pain consequent on sickness and old age, seems to have been a fairly late development, though Rameses the Great, as far back as 1250 B.C., committed suicide in Egypt from despair at the loss of his sight. In Greece and Rome such deaths were not common, until, on the one hand, humanistic ideas had put about the notion of the dignity of the individual, and on the other hand the philosophers had given their sanction to a generous interpretation of what might legitimately be considered unbearable. The deaths of men such as Zeno, Cleanthes, and Atticus were all conditioned by their philosophical principles, and rightly come under the heading of philosophical suicides. It does appear, however, that as early as 500 B.C. it was an established custom in the Island of Ceos (the modern Lia) off Asia Minor, for men over sixty and anyone incapacitated by sickness to take their own lives, to which end the state kept a supply of poison.[1] Those who died in this way, " they did drown with garlands, as triumphers over humane misery ". Seneca, typically enough, thought this sort of self-destruction only worthy when the pain or disease threatened to cloud the mind. Pliny the Elder allowed three diseases, first among them gallstones, so grievously painful that they gave a man colour and countenance to kill himself.[2]

His nephew, Pliny the Younger, speaks in his letters of two prominent suicides who escaped in this way from pain and miserable old age; both deaths are recorded without adverse comment. One is that of Corellius Rufus, a man of great integrity who helped to launch Pliny; his suicide has already been mentioned. The other is that of the luxurious and wealthy Silius Italicus; troubled by an in-

[1] Strabo suggests that this custom originally arose owing to a shortage of food supplies.

[2] It was this Pliny who regarded the existence of poisonous herbs, with which a man might summon death painlessly and quickly, as one of the chief proofs of a kindly providence.

curable tumour, he starved himself to death and so ended a
very fortunate and auspicious life. Such deaths are obviously
sensible, and Diogenes was broad-minded enough to hand a
dagger to Antisthenes when his favourite pupil was in great
pain. Hadrian's physician, however, was afraid to do a
similar kindness for the emperor. When the latter asked for
hemlock he found himself in a dilemma, which only his own
suicide could solve. Before Hadrian's illness Euphrates,
the favourite of Roman society and an ageing stoic, had
secured the imperial permission to end his life with the very
drug which the emperor tried to obtain.

Such, then, are the four types of suicide which seem to have
been commonest in the classical world. How common they
actually were is not to be determined. Probably time and
our knowledge of the philosophic attitude have greatly
exaggerated the numbers of classical suicides. It must be
remembered that philosophic ideas would only directly affect
the educated minority, and that among the people as a whole
primitive taboos and the suicide horror must always have
remained fairly strong. Besides, literature and history then
concerned themselves only with the upper class. There we
do know that suicide was fairly frequent, but what of the
unrecorded populace? This vast majority must have restored
the balance and would show suicide to have been of relatively
infrequent occurrence: perhaps only the privilege and practice of the rich.

There is a last sort of suicide which, though too rare to
cause a type, was by its very nature spectacular—the
exhibitionist suicide. The idleness and the wealth of the
Hellenistic world, and its vastness in which the individual
might well feel his personality swamped, all favoured an
exhibitionist death. Before the eyes of a wondering
Empire the wish for notoriety could be gratified on a more
magnificent scale than ever since. The bid for recognition
made by a certain Sutherland who donned a suit of black

E

and shot himself in front of George III, pales before the public end of a Calanus, or a Peregrinus. Even the death of the unsatisfied nineteenth-century gentleman who attached himself to a rocket, appears as a discreet gesture by comparison with the exhibitionism possible in Greek and Roman times.

The death of Peregrinus was not exhibitionism of the ordinary sort. Like Miss Davison, who threw herself under the feet of the horses at the Derby of 1913, he sought death and notoriety for a particular end. His aim was the further glory and repute of the Cynic doctrines. A native of the Propontis and a man of wealth, Peregrinus had early given away his family fortune; after suffering imprisonment as a Christian he was attracted by the mysticism of the East, and finally ended by adopting the costume and doctrines of the Cynics. Preaching the rule of philosophy, the vanity of pleasure and the contempt of death, he made his way along the shores of the Mediterranean, carrying with him an ever-growing reputation. Eventually his wanderings, or, as it was hinted, his ambition, brought him to Rome, where even the life of Antoninus Pius did not escape his criticisms. Expelled from Italy, he returned to Greece, which henceforward became his headquarters. There his invectives and his reputation both continued to grow. It was at this moment, when his fame was at last world-wide and his position acknowledged among the first Cynics, that he decided to put an end to his life in a way that would rivet the attention of the whole Empire on his philosophy and at the same time demonstrate the true Cynic's contempt for death. Like Hercules, the mythical patron of his sect, he announced that he would die upon a flaming pyre. The date of his spectacular death was chosen to coincide with the Olympic Games, and a vast concourse of people, many of them in a state of religious fervour, collected to watch the great rite. Among them was Lucian, who, as a practical man and an antagonist of Cynicism, has left a very biassed account of the occasion.

To him Peregrinus was simply a determined impostor. Above the roar of the surging crowd Lucian could hear very little of the old man's speech, as he told the people that he was about to bring "a golden life to a golden close". Lucian did, however, notice that he was very pale, and as the moon rose he saw him approach his vast pyre surrounded by his disciples. Taking off his Cynic's robes, he threw incense on the flames, then having invoked the spirits of his ancestors, he passed into the conflagration and was seen no more. It was said that a brilliant phoenix winged upward from the pyre.

The two other mortal conflagrations which caused the greatest stir in classic times are included here as exhibitionist suicides, though since both were engineered by Brahmins they might well be classed as ritualistic and institutional suicides. The death of Calanus, however, has in practice little of the truly institutional about it. Having left India in the train of Alexander, he was disowned by his fellow Brahmins. Corrupted by the life and luxuries of Alexander's court, he gave up the purity of his vocational life and seems to have degenerated into the flatterer of a prince. At the age of thirty-seven he contracted a disease, probably due to his excesses. Threatened with blindness and finding his malady going from bad to worse, he decided on a grandiose suicide. An elevated pyre was built and, dressed in magnificent robes, he ascended into the flames in view of the whole Macedonian army, dying, as Strabo says, " in accordance with his ancestral custom ". Three hundred years later a rather similar scene was repeated before the Emperor Augustus. The chief actor was again a Brahmin, but the motives this time seem to have been almost purely religious. The exhibitionistic element is fortuitous. Porus, the Indian king and descendant of Alexander's ally, had sent to the Emperor, along with an embassy, a selection of curious gifts likely to intrigue a Western eye: " The gifts "—Strabo is quoting from an older historian—" were presented by eight naked servants, who were clad only in loin-cloths besprinkled with sweet-smelling odours." They consisted of a man who was born without arms (" whom I have myself seen," says Strabo), large vipers, a serpent ten cubits in length, a river tortoise three cubits in length, a partridge larger than a vulture,[1] and lastly a Brahmin who had been sent all the way from India expressly to commit suicide for the delectation of the Emperor.

Augustus was at the time in Athens, and there the public and voluntary immolation of the Brahmin took place before a large crowd.

> Whereas [says Strabo] some commit suicide when they suffer adversity, seeking release from the ills at hand, others do so when their lot is happy, as was the case with this man; for . . . although this man had fared as he had wished up to that time, he thought it necessary then to depart this life, lest something untoward might happen to him if he tarried here . . . therefore, he leaped upon a pyre with a laugh, his naked body anointed, wearing only a loin-cloth.

This Brahmin's excessive caution and desire to liquidate his earthly happiness were recorded by the following inscription : " Here lies Zarmanochegas, an Indian from Bargosa, who immortalized himself in accordance with the ancestral customs of Indians."

It was an ardent desire for a more earthly immortalization than the Brahmin's which caused Empedocles to jump unseen into the crater of Mount Etna. This was an odd exhibitionism, a desire for the permanence of his memory and not for a temporary limelight on his personality. He hoped that his absolute disappearance, coinciding with his own prophecies, would establish the legend that he had never died but had ascended to join the gods. Unfortunately the volcano would have us part in the deception, and soon after

[1] Presumably a bustard.

belched forth his sandal. This, together with the testimony
of a shepherd who had seen him near the rim of the crater,
betrayed his conspiracy. This revelation, though it ruined
his reputation, by a curious paradox provided him with the
immortality for which he had shown himself so avid.

Two other exhibitionists of classic times are worth men-
tioning. First, there is that King Ptolemy of Cyprus whom
Cato was sent to deal with. Hearing of the Roman's
approach Ptolemy determined to die in avaricious style,
destroying at the same time his fabulous treasures, himself,
and his servants. All were ceremoniously embarked on a
large vessel, and the king put out to sea with the intention
of boring holes in the ship's bottom. The thought of wast-
ing such gold was, however, too much for his resolution.
Returning to port he procured a less dramatic death, and his
treasure found a lease of life in Rome.

Sardanapalus, the Persian king, conceived of death on a
yet grander scale, and was more determined in his resolution.
Arbaces, one of his generals, having seen the king " painted
with vermilion and adorned like a woman, sitting among his
concubines carding purple wool and sitting among them with
his feet up, wearing a woman's robe and with his beard carefully scraped and his face smoothed with pumice-stone (for he
was whiter than milk, and pencilled under his eyes and eye-
brows)", was overcome with moral indignation, revolted,
and gathered a large army. Sardanapalus, defeated in battle,
determined none the less on a magnificent death. Within
the precincts of his palace he ordered a vast pyre to be made
and on it he set a hundred and fifty golden couches and
tables.

And he also erected on the funeral pile a chamber a hundred feet
long, made of wood; and in it he had couches spread, and there
he himself lay down with his wife, and his concubines lay on
other couches around. . . . And he made the roof of this apart-
ment of large stout beams, and then all the walls of it he made of

numerous thick planks, so that it was impossible to escape out of it. And in it he placed ten millions of talents of gold and a hundred millions of talents of silver, and robes, and purple garments, and every kind of apparel imaginable. And after that he bade the slaves set fire to the pile; and it was fifteen days burning. And those who saw the smoke wondered, and thought that he was celebrating a great sacrifice; but the eunuchs alone knew what was really being done. And in this way Sardanapalus, who had spent his life in extraordinary luxury, died with as much magnanimity as possible.[1]

Amongst these stylists there should be a place kept for Heliogabulus, unsuccessful as an emperor but unrivalled as an eccentric. The man who combed Arabia that the phoenix might grace his table, also prepared the instruments of his own death with meticulous forethought. Syrian priests had told him that he would end his life by suicide; and for this purpose he provided himself with a golden sword, poison enclosed in a priceless ring, and a rope of imperial purple and gold. Finally, in case none of these methods should suit his mood, he ordered a pavement of jewels to be laid beneath one of his towers, considering that only precious stones could decently receive an imperial precipitate. His forethought was unfortunately wasted, as his own guards murdered him.

II. LIBER MORI

Mori licet cui vivere non placet, he is at liberty to die who does not wish to live : this, with qualifications, became the final attitude of most classical philosophers. Cynic, Stoic, and Epicurean philosophies all led to an acceptance of suicide. In spite of this, however, there were always two main lines of thought in opposition, one deriving from Pythagoras, the other from Aristotle. The Orphic or Pythagorean doctrine viewed life as a penitential journey, a

[1] Athenaeus. *The Deipnosophists.*

discipline imposed by the gods to which a man must submit himself. The measure of his humility and submission was the measure of his virture.

Athenaeus, writing in the third century, gathered together some Pythagoreans at an imaginary banquet. Their spokesman, stating the Pythagorean position, said

> that the souls of all men were bound in the body, and in the life which is on earth, for the sake of punishment; and that God has issued an edict that if they do not remain there until he voluntarily releases them himself they shall fall into more numerous and more important calamities. On which account all men, being afraid of those threatenings of the gods, fear to depart from life by their own act, but only gladly welcome death when it comes in old age, trusting that the deliverance of their soul will take place with the full consent of those who have the power to sanction it. And this doctrine we ourselves believe.

Suicide was thus a rebellion for the Pythagoreans, an unruly escape from a destiny laid down by the superior powers. "We must wait," they said, "to be set free in God's appointed time." Pythagoras's own theory of numbers further strengthened this feeling about the wrongness of suicide. There were, he said, just so many souls available for use in the world at any given moment. By suicide you upset the spiritual mathematic; for it might well be that no other soul was ready to fill the gap caused in the world by your so sudden and arbitrary exit.

Plato in the *Phaedo* makes Socrates echo and extend the Orphic idea about suicide. Man is God's chattel: self-destruction is a mutilation of divine property. The passage has played so great a part in the moral history of suicide that it is worth quoting at some length.

> The reason [against suicide] which the secret teaching [1] gives, that man is in a kind of prison, and that he may not set himself free, nor escape from it, seems to be rather profound and not easy

[1] The esoteric system of the Pythagoreans.

to fathom. But I do think, Cebes, that it is true that the Gods are our guardians, and that we men are a part of their property. . . . If one of your possessions were to kill itself, though you had not signified that you had wished it to die, should you not be angry with it? Should you not punish it, if punishment were possible? . . . In the same way perhaps it is not unreasonable to hold that no man has a right to take his own life, but that he must wait until God sends some necessity upon him, as has now been sent upon me.

Further, in the eyes of Socrates, a mortal is not merely the property of the gods; he is their soldier too. A man's life is like a soldier's watch, and for this reason suicide is tantamount to desertion. Neither men nor soldiers should leave their posts without orders from their superior. Plato, however, can by no means be ranked altogether in the anti-suicide camp. The extreme desirability of death and the ideas of immortality expressed in the *Phaedo* have been a strong pro-suicide force. So moved was Cleombrotus, a young Greek philosopher, by the very reading of it, that the dialogue is said to have been directly responsible for his throwing himself into the sea.[1] Further, Plato admits that in certain cases of *necessitas*, such as extreme and incurable illness, suicide may be justified. "If any man," he says, " labour of an incurable disease, he may dispatch himself, if it be to his good." Plato represents, in fact, a guarded middle position. This position the later philosophers did not try to take by storm. It was unnecessary to do so. By simply extending Plato's *necessitas*, by making it a question of in-dividual decision, they made it applicable to any and every case. After all, they argued, only the suicide knows when

[1] Cf., *Paradise Lost*, Book III.
> " And he who, to enjoy
> Plato's Elysium, leaped into the sea,
> Cleombrotus."

Milton has allowed Adam to express his adverse attitude to suicide at some length in Book X.

life is absolutely insupportable to him; he is the judge of
what situation constitutes a *necessitas* for his own suicide.

The true interpretation of Plato's attitude was kept alive
by his spiritual successors, the Neo-Platonists. Though
Plotinus also speaks of a " stern necessity " which may
sometimes excuse suicide, his outlook, if anything, is more
severe than Plato's own. " The soul," he writes in the
Ennead, " will wait for the body to be completely severed
from it; then it makes no departure, it simply finds itself
free. . . . There must be no withdrawal as long as there is
any hope of progress." These ideas were for Plotinus
maxims to be put into practical application. Suspecting his
friend and biographer, Porphyry, of wishing to commit
suicide, he went out of his way to dissuade him. Porphyry
tells how Plotinus " came unexpectedly to my house where
I had secluded myself, and told me that my decision to
commit suicide sprung not from reason but from mere
melancholy ". Plotinus's counsel was altogether practical; he
prescribed rest and departure from Rome, a treatment that
proved successful.

The Aristoteleans in their condemnation of suicide used
very different arguments from the Pythagoreans. Their
attitude carries a certain weight to-day. In his review of
justice, Aristotle is led to consider whether a man can do an
injustice to himself, and this brings him to suicide. Suicide,
Aristotle says, is a voluntary injury not committed as a
lawful retaliatory act.

> Therefore the suicide commits injustice; but against whom?
> It seems to be against the state rather than against himself; for
> he suffers voluntarily, and nobody suffers injustice voluntarily.
> This is why the state exacts a penalty; suicide is punished by
> certain marks of dishonour, *as being an offence against the state.*

The validity of this argument depends on the old question whether the individual exists for the state or the state
for the individual. Even the later philosophers rightly

recognized the suicide's social responsibility, and Seneca admitted the wrongness of the act where duties to the state, or even to the family, were sacrificed. Cicero, realizing that the same course might be right for one man and wrong for another, makes a more subtle distinction, based not on circumstances but on character. " Diversity of character," he says, " carries with it so great significance that suicide may be for one man a duty, for another [under the same circumstances] a crime." Cicero's position, like that of certain other practical writers, is equivocal. He devoted a whole essay to the praise of Cato's life and death, and he often shows a sympathy for suicide. " The true point of time," he says, " in which a man should die, is when he can do it opportunely or with dignity to himself, without paying any regard to the length or shortness of his life ". On the other hand he as often condemns it : the suicide leaves his post; he shakes off the destiny with which the divine will has charged him. In the *Somnum Scipionis* the shades of his ancestors even tell the young Scipio that he can never rejoin them in the next world if he commits suicide. Both Caesar and Plutarch were more definitely opposed, though the only thing that the latter could find to account for man's attachment to life was " the fear of death ". He was, however, antagonistic to the whole Stoic position and went so far as to write an attack on their practice and doctrine.

As time went on philosophy retreated from Aristotle's extreme position. The duty to the state was not considered to be so exclusive that the *private* individual must be responsible to the latter even for his manner of dying. The official, indeed, must stay the course while he could still be useful; but the private citizen might leave when he wished.

Elsewhere when speaking of courage, Aristotle condemns suicide as an uncourageous act.

> To seek death [he says] in order to escape from poverty, or the pangs of love, or from pain or sorrow, is not the act of a

courageous man, but rather of a coward; for it is weakness to fly
from troubles, and the suicide does not endure death because it is
noble to do so, but to escape evil.

Seneca himself agrees with him to the extent that, if it is
brave to seek death, it is even braver to stay and endure
evil. The whole question of the bravery or cowardice of
suicide is always being rehashed, and the truth lies somewhere between the idea of the suicide-hero and the dictum
of Sir Thomas Browne, that the suicide is not one who disdains death, but one who fears life. To face any form of
death voluntarily obviously demands great bravery from
most people; conversely it is often an act of cowardice to
turn one's back on life. We are up against an irresolvable
antinomy, and we have to decide each case on its own
merits. There will nearly always be a quaint mixture, fear
and bravery going hand in hand.

As one would expect, the primitive and popular hate of
suicide barely makes its way through to philosophy, though
the Orphic beliefs with their religious basis must have preserved something of this feeling and of the idea that the
suicide was unclean and tainted by his violent death. It is
interesting, however, though not surprising, to find the instinctive horror coming out in literature. Vergil, in the
Aeneid, clearly represents the popular attitude. Having
crossed the Acheron and penetrated into hell he finds
there the ghosts of those who had committed suicide when
mad, together with the spirits of infants (cf., the unbaptized infant of Christianity and the dead children of the
Baganda tribe; see page 38), and certain others. Here is
the passage referring to the suicides:

> *Proxima deinde tenent maesti loca qui sibi letum*
> *Insontes peperere manu, lucemque perosi*
> *Projecere animas. Quam vellent aethere in alto*
> *Nunc et pauperiem et duros perferre labores!*

Fas obstat, tristisque palus inamabilis undae
Alligat et noviens Styx interfusa coercet.[1]

There is obviously no moral bias here, any more than
where dead infants are concerned, for the suicides were of
" guiltless " mind. The condemnation and horror are
irrational, primitive, and semi-religious.

The opposing philosophic forces which condoned and
even tended to promote suicide were mustered under the
three banners of Stoicism, Epicureanism, and Cynicism. The
Cynics, the earliest of these philosophical sects, exerted
the least direct influence. A certain pedantry, of which
Diogenes's actions are typical, and an absolute disregard for
science and liberal culture, sidetracked the movement. It is
interesting none the less to find that Diogenes himself apparently committed suicide by holding his breath. Stoicism,
which developed certain cynical features such as personal
reliance and the discipline of character, exerted a wider actual
influence and is more intimately connected with our subject.
" To live consistently with nature " was the reasonable aim
of the Stoics and the goal which men such as Attalus, Seneca
and Epictetus, set themselves in the first century A.D. These
philosophers did not separate body from soul into an absolute duality, nor did they expect to retain a personal
individuality after death. Believing in the certainty of know-

---

[1] *Aeneid*, vi, 426.

> And next are those, who, hateful of the day,
> With guiltless hands their sorrowing lives have ta'en,
> And miserably flung their souls away.
> How gladly now, in upper air again,
> Would they endure their poverty and pain!
> It may not be. The fates their doom decide
> Past hope, and bind them to this sad domain.
> Dark round them rolls the sea, unlovely tide;
> Ninefold the waves of Styx those dreary realms divide.
>
> *Translation by* FAIRFAX TAYLOR.

ledge and the possibility of appropriate action, they allowed themselves to be guided by reason, and supported by will.

Epicureanism, developing coincidently with Stoicism, equally concerns our subject. It can fairly be called the first materialist philosophy. Nature, escaping from capricious providence, was for the first time ruled by scientific law, and the soul putting off incorporeality became compounded of four atoms. Pleasure and pain were the only human driving forces; the only use of knowledge was to promote happiness, and the only point of the virtues was that they tended to maintain it. A reasonable utilitarianism was the keynote of the movement, and Epicurus himself said, " Vain is the discourse of that philosopher by whom no suffering is healed."

As touching suicide there are two points in these advocate philosophies which are worth noting. First of all there is the emphasis and responsibility which is placed in each case upon the individual. The decline of the small city state in Greece, and later in Rome, left the individual in isolation, without precedents for conduct or rules for thought; he had nowhere to turn but inward to himself. Thus the individual became of importance, and such isolation together with the necessity for thought leads, as we shall see, to suicide. Secondly, these philosophies are pronouncedly rational; they mark, in fact, the first triumph of reason. And reason, like isolation, leads to an increase in suicide, for reason sees a variety of situations in which death is preferable to a painful or dishonourable life. In classical times, as later after the Renaissance, the birth of reason meant an increase in self-destruction. Epictetus admirably voices the reasoned attitude, as it bears on suicide. " Above all things remember that the door is open. Be not more timid than boys at play. As they, when they cease to take pleasure in their games, declare they will no longer play, so do you, when all things begin to pull upon you, retire."

These Stoic and Epicurean philosophers looked on suicide
as a purely personal affair, lawful under almost any circumstances, and surely wise where honour, or disease and old
age, were involved. Of the last, Seneca says:

> I will not relinquish old age if it leaves my better part intact.
> But if it begins to shake my mind, if it destroys its faculties one
> by one, if it leaves me not life but breath, I will depart from
> the putrid or tottering edifice. I will not escape by death from
> disease so long as it may be healed, and leaves my mind unim-
> paired. I will not raise my hand against myself on account of pain,
> for so to die is to be conquered. But if I know that I must suffer
> without hope of relief, I will depart, not through fear of pain
> itself, but because it prevents all for which I would live.

Musonius, a fellow Stoic, puts a similar idea with graphic
clearness:

> Just as a landlord who has not received his rent, pulls down the
> doors, removes the rafters, and fills up the well, so I seem to be
> driven out of this little body, when nature, which has let it to
> me, takes away one by one, eyes and ears, hands and feet. I will
> not therefore delay longer, but will cheerfully depart as from a
> banquet.

The way a man died was his own affair: a serious affair certainly and to be approached with wisdom and gravity, but
none the less a private matter. "As I choose the ship," Seneca
says, " in which I will sail, and the house I will inhabit, so I
will choose the death by which I leave life. . . . In no matter
more than in death should we act according to our desire."

Suicide became in time the final resource, and the last
weapon in the battery of Stoic argument: Man was uncon-
querable, the dignity of human personality, the determination of the human will, need never be broken, for the door
was always open; man's last and most faithful ally, death,
would never desert him. Thanks to the proximity of death,
man stood invincible on earth: his spirit need never be
subdued, his body need never be tamed. Amid the treach-
ery, corruption, and horror, that surrounded the Imperial

Court, the philosophers clung to their right to die with a strange joy and pathetic tenacity. Seneca, again their most eloquent spokesman, and eventually the victim of Nero's malice cried:

> To death alone it is due that life is not a punishment, that, erect beneath the frowns of fortune, I can preserve my mind unshaken and master of itself. . . . I see the rack and the scourge, and the instruments of torture adapted to every limb and to every nerve; but I also see Death. She stands beyond my savage enemies, beyond my haughty fellow-countrymen. Slavery loses its bitterness when by a step I can pass to liberty. Against all the injuries of life, I have the refuge of death.

And again he says:

> Foolish man, what do you bemoan, and what do you fear? Wherever you look there is an end of evils. You see that yawning precipice? It leads to liberty. You see that flood, that river, that well? Liberty houses within them. You see that stunted, parched, and sorry tree? From every branch liberty hangs. Your neck, your throat, your heart are all so many ways of escape from slavery. . . . Do you enquire the road to freedom? You shall find it in every vein of your body.

Viewed from this angle, suicide appears as a keynote of the Stoic doctrines.

These philosophers, unlike many others, practised nobly the death they preached. There is something almost amusing about Zeno's end. Founder of the Stoic philosophy, he had always preached that a man was at liberty to abandon life and should be ready to do so if ever he found it not worth living. He had lived to the age of ninety-eight without meeting any *contretemps* sufficiently serious to warrant his departure; at that advanced age, however, as he was leaving his school of philosophy, he fell down and put a toe out of joint. So disgusted was he at this, and so convinced of the vanity of the world, that he went home and hung himself on the spot, bearing honourable but tardy witness to his own credo.

Cleanthes, his successor, lived up to his beliefs in a less impetuous fashion.

As a cure for some trifling indisposition—a gumboil apparently—his doctor ordered him to knock off food for two days. The treatment having proved effective, he was told that he might return to a normal diet again; he continued, however, to refuse food, saying that " as he had advanced so far on his journey towards death, he would not retreat ", and so in due course he starved himself. The tradition did not die with these early Stoics. Cocceius Nerva, the favourite of the Emperor Tiberius, staging his death as a philosophic protest against the extravagance of the Imperial court, imitated Cleanthes in self-starvation.

Attalus, another Stoic advocate of suicide, also flourished in the reign of Tiberius—if one can be said to flourish on bread and water. Even this diet he only continued owing to the persuasion of his friends, among whom was Seneca. The latter records Attalus's advice to Marcellinus, who, suffering from an incurable disease, was contemplating suicide.

> Be not tormented, my Marcellinus [he said], as if you were deliberating of any great matter. Life is a thing of no dignity or importance. Your very slaves, your animals, possess it in common with yourself : but it is a great thing to die honourably, prudently, bravely. Think how long you have been engaged in the same dull course : eating, sleeping, and indulging your appetites. This has been the circle. Not only a prudent, brave, or a wretched man may wish to die, but even a fastidious one.

As a result of his counsel, Marcellinus quietly starved himself to death.

However, it remained for Seneca—more of a philosopher in his death than in his life—to create the final type and example of Stoic suicide. Having fallen from the Imperial favour, the only course open to him was to forestall Nero's vengeance with his own hand. He was at his villa when the news came that the Emperor desired his death. Far from

L. ANN. SENECA

(Anonymous 17th century engraving)

THE DEATH OF SENECA

being upset, he devoted himself to rallying the friends who
were gathered round him. While he restrained their tears
by words, threats, and exhortations, he asked :

> " Where is now your philosophy ? Where are now those well-
> considered precepts which for so many years you have kept against
> adversity ? Who has not suffered from the ignoble cruelty of
> Nero ? Nothing else was to be expected but that, after killing
> his mother and his brother, he should send to death his teacher
> and preceptor."

Having determined to take his life, he embraced his wife
Paulina, but she, refusing to be left alone, insisted on sharing
his death. Their embraces, as Tacitus says, were loosened
only by the steel which freed them.[1] At the very last Seneca
showed the courage and consideration of the true Stoic.
Exhausted by the pain of a clumsy wound, he persuaded his
wife to be carried into a neighbouring chamber, " lest by his
torments he should disturb her and lest he should himself
slip into an unworthy impatience at seeing her suffer ".

Epicurus had said that one must weigh carefully whether
one preferred to wait for death or artificially to forestall it.
His followers believed that the door was always open and
were hardly behind the Stoics in living up to their beliefs.
Lucretius, the Epicurean poet, had written :

> If one day, as well may happen, life grows wearisome, there
> only remains to pour a libation to death and oblivion. A drop
> of subtle poison will gently close your eyes to the sun, and waft
> you smiling into the eternal night whence everything comes and
> to which everything returns.

In due course the wearisome day came and the poet's suicide
followed. Atticus, the friend of Cicero, and the philosopher
Diodorus, were other eminent Epicureans who took their
own lives. It is Petronius, however, who strikes the typical

---

[1] Paulina did not, in fact, die. Nero insisted on her rescue and
treatment.

F

Epicurean note in a death that may be contrasted with Seneca's. Petronius, the Beau Brummel of his time, the *arbiter elegantiarum* of the court and the model of Imperial voluptuaries, was an extraordinary figure. Not satisfied with being a person of exquisite manners and perfect taste (and possibly the author of the *Satyricon*), Petronius was also an admirable provincial administrator and an able consul. Thrown out of favour by a court intrigue, and believing that Nero had decided on his death, he resolved to forestall the blow. Gathering his friends at his villa, he opened and closed his veins at pleasure; in the intervals he slept or sauntered round in conversation. His last hours character-istically enough were not spent in consideration of the immortality of the soul, but in an exchange of witticisms, scandal, and the important nothings of the hour. Finally, having settled all his business, his veins were opened for the last time, and in the midst of a cheerful and magnificent banquet he died as gracefully as he had lived.

Petronius was a sophisticated person, influenced by and conversant with contemporary and philosophical ideas. His death is understandable. One may say the same of people like the poet Lucan. The latter opened his veins and as the moment of death approached began to repeat some lines from his own *Pharsalia*, descriptive of a similar suicide. But what of the other people?—the nonentities whom philosophy guided to one suicide or another? That remarkable figure Hegesias, who wrote a work on self-starvation and was known to antiquity as the " Orator of Death ", proclaimed that the fleeting pleasures of life were worthless and that death was the only wise alternative. So successful was his teaching that he initiated an *epidemic* of suicide. The civil authorities were forced to take steps, and Ptolemy Philadelphus expelled the dangerous advocate from Egypt. In what way and for what reasons did and could such philo-sophies make death palatable to the man in the street?

Stoicism [says Lecky] taught men to hope little, but to fear nothing. It did not array death in brilliant colours as the path to positive felicity, but it endeavoured to divest it, as the end of suffering, of every terror. Life lost much of its bitterness when men had found a refuge from the storms of fate, a speedy deliverance from dotage and pain. Death ceased to be terrible when it was regarded rather as a remedy than as a sentence. Life and death in the Stoical system were attuned to the same key.

A conception of death the same, or similar to this, extended far beyond philosophical circles. Death did not present the haunting and fearful uncertainty which had characterized it in earlier and more superstitious times and which it was again to assume later. There was no idea of hell, and the absence of all sense of sin left people free from the fear of a later and eternal retribution. Death was indeed a problem, something to be argued about objectively, but it did not enter people's heads that once the transit was over anything unpleasant or worthy of fear might be in store for them. Cicero crystallizes the feelings of the educated man. " Souls either remain after death or they perish in death. If they remain they are happy; if they perish they are not wretched." the tone of such arguments reminds one of the end of Antoninus Pius. When the dying Emperor was asked by a tribune what was to be the watchword of the night, he replied magnificently, " *aequanimitas* ".

Current ideas about life and the after-world we may say tended to make equanimity a possible mood in which to approach death. But that is only one side of the picture. The other is the contempt for pain characteristic of the ancient world, and which we have met in an even greater degree among primitives (see page 19 *et seq.*). It is difficult for the modern European with his extreme sensibility to realize this indifference to pain, though the examples that follow prove its existence clearly enough. Athenaeus, for instance, relates that some of the Thracians at their banquets used to *play the game of hanging*. They fix a round noose to some high place, exactly beneath which they place a stone . . . then they cast lots, and he who draws the lot, holding a sickle in his hand, stands upon the stone, and puts his neck into the halter. Another person then moves the stone from under him, and if he cannot cut the rope in time with his sickle, he is hung; and the rest laugh, thinking his death good sport.

There is a natural and lighthearted contempt of danger here, that outdoes the Stoics themselves.

Secondly, Frazer tells us that at Rome in the time of the Punic wars it was not only possible but easy to secure candidates for execution at the cost of 5 *minae* (about £20), to be paid to the dead man's heirs. Such competition was there to die at this price that many people secured the privilege by offering to be beaten to death rather than executed—a more painful and spectacular bargain. As far as can be judged these candidates for execution were beheaded or cudgelled solely to provide amusement and a good " turn " for jaded spectators. Real death could thus be the fare of the " theatre-going public ". Other explanations are that these candidates were either offering to act as living funerary sacrifices, or as substitutes for condemned criminals. At all events the facts remain. They prove an absolute disregard for pain and death.

Added to this almost physiological insensibility, there were contributory influences, active at the time when the Stoic and Epicurean doctrines were at their height, and tending to make suicide easy and acceptable. In the century that preceded, and in that which followed, the birth of Christ, the upper stratum of society was in a state of turmoil. Civil wars followed one upon another, spilt blood was not remarkable, and victory was usually to the strong and unscrupulous. The despotism and irrational cruelty of a Nero left none of the upper class in security. Unless it were possible to develop an indifference to death, life for these people would have been an intolerable nightmare of fears, tremors, and tortured expectations. To live at all it was necessary to be brave.

Thus both a natural disregard of pain, and a temporary state of social uncertainty and danger, predisposed the educated to accept the doctrines of suicide contained in the Stoic and Epicurean philosophies. These provided a rational and dignified basis from which to face a very difficult situation. Physical courage and the state of society needed only the stimulus of philosophy to elevate suicide to the place and popularity which it enjoyed in the time of Seneca.

III. LAWS AND PENALTIES

Broadly speaking, law and custom regarding suicide in the ancient world divides conveniently into two types, one deriving from religion and popular superstition, and the other having a practical and economic basis. The first type, being typical of primitive periods, is commonest in early Greece; later, as the rationalization of the Mediterranean progressed and intelligence was exalted as against the other faculties, this type tends to decrease, and among the educated in Rome only survives in the pontifical law, whose authority in the Empire received a tolerant and half-humorous acknowledgment. By contrast the penalties with an avowedly economic basis, not recognized in the Periclean age, increase as time goes on. With the development of standing armies and large slave estates they become of considerable importance.

The religious prejudice against suicides, as we have shown, derives from the fear of the ghost and the idea of blood guilt; this prejudice found expression in various laws and customs in the Greek cities. First it is interesting to discover that usually such laws and customs were inapplicable to suicides who died through voluntary starvation. This death was presumably a calm and considered action and, as such, was believed to be free from all the agony, rancour, and perturbation which made the ordinary suicide haunt his fellow-men after death. Secondly, and more obviously important, there was no physical violence, no blood guilt, no idea of the sudden and protesting wrench of the soul from the body, a parting of which the ancients were most apprehensive.

The first case of discrimination against a suicide occurs in the *Iliad*, where Ajax after his suicide before Troy is *buried*, and not cremated as would have been the ordinary procedure with so illustrious a warrior. There seems, however, a certain amount of doubt whether the denial of cremation was ever the usual penalty for Greek suicides. At Athens criminals, and more particularly those convicted of pillaging the temples, were refused cremation and buried in a sort of open ditch; but there is no evidence to show that this usage was generally applied to suicides. If such a penalty existed it would have arisen owing to the primitive idea that fire is holy and must not be contaminated with anything unclean. The regular Athenian punishment visited on the suicide's corpse was the cutting off of the hand which had been the instrument of death. Even this penalty, founded on primitive ideas of superstition, probably had a limited application. Plato, in his *Laws*, says that the man who commits suicide " when he is not compelled to it by the occurrence of some intolerable and inevitable misfortune, nor by falling into some disgrace that is beyond remedy or endurance " must be buried according to religious law, and adds,

> for those thus destroyed the tombs shall be, first, in an isolated position with not even one adjacent; and, secondly, they shall be buried in those borders of the twelve districts [of Athens] which are barren and nameless, without note, and with neither head-stone nor name to indicate the tombs.

Demonassa, Queen of Cyprus, who herself committed suicide, enforced even stricter laws against self-murderers. They were allowed no funeral rites at all and were left unburied (the second penalty probably being a product of the primitive superstition that no soul could find rest until covered with soil.) In Thebes they were equally uncompromising, and the Spartans even refused an honourable burial to Artemidorus, who sacrificed his life unnecessarily fighting against the Persians at the battle of Plataea. The Spartans are certain to have at all times been most antagonistic, and within the close and compelling framework of their state so individualistic an action must, at best, have been an exceptional occurrence. Montaigne tells the following story of a Lacedaemonian child who was sold as a slave. Rather than perform abject and servile tasks (he was apparently sent to fetch a chamber pot) he flung himself headlong from the top of his master's house, saying, " Thou shalt see whom thou hast bought; for it were a shame for me to serve, having libertie so neere at hand." It is worth noticing, however, that this sort of suicide takes place outside the social framework. The suicide of the Spartan king, Cleomenes, also took place under peculiar circumstances. He had just returned from a compulsory exile; he was cordially hated by the citizens; and he was in no sense a real member of the community. The same may be said of Pausanias, who fled to sanctuary and there starved to death. Like Cleomenes, he had turned his hand against the Lacedaemonians and stood outside the Spartan framework. The voluntary death of the Spartan as citizen and soldier comes, as we have seen, under the heading of institutional suicide.

Plutarch, in his *Mulierum Virtutes*, tells how the inhabitants of Miletos, where apparently no anti-suicide legislation existed, combated an epidemic of self-destruction among the women of the island by ordaining that those " who hanged themselves should be carried out to burial through the market place ". The fear of shame and exposure in this case had the desired effect, and the epidemic ceased without the imposition of further penalties.

Parallel to the suicide opposition which from scattered references we can trace in most parts of Greece, there was undoubtedly a line of opinion, strengthening as we approach the Roman period, favourable to judicious self-destruction. Such self-destruction is obviously closely connected with euthanasia and one is reminded of the regularity with which the Spartans, and others to a lesser degree, exposed their weak infants, leaving them to die on the mountains rather than to continue a sick and miserable existence. At Ceos, the home of Simonides, whose people were responsible for achieving the improvements in lethal drugs which eventually made hemlock a practical instrument of state execution, suicide was a legally recognized death. It is reliably reported that those over sixty were allowed, or perhaps even expected, to take their own lives by poison. In defence of this practice Donne pointed out that if the state may take life, if it may dispose of the criminal and the traitor, it surely also has power to give permission to the individual to dispatch himself.

Montaigne recounts how Pompey witnessed the end of an aged Cean lady who availed herself of the island privilege.

A woman of great authority, having first yeelded an accompt unto her Citizens, and shewed good reasons why she was resolved to end her life, earnestly entreated Pompey to be an assistant at her death, that so it might be esteemed more honourable . . . She had lived foure score and ten yeares in a most happy state of minde and body, but then lying on her bed, better adorned than before she was accustomed to have it, and leaning on her elbow, thus she bespake : As for my part, having hitherto ever tasted the favourable visage of fortune, for feare the desire of living over-long should make me taste of her frownes, with an happy and successful end, I will now depart, and licence the remainder of my soule. . . . That done, having preached unto, and exhorted all her people and kinsfolks, to an unitie and peace, and divided her goods amongst them . . . with an assuredly-staide hand she tooke the cup, wherein the poyson was, and having made her vowes unto Mercurie, and prayers, to conduct her to some happy place in the other world, roundly swallowed that mortal potion . . .

The Greek colonists who founded Marseilles brought with them a similar usage. There the magistrates kept a supply of poison always at hand for those who, upon alleging adequate reasons, obtained permission from the Senate to kill themselves. It seems probable that in many other places, Athens included, the right to commit suicide must have been similarly granted under especially trying circumstances. Plato speaks of suicide as culpable only " when not legally ordered by the state ", and a classical writer sums-up the general position as follows:

> Let the man who wishes to live no longer explain his reasons to the Senate, and, having obtained their permission, leave this life. . . . Let the unfortunate recount his sorrows, so that the magistrate may furnish him with a remedy and put an end to his misery.

Perhaps even later in Rome, some arrangement of this sort may have at one time existed, for we find the orator Quintilian demanding of the Senate leave to die, as though this was recognized as a natural prelude to lawful suicide. It is probable that such permissions were sometimes granted on inadequate grounds, as Libanius of Antioch, the friend of Julian the Apostate, pokes fun at the practice. Amongst other things he makes Timon the Misanthrope ask leave to commit suicide since, though he is pledged by profession to hate all the world, he can't help loving Alcibiades.

With the decline of the city state and the growth of the Roman Empire, measures against suicides, based either on politico-ethical grounds as at Sparta, or on religious grounds as at Athens, tend to disappear. In Imperial Rome the last, and apparently the only vestige of the latter, survives in the pontifical law. This canonical legislation, whose authority was symbolized in the person of the Pontifex Maximus or chief priest (who in Imperial times was usually the Emperor) laid down that suicide by *hanging* involved both a punishment and an expiation. The former consisted in the refusal of burial; the fact that a similar privation was the penalty for being struck by lightning, shows the superstitious and non-moral nature of the punishment. The rite of expiation was more curious. On the day when the dead man's children celebrated their yearly remembrance—the *parentalia*—a doll was strung up. The connection of this imitative hanging with religious sacrifices, and more particularly with the swinging festival at Athens, has been shown above. It was a primitive and protective measure.

With this exception, custom and law in Imperial Rome were moved by no anti-suicide prejudices of ethical or religious origin. Where practical and economic issues were not involved, Rome recognized the *liber mori*. However, as time went on, certain developments increased the economic repercussions of suicide, and the right to die became strictly modified for certain classes of people. Suicide *per se*, however, never at any time became a penal offence in Rome; no civil statute declared it to be either a crime or a misdemeanour, and for the general citizen no punishment or penalty attended an unsuccessful attempt. Such legislation as dealt with suicide, approached the subject either from a military or a fiscal point of view. It considered the act not as a crime abstractedly, but rather weighed how far its commission affected the army or the treasury. It is important, however, to notice that to the man in the street, ignorant of the facts and causes, it would appear as though punishment *was* imposed on suicide *per se*. This in its turn would help to strengthen any prejudice against it and reinforce the primitive horror.

For three classes in Italy suicide was punishable—people accused of crime, soldiers, and slaves. In each case it is easy to detect the purely practical and economic causes underlying the deterrent. As to the first class: felony was usually punishable by death and the confiscation of property. Suicide when under arrest thus robbed the treasury of the goods which would have accrued to it in the case of a conviction, and also secured the suicide's property and chattels for his family. Domitian effectively closed this leak in the revenues by decreeing that those who killed themselves to escape a conviction were without legal successors, and that their goods were to devolve upon the state. Roman justice, however, provided that this penalty should only be applicable in cases where the suicide was accused of a crime which in itself was punishable by confiscation. As a rider to this law we find a note added to the *Digests* to the effect that it is not customary to wear mourning for those who thus kill themselves not *taedio vitae* but *mala conscientia*. (The same also applied to suicide by hanging, but here the basic prejudice was religious.)

That some injustice existed in this law of confiscation is evident, for no loophole was provided for the accused yet *innocent* man who committed suicide. Under Antoninus Pius the law was readjusted to remedy this unfairness. In its final form it allowed the relatives of accused suicides to plead in their defence. If their innocence could be established, the state had no claim upon their property which passed to the natural heirs.

The second class discriminated against were soldiers, and this is perhaps natural, for the state would wish to have an absolute control over its defensive arm. The suicide of a soldier was regarded not as an individual death, but as an action which weakened by a tiny fraction the effective force of the Roman armies and which, if it spread and was encouraged, might easily become a serious menace to the legions. The first reproof of suicide in this connection occurs under the Emperor Marcian, when it is laid down that a soldier who commits suicide is in every way worthy of punishment " unless his act is compelled by weariness of life or the impatience of pain; for he who does not spare himself will hardly spare another ". Excuses such as pain and weariness of life provided large loopholes, and it is not surprising to find the law restated later with more precision and severity. This change may have been partly stimulated by the growing difficulty of raising voluntary troops from among the native Italians and by the decline of the martial spirit at home. At all events we find Hadrian assimilating suicide to desertion : a departure from life is considered to deserve the same penalties as departing from the standard. In the *Digests* the whole position is finally regulated as follows :

1. The *attempt to commit* suicide for no good reason, or merely to escape from military service, is punishable with death.

2. The *attempt* on grounds of depression, great sorrow, madness, etc., is punishable with dismissal from the service.

3. If the successful suicide takes his life in shame or fear on account of some military misdemeanour, his will is invalid, his goods go to the state, and his name and memory are dishonoured.

4. Conversely, his will is valid if he takes his life for any good personal reason, such as extreme pain, madness, etc. If he has made no will, his goods go to his next of kin or to the Legion.[1]

The last class for whom suicide was illegal were the slaves. In this case, naturally enough, not the Digests of Roman Law, but the anger or clemency of the master appointed the punishment. Usually burial was denied to the dead slave, and he may be supposed to have been thrown into the infamous pits which received the bodies of criminals. The statutes of the famous funerary college or sodality of Lanuvium, drawn up with the approval of the ruling class for a body of very poor men, largely recruited from the slave population, throw an interesting light on this aspect of suicide. They declare that the alumni are not to contribute to the expenses of a funeral for one of their members who

---

[1] An inscription recording the gift of a free burial ground, is quoted by Adams from *Spons Miscell. Erudit. Antiquitatis.* Discharged soldiers who have hanged themselves are here classed with those who have taken to prostitution.

has committed suicide, *whatever his reasons*. When one considers what a savage punishment non-burial constituted at
that time, and what importance certain classes always attach
to a " decent funeral ", the deterrent effects of such a statute
are obvious. By every means in his power the master was
determined to secure the use of his slave until a natural
death should part them. A slave's suicide might represent
considerable financial loss to him and was to be discouraged
in every way possible.

On the other hand, it appears that if a slave attempted
suicide, his master could not deduct his wages as a punishment. He could only deduct the money which he spent in
restoring his slave to health. The legal basis for this leniency Ulpian states as follows : *licet etiam servis naturaliter in
suum corpus saevire*. Even the worm has a right to turn
against itself. This right, though legally claimed, can hardly
have been a social axiom. Symmachus, who bought twenty-
nine Saxon prisoners to grace the public games that he was
giving in honour of his son, was outraged when they all
strangled themselves on the very day of the celebrations.
He refers in a shocked way to the "impious hands" that had
robbed Rome of her sport. The values involved in this story
make it interesting to reflect that Symmachus was one of the
finest of the late pagans, and living in the fourth century is
said to have embodied most of the old aristocratic and republican virtues.

In another aspect suicide by a slave fell directly under the
civil code. The latter decreed for the protection of the
master that any slave who killed, or tried to kill, himself
within six months of purchase, might be lawfully returned
to his former owner, and the transaction declared null and
void. Suicidal tendencies were thus classed among the
other serious blemishes, such as hidden physical infirmity
or a criminal nature, which in a slave were considered good
enough reason to invalidate a deed of sale. Rome, altogether

practical, begins and ends its suicide penalties with a strict eye to the main chance. Denarii are at the bottom of their morality; the state treasury and the master's pocket create the criminality of self-destruction.

Classical times gave prominence to another type of suicide —the compulsory suicide—which has a legal and penal aspect. The germ of this compulsory suicide can be traced in the cup of hemlock and the principle that it represented, whereby the condemned took his own life almost with an air of volition. There was to be no wrenching of soul from body. By a sort of sophistry the state was able to disclaim responsibility for death, and evade the attentions of wronged and bitter ghosts. The first use of hemlock to which there is any reference is apparently the cup given to Theramenes, one of the thirty Tyrants, in 403 B.C.; thus when Socrates took it four years later, the custom in Greece was probably still young.

In Imperial Rome the idea of compelling a man to take his own life was abused and extended. It reached its culmination under Nero who, hoping to shift a burden of direct guilt from his shoulders, dispatched numbers of people by this expedient. Among them were Seneca and, virtually, Petronius. The choice of death, or *mortis arbitrium* as it was called, consisted usually of throwing a dagger and sword into the cell where a prisoner was confined, or even of presenting them by polite messenger at a man's villa or dinner table. It is cited as an example of Nero's cruelty that with these gifts went the tacit understanding that they must be employed within the hour. More considerate rulers had been accustomed to allow a day or at worst a forenoon. The tradition of the *mortis arbitrium* has by no means died out; it is a useful device still employed by rulers or governments doutful of the justice of their cause and unwilling to give their opponents a handle for retaliation such as an open execution would provide. Effective use of the *mortis arbitrium* was made in the Nazi

" clean-up " of June 1933, when Heines and others committed " suicide " in their cells. Another milder variant
of the same phenomenon, not always resulting in death, is
the " confession " of Russian political trials, when prisoners
are forced to condemn themselves out of their own mouths.

IV. CATO AND ANTONY

No mention has been made of the two most famous
suicides of the Ancient World—Cato and Antony. Opposed
in every sense, the contrast of their deaths is illuminating :
they stand at opposite poles, representing the philosophic
and the profane suicide.

Marcus Portius Cato " Uticensis ", great-grandson of the
Censor whose reiterated phrase, *delenda est Carthago*, for so
many years disturbed the business of the Senate, was born
into the revolutionary period which preceded the fall of the
Republic. Rarely have the will, the character, and the opportunity, been granted any man as they were granted Cato,
to make the facts of his life conform with his own ideal
pattern. Among lives that waver and change direction, that
calculate their aims upon opportunity, and cancel them with
altering circumstance, that have no port and only drift into
death, Cato seems almost inhumanly constant. He, if anyone, was impervious to circumstances, troublesome or advantageous; he was, what from the first he had decided to be, a
Roman in his own sense of the word : scrupulous, simple,
courageous, and above all and through all, absolutely just.
Such faults as he had were mostly inherent in the pattern
that he had chosen; he would not himself have wished to
alter them. To do so would have been in some degree to
modify the ideal which he had set himself. He was a man
whom history could flatter with plausibility. Sallust wrote :

He was one who chose to be, rather than to appear, good.
He was the very image of virtue, and in all points of disposition

more like to the gods than to men. He never did right that he might seem to do right, but because he could not do otherwise. That only seemed to him to be reasonable which was just. Free from all human vices, he was superior to the vicissitudes of human fortune.

One may question the relevance and practicability of Cato's life at the moment when he lived; its perfection as a pattern, however, and its value as an inspiration to later men, are certain. His life he moulded to a preconceived form, and this form he placed at the service of the Republic in a day when it was threatened by the illicit ambitions of both Caesar and Pompey. His career was consecrated to nothing but this—the maintenance of the liberty of the citizen and, thus, to the preservation of the traditional Roman virtues. Both his tactics and the vehicles through which he chose to work—the old Aristocratic party—can be criticized; Cato himself cannot. The Aristocratic party had no policy, and Cato was not the type of man to create one suitable to the times. A cleverer, quicker witted, more scheming and conciliatory politician, might have played off the opposing dictatorial forces one against the other, and have avoided the final catastrophe. Cato was not a politician. His austerity and integrity were not calculated to win approval; his denunciatory speeches were not oratory. Judged by common standards he was obstinate, short-sighted, and often intolerably rude; yet the obscure wisdom which directed him was not at fault, only by living as he did could he conform to the pattern which he had set himself.

His life is the same as his ideal. They do not diverge, and even Cato the boy fits into the pattern. Plutarch says that even in childhood he " displayed in speech, in countenance, and in his childish sports a nature that was inflexible, imperturbable, and altogether steadfast ". Even at that age he inspired among his friends and fellows the same personal devotion which he always aroused later.

When Cato was hauled off to prison from the Senate House, it was this devotion that prompted one of the Senators, as he stalked out angrily after him, to turn to Caesar saying that he preferred to be with Cato in prison than with Caesar in the Senate. Cato first distinguished himself in the fighting against Spartacus; after the operations, however, he refused the prize of valour that was bestowed on him, and thus set a precedent for the rest of his career. No honour did he ever accept, not even the right to wear the purple-bordered robe which a grateful Senate voted him many years later. His dress and habits were in keeping with his modesty; he never rode when he could walk, and to the horror of the *bourgeois* citizens often appeared to transact business barefooted and without his toga. The only indulgence which he allowed himself was the wine he took with his philosophy, for at his country villa he would sit up all night with his friends drinking and discoursing. In a person of so austere and determined a character, who was reputed never to smile, it is pleasant and almost unexpected to find extreme liberality and humane kindness. When he gave up his military tribuneship in Macedonia, men of the legion actually wept, and, sinking on their knees, kissed his hands as he left them. Dio Cassius says that though he was proud and unbending to his enemies, " he loved any one of the common people through pity for his weakness ". When the civil war broke out he laid it down as a maxim, with a clemency astounding in those times, that no Roman should be put to death except actually in battle, and that no hostile Roman town should be plundered.

His career as a public man was an exact illustration of his character. As Quaestor he reformed the city's finances and put down bribery; sent on a mission to Cyprus, he subdued the island peaceably and brought intact to the Senate more treasure than Pompey had done in all his triumphs;

G

forced to assume the tribuneship he combated the demagogic rascality of Metellus Nepos; lastly, to stem the anti-Republican tide he proposed himself consul, and characteristically failed in the elections for the simple reason that he refused to flatter or bribe the electors.

But time was moving on. Despite Cato's exhortations, the Senate quarrelled and wavered. There was little of the old virtue left to which he could appeal, and when in 49 B.C. Caesar crossed the Rubicon, no adequate force could be rallied to oppose him.

Thinking opposition from abroad was the only possible policy, Cato now followed Pompey into Greece. At the victory of Dyrrhachium, which is said to have been largely inspired by Cato's presence among the Republican soldiers, he actually wept when he saw the dead. Far above partisan issues, it was the suffering of Rome that made a settled sorrow rule his face in victory or defeat. Since Caesar's arrival in Italy he had not trimmed his beard nor worn a garland on his head, and subsequent to the battle of Pharsalus he never again reclined at meals in the Roman fashion, but sat, in sign of mourning.

Pompey's defeat left only one hope to the Republicans, a conflict in Africa. Cato accordingly set out for Libya. Having arrived, he made his headquarters at Utica and tried to rally the Republican party. His policy might have brought success, but Scipio's rashness and utter defeat at Thapsus put an end to his hopes. The old virtues, liberty and Republicanism, the things to which he had devoted his life, were dead and not to be resurrected. There remained nothing for him to do but die himself. Cato without his ideals, living in a sycophant and subservient Italy, could have no point or meaning.

> He had been endued by nature [says Cicero] with an austerity beyond belief, and he himself had strengthened it by unswerving consistence, and had remained ever true to his purpose, and fixed

resolve; and it was for him to die rather than look upon the face of a tyrant.

Caesar was now approaching, and perhaps the most touching thing in Cato's impressive life was his solicitude at this moment for his fellow Republicans and for the citizens of Utica. The latter he advised to make their peace with Caesar. When, however, they announced their intention of interceding for Cato, he replied that

> they must make no prayer for him; prayer belonged to the conquered, and the craving of grace to those who had done wrong; but for his part he had not only been unvanquished all his life, but was actually a victor now as far as he chose to be, and a conqueror of Caesar in all that was honourable and just.

His last three days he spent in evacuating the Senators and the Republican forces. Stationing himself at the gate of the city leading to the sea he assigned transports to the troops, many of whom were going on to Spain, supplied stores and provisions to those who were destitute, and with his usual passion for justice, saw to it that the natives were not plundered or abused.

On the last evening of his life he supped with the few friends that could not be persuaded to leave him, chief among them being the philosophers Apollonides and Demetrius, and his own son. After arguing long over the everfresh philosophical questions with which they were all familiar, and after counselling his son to retire from politics into the country as there was now no party worthy of a Cato's allegiance, he gave a few necessary instructions and retired to his chamber. There he lay down and began to read the *Phaedo*; chancing to look up, however, he noticed that his sword was not hanging in its proper place on the wall. Suspecting Cato's designs, his son had, in fact, removed it. When a servant, whom he sent, failed to bring it, Cato rose in great anger. Confronting his friends, he taxed them bitterly with trying to alter his fixed intention and with betraying those very stoic ideas in which they had always pretended to believe. "When I have come to a resolve," he said, "I must be master of the course which I decide to take." Bursting into tears and speechless, his friends withdrew. Soon the sword was sent to him, carried by a little child. Having tried its point, he laid it down and returned to Plato's dialogue on the soul. He is said to have read it through twice, before falling into a sleep so deep that those outside heard his breathing. About midnight he called for Butas, one of his freedmen, and sent him down to the sea to find out if all had set sail according to plan. Hearing that the embarkation had gone off successfully, but that a heavy storm was raging with a high wind, Cato "groaned with pity for those in peril at sea, and sent Butas down again, to find out whether anyone had been driven back by the storm and wanted any necessaries".

Such consideration for his friends was typical, and particularly touching since the night of his own death was already far gone.

> And now the birds were already beginning to sing, when he fell asleep again for a little while. And when Butas came and told him that the harbours were very quiet, he ordered him to close the door, throwing himself down upon his couch as if he were going to rest there for what still remained of the night. But when Butas had gone out, Cato drew his sword from its sheath and stabbed himself below the breast.[1]

Death did not come at once. His over-zealous friends again tried to save him; and again their efforts were thwarted by Cato himself. Hardly was this Roman dead before the whole people of Utica had assembled.

> With one voice they called Cato their saviour and benefactor, the only man who was free, the only one unvanquished. And this they continued to do even when word was brought that Caesar was approaching. But neither fear of the conqueror, nor a

[1] Plutarch.

desire to flatter him, nor their mutual strife and dissension, could blunt their desire to honour Cato. They decked his body in splendid fashion, gave it an illustrious escort, and buried it near the sea, where a statue of him now stands sword in hand. Then they turned their thoughts to their own salvation and that of their city[1]

Such, briefly, was the life and death of Cato of Utica. Rare among men he lived as he had intended; and died as he had lived. His death is a classic example among considered suicides. Gravely and sanely undertaken, it was the result not of passion, circumstance, or weakness, but of a certain philosophical upbringing shared by many men of his time, and of a way of life common to himself alone. It is in the " high Roman fashion ".

It would be hard to find a greater contrast than that provided by the lives of Cato and Marc Antony. Antony, with his shapely beard, broad forehead, and acquiline nose, an adept in the Asiatic style of oratory, proud to be called " Philathenian ", affecting a dress like Herakles, and driving around the Italian countryside with a yoke of lions in his chariot: Cato, unattractive looking, forceful and bald as a speaker, proud to own no other title than " Roman ", ascetic in habit, simple in dress and carriage. Fastidious in his friends, Cato knew only honest men. Antony, on the other hand, knew anyone who would amuse him, great and small, good and bad, and, as Cicero says, " often went about Italy at the head of pimps, prostitutes and buffoons ".

Cato never gave a thought to his future, but valued infinitely his good name; Antony, led by a world-wide ambition, cared not a jot for his reputation. Cato was just, Antony unjust both in his astounding liberalities and in his punishments (in this context, the murder and mutilation of Cicero are unforgivable). Cato was hardly capable of physical passion; Antony was a womanizer. The antitheses can be numbered indefinitely, for they only seem to have

[1] Plutarch.

shared courage and the ability to inspire devotion. Yet every comparison is unfair to Antony. There is a certain quality in all his actions which is lost in such comparison, but which throws a light and brilliance over his whole life. This quality will not allow him to be dull, petty, or predictable, residing in his caprice as much as in his courage, in his licentiousness as much as in his magnanimity, it makes everything that he does dramatic, poetic, and important. This is the indefinable quality that attracted Shakespeare and that makes Cleopatra say on his death:

> . . . Young boys and girls
> Are level now with men; the odds is gone,
> And there is nothing left remarkable,
> Beneath the visiting moon.

Standing so far apart, not even their suicides will unite these two men: there is only the link of a weapon between the cool, philosophical end of Cato, based on belief, and the passionate suicide of Antony. The latter does in fact exemplify a new type. Self-conscious and self-pitying, jesting and introspective, in disaster alternatively gay and melancholic, Antony seems like a Renaissance figure, and his death is of a sort that becomes familiar only with the Renaissance. Suicide that springs from one ruling passion, and the blankness that supervenes when that passion is thwarted by man or death, is not natural to classic times. The balance of the Roman world, the shrewd poise of the enemy Octavius, the caution of a Cicero, were not conducive to this sort of self-destruction. The Roman was a social animal and he rarely forgot that he was a Roman citizen; Antony never remembered it. It is this lack of a sense of proportion, of social and human dynamics, that hopelessly alienates him from men of the old Republican type. Not only was passionate suicide unusual, but when this passion, like Antony's, was love, the case became rare, anomalous, a matter for wonder. His contemporaries thought his conduct inexplicable. Passionate

love was to them a limited affair with known and compass-
able objectives. Where was Cleopatra's attraction, since (as
Plutarch astounded and uncomprehending, says) she " was
superior to Octavia neither in youthfulness nor beauty "?
The psychological complexity of Antony's passion, strange
to the old world, but not surprising to us, altogether
escaped them. At Actium his fleet simply would not believe
that he had left an empire for a woman. Besides his ships,
they knew that he could count on nineteen undefeated
legions and twelve thousand horse, and for seven days his
infantry waited, disregarding Caesar's messengers, and believing that he must return. Only on the eighth day, when
Canidius, their general, had fled, did his devoted troops in
bewilderment go over to Octavius.

There is a self-consciousness about Antony's relations
with Cleopatra which makes it seem almost as if he knew
that he was creating something unparalleled. There is a
tendency to dramatize himself, to fix the new complexity of
this passion on his own and the world's memory. Love is
not what Rome thinks; it has to do with more than the
Senate ever imagined, and not least with all sorts of colours,
shapes, tastes, verses, gold, and music. He is willing to give
his life to prove it; in fact he can do nothing else, since love
now stretches so far and embraces so much that there is no
evading its orders. This lover sees himself; and, as people
find who watch their own actions, all he does seems both
curiously sweet and strangely melancholy. Like the first
romantic, Antony labels Cleopatra and himself *The Inimitable Livers*, and when fortune changes he as solemnly hangs
out a new flag, inaugurating the society of *The Partners in
Death*. Intensely passionate, yet complex, Antony sees the
pathos of his own situation; he even sees that his passion is
making history.

The story of Antony's end is well enough known. But
there are several passages in Plutarch's account which are

worth noting as they emphasize the mixture of passion, romanticism, and the new complexity to which we have been referring. Taken on board Cleopatra's vessel as she scudded away from Actium, Antony " neither saw her, nor was seen by her. Instead, he went forward alone to the prow and sat down by himself in silence, holding his head in both hands ". And there he sat for three days without stirring and always in the same posture. Arrived in Africa, he sent Cleopatra forward into Egypt, but he himself wandered off along the Libyan coast, roaming from place to place in solitude, and shelving concrete issues. With him went only two friends, one of whom was that Lucilius who tried to save Brutus's life at Philippi. When at last he did reach Alexandria he

> forsook the city and the society of his friends, and built for him-
> self a dwelling in the sea at Pharos, by throwing a mole out into
> the water. Here he lived an exile from men, and declared that
> he was contentedly imitating the life of Timon, since, indeed, his
> experiences had been like Timon's; for he himself also had been
> wronged and treated with ingratitude by his friends, and therefore
> hated and distrusted all mankind.

Here is the ruler of half the Roman world behaving like a creation of Lamartine's. There is this difference, however : where his passion is involved he does not experience a moment's hesitation; he becomes a man of action again, knowing the precise moment when to leave Octavia, when to turn his back on a fleet and empire. Probably in the Libyan wanderings and the Alexandria solitude, for the first time he faced up to the price that he must pay for the new complexity of his love. Everything was demanded of him; in return he got not merely a fascinating and selfish woman's doubtful fidelity, but the romantic's realization of his own sacrifice, and his own realization of the greatness of his passion.

Having promised his enemies the price of his love, his mood changed. He was now decided. His passion was himself, and both should be wound up in a fit manner. The right note must be struck, and the pageant maintained. To the last minute he would watch the course of the strange new disease that he had created. His troops melted away, Herod went over to Octavius, and at last only Egypt remained to him. Now, however,

> none of these things greatly disturbed him, but, as if he gladly laid aside his hopes, that so he might lay aside his anxieties also, he forsook that dwelling of his in the sea . . . and after he had been received into the palace by Cleopatra, turned the city to the enjoyment of suppers and drinking bouts, and distribution of gifts. . . .

Cleopatra and Antony now dissolved their famous society of *Inimitable Livers*, and founded another not at all inferior to that in daintiness and luxury and extravagant outlay, which they called the society of *Partners in Death*. For their friends enrolled themselves as those who would die together, and passed the time delightfully in a round of suppers. From such a supper Antony passed on to death in close and dedicated pursuit of his passion.[1] Cleopatra, he thought, had committed suicide; he would, therefore, follow her in

---

[1] Athenaeus says that Antony once had himself proclaimed as Bacchus throughout the towns and cities of Greece. He also used sometimes to wear the dress of the God, and it was popularly supposed that Bacchus was his tutelary deity. On the night prior to the last engagement when Antony's fortunes were finally lost, a wild, gay, unearthly music was heard passing across Alexandria. The sound moved out through the city's eastern gate directly towards the camp of Caesar. People said that it was the dancing rout of the God, who that night deserted Antony for ever. The idea is used by the modern Greek poet, Cavafy, and provides the necessary excuse to quote a very fine poem :

THE GOD ABANDONS ANTONY.

When at the hour of midnight
an invisible choir is suddenly heard passing
    with exquisite music, with voices—
Do not lament your fortune that at last subsides,

this, as he had followed her from Actium. Brought dying to her monument he was conscious of himself and his role up to the last moment. She was not

> to lament him for his last reverses, but to count him happy for the good things that had been his, since he had become most illustrious of men, had won greatest power, and now had not been ignobly conquered, a Roman by a Roman.

Antony's greatness rests in the empire of the passion for which he has so often been reproached. His suicide is the classic example of dedication to such a passion. Of Cleopatra, shrewd and scheming, one cannot say as much; Dio Cassius suggests that she pretended death, knowing that Antony would commit suicide on receipt of the news and that thus she would be in a better position to negotiate with Octavius. Her own suicide, though characteristically well-staged, is impressive only in Shakespeare's handling of it. It appears that she really died, not to join Antony, but to spare her vanity the humiliation of a Roman triumph.

> your life's work that has failed, your schemes that have
>   proved illusions.
> But like a man prepared, like a brave man,
> bid farewell to her, to Alexandria who is departing.
> Above all do not delude yourself, do not say that it is a
>   dream,
> that your ear was mistaken.
> Do not condescend to such empty hopes.
> Like a man for long prepared, like a brave man,
> like to a man who was worthy of such a city,
> go to the window firmly,
> and listen with emotion,
> but not with the prayers and complaints of the coward
> (Ah! supreme rapture!)
> listen to the notes, to the exquisite instruments of the
>   mystic choir,
> and bid farewell to her, to Alexandria whom you are
>   losing.
>
> *Translation* : GEORGE VALASSOPOULO.

CHAPTER V

THE FATE OF THE WISE MEN

DIOGENES LAERTES believed that suicide was an end that the greatest leaders should counsel to the wisest men. It almost seemed a death that in itself conferred nobility upon the dead. They shared the glory of Cato, the determination of Seneca. Time plays tricks with these and all fancies. Its mutations are often effected in less than a generation. But the translation of Diogenes Laertes's wise men to the last circle of Dante's inferno took a thousand years. The mutilation of their bodies and the desecration of their memories, though whole-hearted, was a slow process. Only when the next turn of the wheel was already promised, and the Renaissance an imminent possibility, did the horror-struck peasants, the last vassals, and the Church, finally hand over the wise men to Dante in hell.

I. THE NEW RELIGION

Christianity, growing too large for the frame which had held it as a slip or seedling, burst the Roman world. Looking back, its disruptive anti-social elements strike one forcibly. It had new values to propound, but its methods were not tactful or economic. Causing infinite disturbance, it provoked in response infinite resistance.

The shortest way was assumed to be the best; the Church invited massacres when it might have brought off diplomatic victories. It blundered into the Roman scheme, an obstinate mother of ceaseless upheavals; needless to say it met with fairly concerted opposition. But one is sometimes bound to wonder not at the sadistic clamour of the anti-Christian mobs but at the restraint of the Roman bureaucracy. Just as significant as the scenes in the arenas is the attitude of people like Pliny, who tried so patiently to find a *modus vivendi* with the Christian communities under their jurisdiction.

The rapidity of the spread of Christianity is noted in history books; it is even given a miraculous interpretation. And yet in 250 the Roman world was still essentially pagan. If this is a rapid spread, it is slow compared to the pace of the Prophet and will hardly keep up with the march of Mrs. Eddy's mystical army through the forty-eight states of the American Union. What seems in retrospect just as remarkable as the succession of Christian victories is the dogged resistance put up by the old pagan hierarchy. When one remembers that Jupiter had to share the honours with Heliogabalus, and that Imperial boys had clambered into Mount Olympus, it seems extraordinary that the gods should have been able to raise any popular feeling. Of course the goldsmiths of Ephesus were not the only people who had investments in established religion. In every city the counterpart of the Ephesians' Diana meant bread and butter; yet granted even the support of interest and the state machine the old gods lasted an extraordinarily long time.

Until A.D. 250 we can therefore regard the moral of the ancient world as pagan and its attitude to suicide the same as before the birth of Christ. But what about the Christian communities which had arisen in the heart of this pagan world? How far had they, by the middle of the third century, modified or altered among themselves the classical ideas and feelings about suicide?

In point of fact we find that these early Christians dis-

regarded suicide completely. Their moral attitude, in so far
as such an attitude existed, was negative and uninterested.
Actually of the four lines of thought which tended among
the pagans to act as moral deterrents only one was relevant
to the Church. The idea upheld by Plutarch, that suicide was
inconsistent with human dignity and the heroic figure,
carried no weight with the Christians, who laid emphasis on
humility and the abject nature of unregenerated man. Aristotle's argument that a man did not belong to himself but to
the state was equally foreign to an anti-patriotic sect that
created the monastic ideal and that for allegiance to a community substituted allegiance to the Kingdom of Heaven.
Lastly, the Neo-Platonists' idea that suicide was a perturbation of the soul and thus reprehensible (the attitude long
after adopted by Schopenhauer) was of too philosophic a sort
to interest the simple convert mentality. Only Plato's
objection to suicide held good for the Christian: that self-
destruction was tantamount to an act of desertion from the
post where a Supreme Being had happened to station one.
Later this idea was worked very hard, and the suicide became
a person who destroyed divine property, a robber of God;
but in these early centuries no definite attitude crystallized
round this point, and suicide is not condemned by a single
canonical text of the period.

Actually there is no real reason why suicide should have
been condemned. One can trace two main characteristics in
early Christianity: a horror of the world as it was, and a
belief in salvation by faith. Neither of these things necessarily entail a condemnation of suicide. In fact, the first
would be likely to encourage it. Later as the Christian
antagonism to suicide developed, it is interesting to notice
that the act was often condemned, not in itself but as proof
that the suicide had despaired of God's grace; in other words,
that he lacked faith. The early Christian found not a single
reference in the New Testament to condemn suicide and St.

Paul's famous chapter on Charity (1 Cor. xiii. 3) classed self-
destruction with other worthy but ineffectual approaches to
grace, such as almsgiving and eloquence: "Though I give
my body to be burned and have not charity, it profiteth me
nothing." St. Paul here apparently refers to voluntary
martyrdom, and the text must have been a justification to the
numberless Christians who compelled the state to take their
lives. In Tertullian these gratuitous martyrs found an
ardent apologist and continual exhortations to seek their own
death. With citations from classic times he spurred them on,
and even held that Jesus Christ on the cross had given up
the ghost freely and voluntarily before the slow end by cruci-
fixion overtook Him. He says, *spiritum cum verbo dimisit
praevento carnificis officio*, and in this intriguing notion he
was supported by Origen. Even St. Augustine said: "His
soul did not leave His body constrained, but because He
would, and when He would, and how He would." Behind
such theories seems to be the idea that for the Godhead
actually to die by the hand of man would be too great an
indignity for spirit to undergo: thinking on rather the same
lines the Docetae denied that the *actual* body of Christ was
ever raised, or suffered, on the cross.

The courage of the early martyrs is beyond belief, and
their disregard of pain is amazing and rather frightening.
Nothing would deter them. The centurion Marcellus, who,
on parade, threw down his arms, crying "I am a soldier of
Jesus Christ," is a single example of what elsewhere con-
verts did by crowds, always with the expectation and hope
of death from a hostile mob. St. Cyprian, who wrote an
apologia in fifteen letters, explaining his flight from martyrdom, nowhere puts forward the horror or sin of suicide as
an excuse for his action. Such an argument would not have
entered his head at the period. Clement of Alexandria, who,
almost alone in those early days, condemns voluntary
Christian suicide, does so not because suicide is inherently

wrong, but because the martyr puts temptation in the murderer's way. This, of course, is a typical line of thought and links up with the horror of murder and of blood-shedding common to the early Christians. What is interesting, however, is that this horror of blood, which was so strong that it made the early Christians refuse military service and so run foul of the authorities on one more point, was not apparently extended to the taking of one's own life.

II. THE EMBRYONIC SIN

With the fourth century, however, the beginnings of a change are visible. The Church wakes up, as it were, to the existence of suicide, and after a period of uncertainty adopts a hostile attitude that grows more and more absolute as the Middle Ages develop. From tentative disapproval, Church teaching drifts to denunciation, punishment and horror.

What were the reasons for this change in feeling? First, no doubt, must come the general decline in world civilization that set in about the third century and grew steadily more marked until the complete collapse of the Empire in the West and the coming of the Dark Ages. The *élite* and the educated, who in the previous centuries had opposed reason to the suicide-horror of the common people, grew fewer and less influential. All through the Empire, and particularly among the common Christians who were drawn from the most instinctive and credulous elements of the people, the old pagan-religious fear of suicide, with its roots in a tribal and almost prehistoric past, found no opposition. As the intellectual impetus and order of society failed, suicide again became a social crime. It is important to emphasize that this was an instinctive movement of the people, a transference of the popular pagan idea into a semi-Christianized world; it was imposed on the Church from below. It was not, as one has been given to understand, a transference of ideas from the

Fathers to the people, an infiltration from doctrinal writing into popular consciousness. It was a reverse movement, common on different planes everywhere in early Christianity and particularly in relation to birth, death, and superstition. In some places the transference of pagan ideas was cloaked; in others it remained unashamed. (In Brittany the Little Saints took over in a whole-hearted and business-like fashion the offices of the local pagan gods; and there are many shrines in Europe with a fine tradition of continuity that leads up to an orthodox saint through Roman worship and Druid sacrifice.)

The bases of such transferences were quite illogical; and revulsion from suicide, on its first appearance in Christianity, had no rational basis. It is interesting to notice that as the opposition to suicide stiffened, the early Christian passion not to shed blood lost strength. The latter might, from a start, have provided a reasoned attack on suicide, but the excellent ideal was forced to modify itself to suit circumstances. Enlistment in the armies became common and recognized, and in 314 the Council of Arles went to the astonishing length of excommunicating deserters.

As might be expected, the horror of suicide first found concrete expression in Egypt, where Christianity was perhaps more than elsewhere a popular religion. The extreme peasant character of the Church and of its monastic developments in the Nile Valley and in the surrounding deserts, led to anti-suicide customs at a very early date. Already in 346 Egypt foreshadowed later procedure in the West by denying funeral rites to suicides. (It is true that this legislation may have had a purely practical and social side as suicide was unusually common in the desert monasteries.)

Once the primitive attitude to suicide was accepted by the Fathers, and the Church had fallen into line, the movement gathered a new and artificial impetus. The mind of the Church was called upon to give both a dogmatic and rational platform to peasant prejudice and to provide the intensifying attack on suicide with a body of respectable arguments. The doctrine of immortality and the writings of the Neo-Platonists were the point of departure chosen by most writers.

If the soul was immortal and due to square its moral account either in heaven or hell, suicide, far from being an escape or a lapse into blessed quiescence, became merely the best possible passport to eternal torment. Life was a gift direct from God, as even the misguided Plato had rightly said, and its rejection must inevitably anger Him. To kill oneself was to frustrate God's purpose, it was to kill one of His specially created beings. It was a sinful act and came in time, perhaps, to be the most sinful of all acts, possible only under the direct inspiration of the devil. For the homicide there might be some mercy, but for the murderer of himself no circumstances were thought extenuating. Judas, theologians came to the conclusion, had not sinned irreparably in betraying Christ; not until he committed suicide had he damned himself out of hand. The Christian idea of the rights and value of the individual life, which led to their attack on the abortion and infanticide generally practised in the Empire, was the chief prop in a rationalization of the suicide-horror. It led to a paradox that lasted twelve centuries: though the life of the individual was valuable only in itself, in relation to its own divine problem and not to the community, yet the individual could not end this life of his if he found it intolerable or useless. In passing, it is worth noting how the sadistic element of Catholicism, its moral rather than its religious side, as it began to develop, would instinctively oppose the early release from pain offered by suicide. As the function of the Church became largely one of compulsion, this attitude would tend to grow more pronounced. Suicide became reprehensible in so far as the command " love one another "

H

was substituted by " believe in this organization and set of dogmas or be damned ".

Beside the prejudice of the people and the rationalizations of the Church, there appeared a third factor ranged against suicide. It was the important economic deterrent, inherited from the slave system of classical times and which the growth of feudalism strengthened and developed. For economic reasons the noble put his whole weight into the balance against suicide at the same time as the priest and the peasant. If he acted for different reasons it was none the less with equal decision. Under the feudal system everyone was somebody else's " man ", so any suicide, however humble, was a robbery of some superior and a breach of fealty. The classical attitude to slave suicide was now *logically* applicable to the whole of society. The nobles saw to it that it was *actually* applied to the lower sections. Fear of losing one's " man " undoubtedly played a large part in the suicide legislation of the Middle Ages, and accounts for the purely deterrent character of many suicide penalties. Public exposure of the corpse and its degrading cartage through the streets (see page 140) are obviously measures intended to create fear and aversion in the people. It is irrational and rather useless to explain them as posthumous punishments, which is the usual reason given; nor do they fit in with expiatory theories and the sort of thing done to cleanse a community from blood-guilt. The economic-feudal pressure brought to bear against suicide was wide and intense, and it is interesting while on this point to notice that nobles were often exempted from the necessary penalties. In France, at any rate, the suicide laws seem rarely to have been enforced against the feudal lords.

The references of Shakespeare's grave-digger to the death of Ophelia in *Hamlet* seem to point to a similar exemption in England at a later date. " Will you h'a the truth on't? If this had not been a gentlewoman she should have been buried out of Christian burial. . . . Great folk shall have countenance in this world to drown themselves more than their even Christian."

Finally, a quotation from the *Connoisseur* shows that a rather similar distinction was still made in the eighteenth century :

> A penniless poor dog, who has not left enough to defray the funeral charges, may perhaps be excluded the churchyard, but self-murder by a pistol genteely mounted, or a Paris-hilted sword, qualifies the polite owner for a sudden death and entitles him to a pompous burial.

Perhaps the most striking instance of the purely economic side of the anti-suicide prejudice is to be found in the measures passed at the Council of Arles in 452. These measures are not, as a casual interpretation might lead one to think, directed against suicide in general. They apply only to servants (*famuli* is the word used) and are simply a repetition of the Roman slave legislation about suicide. The Christian bishops at Arles, in fact, did little but reaffirm the stigma which long before had been attached to suicide in the statutes of the Imperial College at Lanuvium, an institution largely devoted to the education of slaves. The Council really broke no new ground and it gave no expression to the growing psychological horror of suicide as such. Not the act, but dislike of its repercussions as they effect the master and landowner, provides the motive which makes the act criminal in certain cases and envisages the suicide as *diabolico repletus furore.*

But though bishops, landowners, and land-tillers came for different reasons to range themselves against suicide, the change in opinion took time. The intelligent tradition of the old world and probably a small and living minority of educated people in the new, formed a bulwark difficult to break down. There seems to have been no canonical legislation against suicide generally (the *act* condemned rather than a class of persons committing the act) until the Council of Braga in 563 and no civil legislation until even later.

The writings of the ecclesiastics in the fourth and fifth centuries, mirror the uncertainty that existed even in the Church. Though these writers generally condemn the act, they do not yet demand penalties. The question is still in the melting-pot; fit for discussion rather than punishment. While St. Jerome angrily condemns the melancholy of the age which leads to suicide, the old support of a sophisticated society lingered on in St. Athanasius's approval. It is perhaps only the weight and influence of St. Augustine that settles the question. The *City of God* says plainly enough " that suicide is a detestable and damnable wickedness ". St. Augustine produces four arguments to justify his statement which are of great importance, since, for some time, they were the basis of the Church's anti-suicide teaching.

First, Augustine points out that no private individual may take it upon himself to kill a guilty person. The condemnation of murderers and sinners rests with Church and State. Therefore, however aware a person may be of sin and guilt in himself, he has no right to take his own life. As a corollary, the more innocently a man has lived, the more criminally he acts in killing himself; " innocent " blood is on his head. This argument disposed of the idea that certain suicides, as from remorse, might fairly be regarded as expiatory. It countered Petilian's claim, who said that in his suicide Judas showed proof of his repentance and wiped his score clean with his own blood.

Augustine's second line of attack was based on the sixth commandment: *non occides*. The suicide who takes his own life has killed a man. Both logically and in the eyes of God he is no better than a homicide. This argument, because apparently so simple, was eagerly taken up, found general acceptance, and later was chiefly responsible for the classification of suicide as a felony (*felo de se*) in civil law.

Augustine's third line was, oddly enough, stoical in conception, though to give it authority he was forced to deny the Stoics and to attribute Cato's death to weakness. The truly noble soul, he said, will bear all suffering; to escape, even when there is no reason for staying, is testimony of weakness. To this may be added the conception of the " soldier of Christ " which gave a purely religious twist to Stoicism : the pains we suffer are not our own, but are undergone in the service of Christ, either directly as martyrs or in so far as we are part of the plan whereby the world exists only for its own eventual regeneration.

Augustine's last argument had to do directly with the contemporary scene, as many Christians in the early centuries committed suicide for fear of falling before temptation. They preferred to sacrifice a score of years on earth, rather than lose eternity in heaven. Augustine argued, however, that suicide was a sin greater than any they could avoid by its commission, and that the suicide died the worst of sinners. The logical outcome of their line of thought would be, as he pointed out, suicide immediately after baptism : only so would a direct passage to heaven be absolutely certain.

In spite of the diatribes of the Fathers and of the anti-suicide prejudice which was hardening into a set mould throughout the fourth and fifth centuries, three points remained unsettled and three types of suicide, even if officially condemned, were excused by the man in the street. The cause of endless controversy and fairly common in occurrence, these three types strike the characteristic note of the early Christian centuries. Suicide, in so far as it was acknowledged or allowed to come before the public eye, appeared in one of these three forms.

First in importance, frequency, and respectability, came voluntary martyrdom.

III. THE GLORIOUS COMPANY OF MARTYRS

Accounts vary infinitely as to the number of the early
martyrs. It has been said that " As in the passover from
Egypt every door was sprinkled with blood ", and again,
that in the Roman Martyrologia " there is no day which
hath not five hundred martyrs ". Such estimates, however,
are too vague. Sozomen, writing of the Diocletian persecutions in the fourth century says that in Syria and Persia alone
there were 16,000 martyrs " whose names had been ascer-
tained ", not to mention legions who were nameless. Gibbon,
with more probability, puts the total number for the Empire
during the same period at 1500, nine of whom were bishops.
The truth must lie nearer Gibbon's figure when it is remembered that only one man in twelve was a Christian
before the conversion of Constantine and that on the whole
no law could have provided more loopholes than the Roman.
The life of a bishop, as facts show, was often safer than that
of an Emperor : during the ten years in which Cyprian
successfully ruled the see of Carthage, four Emperors were
killed, sharing their violent deaths with their families,
favourites and slaves.

Whatever the number of the Christian martyrs, one fact
at any rate is certain, a very large percentage of them gave
up their lives voluntarily, going out deliberately to procure
their own self-destruction. It was hardly an unusual thing
to journey, as did St. Anthony, in the persecutions of
Diocletian, a full 200 miles with no object in view but to
secure one's own death. The corollary of eternal life, the
other side of the picture, hardly obtrudes itself in the endless
account of knives, fires, roastings, mutilations, and wild
beasts. The overwhelming desire to suffer voluntarily, " to
testify to the faith ", ousts every other consideration. In
modern jargon we might call this masochism and quote
Ignatius's words when he writes of the arena : " Let me

enjoy these beasts whom I wish much more cruel than they are; and if they will not attempt me, I will provoke and draw them by force."

Contemporary thought and custom enhanced the desirability of martyrdom. For the martyr, his sacrifice secured honour and perpetual commemoration; for his family it meant support and an income from the Church funds. Such a death, better than any other, opened the road to heaven: baptism purged a Christian from original sin, and martyrdom cleared him from the sins of a lifetime. In addition, martyrs were the popular figures of the period. A general enthusiasm for the state of martyrdom extended the honour to a child " which dies in his mother's womb if she be a martyr ", to all the infants slain by Herod,[1] and later to eleven thousand virgins. Some even, among them Ignatius in his epistles, styled themselves martyrs, though they never died. Finally, martyrdom came to be regarded as a trenchant form of argument, and heretics calculated the virtue of their sect by the number of their dead.

The Christian desire to seek out voluntary martyrdom, rather than to have it imposed by force, was met half-way by the gentleness of Imperial policy and the tenor of Imperial legislation. Rome did not eagerly seize the heretics and rarely *forced* martyrdom on the Christians. It was the latter who insisted that Roman governors should inflict the full powers which they possessed. Until personally insulted and angered, the attitude of the average Roman official in the execution of his duties was one of deprecation or perplexity.

---

[1] The cult of the Innocents seems to have been widespread and important. Saint Louis presented to Nôtre Dame in a crystal bowl *un innocent entier*. The adjective is amusing and indicates the relic-hunting snobbery that prevailed. It was essential to procure a fine ' specimen '. In the fifteenth century a procession of children estimated at over twelve thousand escorted the body of one such Innocent across Paris.

Pliny the Younger is a typical example. He was reluctant to convict the Christians under his jurisdiction, and with the Imperial tradition of toleration behind him, he could see nothing wrong (though much fantastic) in their beliefs. It was only their self-sufficiency, priggishness, and isolation from the community, their refusal to play at the game of God-Emperor, that he found dangerous and anti-social. In a letter to the Emperor Trajan, asking for a clear line of policy on the subject, he says that not their conduct "but their inflexible obstinacy appears deserving of punishment". Nine out of ten of his contemporaries must have thought more or less the same. It is on record that a frantic pro-consul faced by a mob of Christians demanding martyrdom, shouted, "Goe hang and drown your selves and ease the Magistrates."

The policy outlined by Trajan in his reply to Pliny is characteristic of the pagan attitude which, with short breaks, prevailed until paganism itself went under. It makes every attempt to meet Christian obstinacy half-way.

> No charges against Christians [he says] are to be anonymous, and when made must be supported by circumstantial evidence. When finally guilt is proved, Christians are still to be offered life and freedom. All that is asked is that they shall prove their good faith by a single sacrifice to the orthodox gods. The duty of the judges is not so much to punish as reclaim and only when every effort has failed are the punishments to be applied.

A final point in the application of anti-Christian laws seems to us now lenient to the point of foolishness. Between the accusation of a Christian and his appearance for trial, there was generally a liberal lapse of time granted, ostensibly for the preparation of a defence, but tacitly is was regarded as a good opportunity for flight until trouble blew over. The existence of such a clause, though it was not always in force, proves both an unwillingness to convict and the self-inflicted nature of many martyrdoms. Though under Diocletian the laws were temporarily stiffened, and to hold a Christian service was directly punishable by death, yet the same element of volition appears in the accounts of martyrdoms at that time.

This suicidal element in martyrdom is perhaps natural if one takes into account the psychology of the Christians. Eusebius tells of a man who, having been condemned to death over a slow and lingering fire, " leaping and exulting with joy gave thanks to God with a loud voice, who had honoured him with a martyrdom ". In Phrygia three Christians who had destroyed pagan idols voluntarily gave themselves up to authority, and refusing to sacrifice, were duly ordered to die on gridirons. As the process went forward, they called to the governor, " Amachus, give orders that our bodies may be turned on the fire if you do not desire to be served with meat cooked only on one side." Donne tells of an old wretched man, who passing by after the execution of a whole legion of 666, by iterated decimation, under Maximianus, " wish't that he might have the happiness to be with them and so *extorted* a Martyrdome ".

Such an attitude was hardly likely to take advantage of Roman clemency, and time and again we see suicidal tactics forcing the hands of a reluctant governor. Numberless stories witness the aggressiveness of these early Christian martyrs, many of whom died not for their religion but for their insolence. The destruction of Diocletian's edict at Nicomedia is famous. Less well known perhaps is the story of the lady who, when called upon in the presence of the governor to contribute her pinch of incense to the gods, kicked over the altar. Not unnaturally she was beheaded.

Though they can have had no doubt about the penalties, it was common enough for Christians even to disrupt pagan services and to desecrate the public idols. In Phrygia a whole congregation of Christians preferred to be burnt alive in the walls of their church, rather than give up the building to the Roman authorities. On another occasion Babylas, whose church was visited by Decius in a moment of curiosity, barred the door to the Emperor, saying that no wolf should enter his fold. The Emperor went away, but the Christian, as he must have expected, lost his life.

Stories of less actively aggressive but quite effective suicide-martyrdoms are equally common. Few people took the legal opportunity of removing from areas of persecution and cases of actual self-accusation abound. Once condemned it was usual to court the flames, to exasperate lions, or, like Agapius, to hug the oncoming bear. One story in the typical tradition illustrates this semi-suicide. Six young men, having bound their hands together to forestall individual changes of opinion, rushed before a provincial governor presiding over the games, and confessed their faith. Their disappointment was intense when they were not thrown to the animals, and their wishes were only partially gratified by a later decapitation.

Perhaps, however, the strangest suicidal deaths of the period occurred among the heretical Donatists and Circum-celliones in North Africa. When threatened with persecution they killed themselves in vast numbers. St. Augustine says that " assembling in hundreds they leaped with paroxysms of frantic joy from the brows of overhanging cliffs, till the rocks below were reddened with their blood ". The Father thoroughly disapproved of their precipitations and added that they consecrated their martyrdom to the Devil who tempted Christ to throw Himself down.

This whole question of martyrdom and suicide is strange, and histories of the times fill one alternatively with horror and admiration. Faith and courage have perhaps never existed in such degree among large numbers of people as among the early Christians. One can only admire these virtues. Their passionate disregard for life, however, involves other questions : there seems something a little perverted in their welcome of pain and a sort of biological insanity in their determination to destroy their flesh and root out their own lives. As Donne says, that age was so hungry and ravenous of martyrdom, " that many were baptized only because they would be burnt ".

Contemporary thought, also, realized that there were two sides to the picture. As voluntary martyrdom increased people began to doubt its use and validity. Though popular praise was always active for the suicide-martyrs, the official Church attitude became more and more disapproving. In the third century Tertullian had been strongly in support of Christians remaining to await martyrdom, rather than of their availing themselves of the chance of escape generously provided by the law; and even St. Augustine had said that the Good Shepherd must give His life for His flock and not remove to a neighbouring town. By about 450, however, Sozomen in his ecclesiastical history could posit, without comment, " the divine precept which commands us not to expose ourselves to persecution ". Such suicide was no longer recognized as martyrdom. Neither were the deaths directly provoked by Christian aggression, for the Council of Illiberis refused to honour those who procured their own death by publicly desecrating the idols.

Opposition to the suicide-martyr had a further basis. By A.D. 300, as Eusebius perhaps overstates, the Church had " sunk into negligence and sloth, one envying and reviling another in different ways . . . and hypocrisy and dissimulation had arisen to the greatest heights of malignity ". In such communities people burdened with poverty and debts often found suicide-martyrdom their most honourable and practical exit, ensuring as it did support and provision for their family. Other even subtler rogues adopted the procedure of suicide-martyrdom in order to obtain the alms and gifts showered on such faithful sufferers in prison; they took care, however, that the machinery of legislation did not take them farther than their cells whence timely recantation eventually restored them to liberty.

IV. IN DESERTS, CAVES, AND CELLS

The second type of suicide which the Church could not bring itself to condemn unanimously was that which the ascetics inflicted on themselves by intense privations. The whole question was a little delicate and uncertain, because an extremely and even morbidly rigorous rule tended in certain cases to produce paradoxically long life. St. Anthony, foremost of the Egyptian hermits (who were the ascetics *par excellence*) lived to be one hundred and four, and St. Jerome's monk who existed in a hole on a diet of four figs a day apparently was none the worse for it. It was a kill-or-cure procedure.

However, there is no doubt that suicide either indirectly through starvation and maceration of the body, or directly as a result of manias and depression was fairly common, particularly in the Eastern monasteries. St. Palaemon apparently died of his asceticisms, and St. Simeon Stylites is a yet more famous example of a long life finally terminated by direct privation and mistreatment. For thirty years the saint stood on his sixty-foot pillar near Antioch with a magnificent disregard for his person. Eventually an untreated ulcer killed him. Gibbon makes a typical pun on the subject: " The progress of an ulcer in his thigh might shorten, but it could not disturb this *celestial* life." The brutal self-disciplines and strange ascetic practices of the early monks and hermits were various and always severe. From the βόσκοι, or grazers of Syria (" they each took a sickle and cut some grass on the mountains; and this served for their repast ") to monks, like a certain Valens who would neither eat nor even take the communion, saying " I need not the supper, for I have this day seen the Lord ", their intense privations led to madness and death.

More frequent, however, were the suicides that occurred from remorse, hopelessness, and despair of virtue, among those who were unable to live up to the monastic ideal. These deaths took place chiefly among young men who tried in vain to twist a normal nature into the unnatural moulds of celibacy and solitary seclusion. In innumerable instances the fight between chastity and nature was too exhausting, and as the weight of repressions piled up the victim committed suicide to escape inevitable defeat. In this struggle the great Pachomius applied asps to himself—luckily in vain—and St. Anthony, with apparent equanimity, saw a despairing brother fling himself into a baker's oven. Pachomius's contemporary biographer says that in this fight with the devil " many have destroyed themselves; some, bereft of their senses, have cast themselves from precipices; others laid open their bowels; others killed themselves in divers ways ". There is no doubt also that into these suicides there often entered an element of martyrdom, the notion that a man would rather die than suffer the loss of his virtue. Though never countenanced by the Church, these curious heroic suicides were common enough to attract the attention of St. Chrysostom. In a letter to a rich young man, named Stagirius, who had turned monk but was unequal to the demands his rule made upon him, Chrysostom gave warning against the temptation of suicide, and pointed out the general wickedness and uselessness of the act in such a situation.

Death as a result of voluntary privations was looked on in a very different light and considered, at any rate in the early days of monasticism, as a blessed ending. Public opinion, however, slowly veered away from extreme asceticism and with the modification of monastic life dangerous privation was no longer a virtue. The coming of the

Benedictines in the West and the restriction of the Egyptian rule completed a revulsion in taste and practice. St. Jerome's story of a certain Blesilla, retailed in delicious language by Lecky, is interesting not only in its typicality but because it shows a certain popular distaste for ascetic excesses even at an early date. By the premature death of her husband this unfortunate lady " lost at once the crown of virginity and the pleasure of marriage ". Struck down with grief, she went into a convent; there, thinking on her sins, she soon came to regret the loss of her maidenhood more than that of her husband. To expiate the former she embarked on a long series of penances, so drastic that they caused her death. On her mother's grief and her own foolish end becoming known, the local populace made a great display of indignation. The scenes at her funeral proved that healthy reactions to such perversion were not absolutely inhibited outside monastic circles.

While on the subject of self-inflicted privations, a note on Origen is perhaps to the point. He, like certain others, doubting the outcome of his combat for chastity, committed a semi-suicide, or, as Gibbon tactfully puts it, " judged it the most prudent to disarm the tempter ". Biologically speaking, castration may well be the only quite effective form of suicide. The father who kills himself makes but half a job of it, and life continues to torment his sons. The Church soon recognized the suicidal element in such an act. His detractors held it up against Origen, and later one of the Apostles, Canons laid it down that " He that gelds himself cannot be a clerke, *because he is an homicide of himselfe*, and an enemy to God's creature ".[1]

---

[1] Antiquity provided two famous but rather different cases of self-mutilation. Democritus was said to have put out his eyes, being unwilling to witness the evils of his day. Leaena, the Athenian courtesan, afraid of betraying the liberal patriot, Harmodius, when put to the torture, bit out her tongue. The grateful Athenians set up to her memory the statue of a tongueless lion (leaena).

V. DE VIRGINIBUS

The last type of suicide which troubled the fathers and called forth the casuistry of the Church, was that committed to save virgin or married chastity. At this remove the whole business seems very odd and it is difficult for us to see how it could have been possible to class such a suicide as either right or wrong. To get the proper perspective one has not only to adopt the anti-suicide ideas of the early Church, but to envisage chastity as something with a *constant* value, quite apart from its possessor. To-day chastity is what a woman thinks it is worth. No more and no less. Its value, great or small, transcendental or practical, depends on the attitude of its possessor. One knows people who would indeed commit suicide to preserve it, and others who for the same reason would hardly walk across the street if it were inconvenient. To-day it would obviously be as impossible as it was in Roman times to say whether or not such a suicide was " exaggerated " and " unnecessary ".

Before going into the question of this type of suicide in early Christian times, we need some sort of explanation why chastity became such an absolute virtue and such an institution. Why did a little mitre-like cap of purple wool, the badge of professed virginity, become an honourable symbol rather than the sign of failure, or the rare curiosity, that it would have been among the pagans? As Gibbon says, " It was with the utmost difficulty that Rome could support the institution of six vestals; but the primitive Church was filled with a great number of persons of either sex who had devoted themselves to the profession of perpetual chastity."

Such a change obviously needs some explaining, and the usual reasons derived direct from the New Testament, though effective, are not quite enough. We read into the gospels too much that we have acquired from our social

environment. " Blessed are the pure in heart for they shall
see God " has acquired an unfortunately limited reference.
Purity, thanks perhaps to the public school tradition, has
come to mean sex; its socially more important application to
business, politics, and so on, is obscured. At the start the
scriptures were not so confined in their application, but the
early Christian found, on the other hand, a situation where
ideals of chastity were socially of the greatest use and importance. First of all the Roman Empire and Roman freedom, by cutting across national and local ties, was leading to
the breakdown of the family. The Church, on the other
hand, wished to increase its solidity and, by using the family
as the cellular basis of its organization, to oppose its
authority and weight to that of the pagan state. The
exaltation of married chastity was certainly the surest way
of rehabilitating family institutions.

In a broader sense chastity was also a necessary ideal and
counterpoise to the licentiousness of the time—a licentiousness that was dangerous in its ruthless methods and lack of
proportion. Chastity was a timely self-preservative adopted
by a wise section of society. The reign of Maxentius produced in Saint Sophronia, perhaps the most famous of the
suicides for chastity, and one has only to look at Eusebius's
account of the morals of the time to see that drastic reaction
was necessary. The Emperor himself was

> sunk into every kind of wickedness, leaving no impurity or
> licentiousness untouched; separating wives from their lawful hus-
> bands, and after abusing these, sending them most shamefully
> violated back to their husbands. And these things he perpetrated
> not upon mean and obscure individuals, but insulting more par-
> ticularly those that were most distinguished in the senate. . . .
> Initiating the soldiers, by luxury and intemperance, into every
> species of dissipation and revelling; encouraging the governors
> and generals, by rapacity and avarice, to proceed with their op-
> pressions against their subjects, with almost the power of associate
> tyrants. . . . There was not a city that he passed through in

which he did not commit violence upon females. And in these he succeeded against all but the Christians. For they, despising death, valued his power but little.

From *some* part of the community a protest had to come against such a state of affairs in this and other reigns—and, as so often, it came from the Christians. As a result we meet, everywhere throughout the Empire, suicide for the sake of chastity. Of course such a line was not new. Leukatas, to escape the unwelcome love of Apollo, had plunged off a cliff into the Aegean, and St. Jerome recalled to the Christians the noble end of Lucrece and Dido. At all events, within the Empire the habit spread.

There are many stories, but it will develop the situation adequately if we look at the cases of two martyrs to chastity who were famous in their time, and around whose example the theoreticians subsequently waged protracted battles.

Sophronia (" far above all the most admirable ", as her historian says) was a married Christian lady of standing and reputation who was unfortunate enough to attract the eye and interest of the Emperor Maxentius. She is said to have been the second Roman woman to take the vow of poverty and chastity, though this does not seem to fit in with the fact of her marriage. At all events she was an exemplary wife and firmly resisted the Emperor's tempestuous advances. At last the latter approached her husband and demanded that she should be given up. He, though Prefect of Rome, valued his life and knew well enough the penalties of refusal. He consented. When the tyrant's creatures burst into the house to carry her off, Saint Sophronia—as she was afterwards to be—met them with a show of resignation and simply asked for a few minutes in which fitly to adorn herself for the Emperor's arms. Having gone into her room, instead of applying cosmetics to her lips, she plunged a dagger into her breast. Her dead body was left for the Emperor.

I

Equally renowned were Domnina and her two beautiful daughters who committed suicide in the persecution of Diocletian when they had fallen into the hands of the soldiery on the road to Antioch.

> The mother . . . being at a loss for herself and daughters, knowing what dreadful outrages they would suffer from the men, represented their situation to them and, above all, the threatened violation of their chastity, an evil more to be dreaded than any other, to which neither she nor they should listen even for a moment.

To cut the story short, they decided that the only hope of delivery was " to betake themselves to the aid of Christ ". A deep and swift river ran beside the road down which they were being escorted. Having asked their guards to retire for a moment, without hesitation they " cast themselves into the flowing river ", and so died.[1]

---

[1] Accounts of this suicide vary. Some writers say that only the daughters committed suicide, and that one of them was that Pelagia who is celebrated in the Church calendar on the 9th of June as virgin and martyr. Donne retails one tradition of her death, with her sister, in a fine passage: " Having drest her selfe as a Bride, and going to the water, Here, sayes she, let us be baptized; this is the Baptisme where sinnes are forgiven, and where a kingdom is purchased: and this is the baptisme after which none sinnes. This water regenerates; this makes us virgines, this opens heaven, defends the feeble, delivers from death, and makes us Martyrs. Only we pray to God, that this water scatter us not, but reserve us to one funerall. Then entered they as in a dance, hand in hand, where the torrent was deepest, and most violent. And thus dyed . . . these Prelates of virginitie, Captaines of Chastitie, and companions in Martyrdome."

The Renaissance comment on such suicides is interesting by contrast, and strictly practical in tone. Montaigne writes: " *Un savant aucteur de ce temps, et notamment parisien, se mette en peine de persuader aux dames de nostre siecle de prendre plustot tout aultre party, que d'entrer en l'horrible conseil d'un tel desespoir. Je suis marry qu'il n'a sceu, pour mesler a ses contes, le bon mot que*

Such honourable and determined women were inevitably examples for imitation, and on the capture of Rome in 410 by Alaric and his barbarian forces the number of such suicides grew alarming. The Church had obviously to define its position. Though Saints Ambrose and Jerome had both written in praise of women who gave their lives for chastity, opinion began to veer, and even here the general prejudice against suicide exerted its influence. As on other questions, it was the authority of St. Augustine that seems to have turned the scale. Augustine's arguments against this sort of suicide are set out at length in the *Civitatis dei* and are worth considering in some detail, not only as an example of the odd angle from which these problems were tackled, but because his ideas were the basis of the ecclesiastical attitude of later times. Augustine begins by arguing that anyway no virgin can lose her fundamental chastity by violation, since real chastity is an attribute of the soul and not of the body. It is, in fact, a thing that no other person can steal. Thus a virgin has no real cause for suicide; and if she does commit it " she commits certain homicide to prevent a crime which is uncertain as yet, and not her own ". He goes on to examine the whole question in the light of Lucrece's death. Approaching the affair from the point of view of the sins involved, he shows the unreasonableness and disproportion of her actions. Tarquin's son, guilty of a serious crime, is merely banished; while she, the innocent, dies. She has, in fact, committed a worse crime against her-self than her violator did: "Lucrece, so celebrated and lauded, slew the innocent, chaste, outraged Lucrece." But *was* she perhaps conscious of some guilt? In that case, though still wrong, her suicide would not have been so shocking a crime as when directed against a more virtuous

j'apprins a Toulouse, d'une femme passee par les mains des soldats: ' *Dieu soit loue, disoit elle, qu'au moins une fois en ma vie je m'en suis saoulee sans peche!* ' "

and innocent self. True virtue, he concludes, is to be found
in those Christian women who, whatever their physical fate,
" within their own souls, in the witness of their own conscience . . . enjoy the glory of chastity ".

To maintain his thesis Augustine was now obliged to
explain the conduct of holy women, like Sophronia and
Domnina, *quorum memoria celebratur in ecclesia.* He did
so by resorting to the idea that a chosen few had acted
under a special divine revelation; but he warns his readers
against presumptuously supposing that they are the recipients of any such revelation. He warns them to stop and
think, " for those who die by their own hand have no better
life after death ".[1]

His attack on this sort of suicide ends with the tenuous
consolation that such troubles produce humility and are good
for the unnatural pride of virgins and chaste women. Also,
he points out that for the barbarian violators, life, even if
merry, is short in the measure of eternity. Their score waits
to be settled. " For some most wicked and flagrant desires
are allowed free play at present by the secret judgment of
God, and are reserved to the public and final reckoning."

However, in spite of Saint Augustine's onslaught,
chastity-suicide was never altogether established as a sin.
Adelhemus, a famous Bishop of Malmesbury, wrote of the
" blessed " virgins who gave up their lives in this way, and
much later a Jesuit historian called Maria Cornelia, who,
when separated from her husband by Pedro the Cruel, killed

---

[1] Though suicide to preserve chastity was condemned, the more
aesthetically unpleasing practice of mutilation apparently escaped
official censure. In 870 Ebba, a Yorkshire abbess, and all the nuns
in her convent, when besieged by the Danes cut off their upper lips
and noses rather than endanger their virtue. Later they were imitated by the Sisters of St. Clare who took the same precautions to
preserve their chastity at the siege of Acre. The infidels, not
unjustly incensed at the sight they presented, put the ladies to
death.

herself for fear that she might not be able to live decently
single, *insigne studium castitas*. A vague sympathy, voiced
now and again by such ecclesiastics, continued for centuries, until in time changes in social manners and opinions
made the problem in Western Europe one of almost purely
academic interest.

VI. THE LAW

Having seen a mounting wave of disapproval wash away
the older Stoic and intellectual bases on which the tolerance
of suicide once rested, it remains to trace this disapproval as
it naturally translated itself into pains, penalties, and legal
statutes. By the end of the fifth century suicide had become
an act tainted with superstitious horror; not even the virgin,
the ascetic, or the martyr could take this way out with im-
punity. Half the distance has been covered between
Diogenes Laertes's elect brotherhood and the seventh circle
of Dante's hell; the suicide is condemned; he is not yet
punished. His fate, however, was only a matter of time : in
a universally Catholic Europe the progress from sinner to
criminal was almost automatic.

The early codes of Theodosius and Justinian show the older
Roman attitude to suicide legally unaltered. In itself it is
not an offence. The law only recognizes its existence when
committed by a slave or when linked to some other criminal
action. Its first appearance in Canon law seems to be at the
Council of Arles, but here again (see p. 115) it is not
penalized in itself, and the Council in practice does little
more than reaffirm the Imperial slave clause. The first real
divergence from the old civil code came in 533, when the
Council of Orleans denied funeral rites to suicides accused
of crime, though it allowed them to *ordinary criminals*. But
it was not until later in the sixth century when the universal
success of barbarism had destroyed the last vestiges of
classic rationalism and the instinctive prejudices of the un-

educated had free play in Europe that the Church legislated against suicide *per se*. It was the Council of Braga in 563 which took the decisive step. *All* suicides were to be penalized. " For those that kill themselves there shall be no commemoration at the oblation [mass] nor shall they be brought to burial with psalms." No exception or distinction of any sort was made. On paper no privileged class could hope for commemoration in the Eucharist or psalms at burial. Every motive and every method—*aut per ferrum, aut per venenum, aut praecipitium, aut suspendium*—were equally culpable. The Council of Auxerre fifteen years later reaffirmed these penalties and the principle of indiscriminate condemnation.

The Antisidor Council of 590 added a further clause which is interesting : " If any kill themselves *istorum oblata non recipiantur*, their offerings shall not be received." This seems to show that there was still some perplexity in the air about the rightness or wrongness of the act and that suicides thought it worth while to make offerings which they hoped would expiate any degree of sinfulness they might be guilty of. This evidently was an inconvenient practice which put the Church in an awkward position; hence its abolition.

The Church had now straightened out its position—to its theoretical condemnation there corresponded a system of penalties to punish and deter. The next centuries saw little alteration of the Canon law and it was not until 1284 that the final ecclesiastical penalty was imposed. The Synod of Nimes then refused suicides even the right of a quiet interment on holy ground.[1] The Church had now done its job, and having indicated the attitude which the secular authorities should take, left them in the certainty that they would carry on her work.

---

[1] The priest in *Hamlet*, speaking of Ophelia, may be supposed to give a very fair picture of the treatment accorded by the Church to less fortunate suicides at a later period. He says :

The Council of Hereford in 673, which ordained that the ancient canonical decrees of the transmarine fathers should be observed in England, brought this country into line with the continent. Theodore, Archbishop of Canterbury, and also Egbert, Archbishop of York, whose *Penitentials*[1] appeared in the middle of the eighth century, restated the position. The former insisted to his clergy that there was to be no mass or Christian burial for suicides unless insane; although, he says, " some allow for mass for suicides through instantaneous distraction ". King Edgar, in 967, finally gave a civil blessing and sanction to these penalties. After this date they underwent no important modifications, and the assimilation of ecclesiastical to civil law which took place at the Reformation did not bring about any change of doctrine on this subject. A rubric in the prayer-book, prefixed to the burial service after the Restoration of 1660, reveals the old outlook unaltered. It reads as follows: " Here it is to be noted, that the office ensuing is not to be used for any that die unbaptized, or excommunicate, or have laid violent hands on themselves." Thus it is fair to say that from the thirteenth century the Canon law of suicide has remained fundamentally unaltered.

Donne's interpretation of the Church's position throws an interesting light on the Canon law. To uphold suicide, he says, was never heretical, and no dogma of the Church con-

---

" . . . But that great command o'er sways the order,
  She should in ground unsanctified have lodged,
  Till the last trumpet; for charitable prayers,
  Shards, flints, and pebbles should be thrown on her;
  Yet here she is allowed her virgin crants,
  Her maiden strewments, and the bringing home
  Of bell and burial."

[1] The *Penitentials* were a sort of manual compiled for the parish priest from the Canon law and other sources. They laid down correct ritual and procedure, and guided him in the imposition of penances.

demns it. Suicide was not unchristian and anyone was
entitled to an opinion on the matter, because it had not been
dealt with by real Canon law but only by the Canons of the
Councils. He goes on to make a wide distinction between
the two types of law, and complains at the attempted usurpa-
tion of authority by the Councils. As he points out, it is out
of all proportion for the Diocesan Council of Antisidor at
which only one bishop was present to presume to dictate on
so important a subject.

Further, Donne argues, Canon law never condemns
suicide as actually criminal. It would have no right to do so.
For instance, it is impossible to deduce the criminality of
suicide from the Council of Braga, because the penalties
which true Canon law imposed against men killed at the tilt
in tournaments—certainly not a criminal death—included a
similar refusal of Christian burial. Donne's conclusion is
that the Canon law against suicide is accorded a very exaggerated respect and that it is the expression of a prejudice
rather than an accepted orthodox dogma.[1]

The development of the secular law with regard to suicide

[1] The Muslim prohibition of suicide is more explicit and
authentic than the Christian. Self-destruction among the true Arabs
is, and always has been, rare. For this the absolute prohibition of
the Koran is partly responsible. " O believers, says the prophet,
commit not suicide. . . . Whoever shall do this maliciously and
wrongfully, we will in the end cast him into the fire." Even more,
perhaps, have the racial propensities of the Arab and the doctrine of
Kismet been influential in preventing suicide. The patience of the
Arab when facing pain, and his acceptance of danger, and trouble,
are notorious. Life to this race is not a matter for speculation or distaste. They identify themselves immediately and uncomplainingly
with its ebb and flow. T. E. Lawrence wrote of the Arabs that he
knew : " The least morbid of peoples, they had accepted the gift of
life unquestioningly, as axiomatic. To them it was a thing inevitable, entailed on man, a usufruct, beyond control. Suicide was a
thing impossible, and death no grief."

in the Middle Ages is more complicated and difficult to trace than the Canon law. It varied from place to place and, as it was based on custom, is without any sort of uniformity. In fact, in many countries, custom remained as the basis of suicide procedure long after one would have expected it to have been given a coherent shape and legal authority. It is in these early and local suicide customs that one sees the vulgar uneducated suicide-horror at its most vindictive. The popular, unreflective, and brutal element persists in the later legal rationalizations of these customs, but there the economic desire to deter, working from above, is also visible, often even intensifying purely popular sentiment.

Though King Edgar, it is sometimes claimed, linked suicide to murder, his union must have been ineffectual because Bracton, the legal authority of his time, writing in the thirteenth century, does not rank suicide as a felony. Thus fifty years after Magna Charta the suicide was not yet legally a criminal in England. His fate, however, was in the melting-pot. Many of Bracton's contemporaries had not agreed with him, and by the middle of the next century, in spite of Bracton's ruling, the person who intentionally took his life had become guilty of *felo-de-se*. This assimilation of suicide to felony came about in two ways. First, the connection between suicide and self-murder had been early established in the Church and among the common people; from these sources it crept into legislation at a later date. Secondly, it is probable that the growing practice of exacting a forfeiture of goods when a sane man killed himself (the same forfeiture occurred when people died obstinately refusing to make a will), had something to do with it. Forfeiture was the special penalty for felonies, and since the suicide forfeited his goods it came in time to be presumed that he must also be a felon.

Primitive superstition, religion, economic pressure, and a legal coincidence, all combined to produce secular penalties

against suicide, yet the law as it develops divides quite
simply into two parts: the first deals with the property of
the suicide, the second deals with his body. Property confiscations after suicide go back, as we have seen, to the Roman
confiscations which took place when a man accused of crime
committed suicide. Throughout our period some similar distinction seems very often to have been made between
criminal and innocent suicides. Although in France Saint
Louis enforced the *general* seizure of suicides' property, this
was probably an exceptional application of the letter of the
law, occasioned by his Christian zeal. In other reigns and
in various districts more leniency was shown. The Constitution of Charles V, for instance, in 1551 readopted the old
Roman distinction, and the law only proceeded against those
who had committed suicide when under accusation of felony.
The same attitude was taken by the Parliament of Toulouse,
and nearly a century later by the Parliament of Paris (1634).

In England, Bracton records a more delicate distinction:
the ordinary suicide forfeited his goods, but the person who
committed suicide to avoid conviction for a felony forfeited
both goods *and* lands. In some cases it was possible for the
heir to buy back the confiscated goods; and in 1289 we find
the widow of one Aubrey of Wystelesburg redeeming her
husband's confiscated property for £300. Finally, Bracton
adds that " the madman, or the idiot, or the infant, or the
person under such acute pain as to produce a temporary distraction, who kills himself, shall forfeit neither lands nor
chattels, because he is deprived of reason". For the ordinary
English suicide, however, as far as his *goods* were concerned,
the law of forfeiture which came in with the Danes remained
theoretically unaltered until the second half of the nineteenth century. In practice it was rarely enforced after the
mid-eighteenth. On the other hand, the right of the law to
confiscate a suicide's *lands* was never absolutely established.
Cowell, writing in 1630, says that there were doubts about

the legality of such confiscation in his time, and Coke's Institutes, fourteen years later, mention only the confiscation of goods and chattels, definitely excluding the forfeiture of land. We can for the whole of Europe only sum up the question of forfeiture in the broadest terms: it is simply true to say that everywhere from the Middle Ages to the eighteenth century suicide of one sort or another entailed seizure of goods or land, or both; the usage was often based upon custom and so varied considerably from place to place.

The second and more severe revenge that medieval law and custom took on the suicide was not on his chattels but on his corpse. Little by little the idea that the sin of suicide *must* be punished gained authority. Since the author of the suicide was untouchable, the next best thing seemed to be to visit the sin posthumously on his body. Thus it arose that the corpse of the suicide fell into the hands of the law, or was subjected by custom to curious indignities. Most of the latter had a definitely religious and superstitious, rather than a legal background, and are obviously of great antiquity. In England, for instance, one custom prescribed that the body should enter the churchyard by the wall and not go in by the gate; another rather similar custom laid down that a suicide must leave the room in which he had died, " not by the door but through some hole or pit made under the threshold of the door ". More often, as in the city of Danzig where the window-frame was subsequently burned, the persecuted corpse had to go out through the window. A gruesome and famous usage, commoner in England than elsewhere, was the burial of suicides by night at a cross-roads; a stake was driven through the breast safely to imprison the spirit that might otherwise have wandered.

Each country and town had its own forms of procedure against the corpse. Thus in some places a distinction was apparently made for women suicides, whose bodies were burnt. In France the connection made between suicide and homicide led to the corpse being dragged, like that of a criminal, head downward on a hurdle through the streets. Fulbecke, writing in 1601, shows the results of the same connection of ideas in England. The suicide, he says, " is drawn by an horse to the place of punishment and shame, where he is hanged on a gibbet, and none may take the body down but by the authority of the magistrate ". At Metz in the fifteenth century we find that attempted suicides were severely beaten, while successful ones were put in a barrel and floated down the Moselle, whence presumably they were eventually carried out to sea. This was evidently a practical way of getting the tainted body, the blood-guilt, out of the limits of the community. The laws of Zürich are perhaps more interesting than any other as their provisions show clearly an underlying primitive desire to imprison the dissatisfied errant spirit at all costs. They ordain particularly that the suicide who has taken his life by throwing himself from a height is to be buried *under a mountain* whose whole weight shall, as it were, press down upon his restive soul; similarly the suicide by drowning is to be buried under sand. The latter penalty is similar to a widespread usage which ordained that suicides were to be interred on the seashore in the sand below high-water mark.

Such degradation of the corpse does not seem to have been legalized until fairly late. In France it does not appear in legal texts before the fourteenth century, though naturally it had been practised very much earlier. In England it seems never to have been properly legalized, and Blackstone, in the eighteenth century, finds no written authority for it, though as a jurist his general attitude to suicide is one of condemnation. He says: " The suicide is guilty of a double offence: one spiritual in evading the prerogative of the Almighty; the other temporal, against the King, who hath an interest in the preservation of his subjects." This being the case, the suicide, he says, forfeits his goods and chattels to the king, and the coroner issues a warrant that the body shall be buried in some public highway. No mention of the stake occurs even in the coroner's warrant, and it seems to have had no vestige of legality.

Though having no legal authority, degradation of the corpse nevertheless existed in England as a practice of the Coroners' Courts for many centuries. By 1823, however, it had long fallen into abeyance[1] and a statute of that year states that no coroner shall issue a warrant for the burial of a suicide in any highway, but that the body shall be buried privately in a churchyard between nine and twelve at night without religious rites.

In a general survey of the treatment accorded to the corpse and goods of the suicide, one thing stands out—the severity of Civil as compared to Canon law. This is perhaps the more curious when one remembers that the crystalization of suicide-custom into secular law is always fairly late, and occurs chiefly from the thirteenth to the fifteenth centuries. Whereas the chief period of the Church's legislative activity against suicide was in the sixth century. This added severity is explained, however, if one looks into the two chief sources of secular suicide legislation. The first source, as might be expected, is the already familiar suicide-horror of the uneducated peasant type. Legislation, deriving on the one hand direct from local custom, incorporated this horror as a very strong element which expressed itself more forcibly than it could hope to do through a barrier of Christian belief and education, and in the framework of the Church.

Secondly, there was the economic factor. To the priest suicide was a sin concerning the soul and God alone; to the

---

[1] In 1823 a suicide named Griffiths was interred at the intersection of Grosvenor Place and the King's Road, Chelsea. This was the last degradation of the corpse in England and must have been exceptional even at that date.

lord it was a sin against society. As the latter it called not merely for condemnation, but for a type of punishment that would act as a *deterrent* to others. It is particularly interesting that secular opposition to suicide should have crystalized into law in the fourteenth and fifteenth centuries when the feudal system was breaking up—when, in other words, the loss of a single one of one's " men " would have been more keenly felt than a century or two earlier. The deterrent element with its economic basis was always particularly in evidence in France, not only in our period but later in the time of Louis XIV (see page 191). In the fifteenth century we find that the body of one Louis de Beaumont was to be dragged " *le plus cruellement qu'il se pourra, pour monstrer l'experience aux autres* ". An indication that the powers were not so much concerned with the sinfulness of suicide as with its prevention among the people, who, no matter *how* they lived, were exploitable *while* they lived.

At a time when it was not usual to search out economic causes for social attitudes, Donne shrewdly pointed to the practical basis of anti-suicide legislation. Discovering that the confusion of suicide with homicide " hath no foundation in Naturall nor Emperiall Law . . . having by custome onely put on the nature of law ", he proceds to the economic root of the matter. Though slavery, he says, has come to an end, the number of wretched labouring men still far exceeds the happy; for this reason it was " thought necessary by lawes and by opinion of Religion to take from those weary and macerated wretches, their ordinary and open escape and ease, voluntary death ". Mahomet, says Donne, " to withdraw his Nation from wine, brought them to a religious beliefe, that in every grape there was a Devill "; similarly, he concludes, was the ordinary man of the Middle Ages frightened away from suicide, an act often harmless in itself.

Such, then, were the secular penalties against suicide. Directed against chattels and the corpse, they were inspired

by twin forces—popular horror and economic fears. Based
on custom, they varied from place to place, but their type
was always the same and they persisted everywhere in
Europe—at least on paper—until the French Revolution.

VII. A HESITATION

In spite of this steadily accumulating mass of legislation
and prejudice there did appear for a brief period the
vestiges of a reasoned attitude. This perceptible pro-suicide
sympathy coincided with that embryonic civilization sketched
out in the dark Middle Ages by Charlemagne. The impetus
which made it possible for him to foster a revival of learning
and to launch his famous palace-academy came oddly enough
from England. There religious influences from Ireland and
Rome had created a certain intellectual artistocracy, and
people like Alcuin and Scotus Ereginus brought to
France a respect for the classics and learning, for order
and reasonableness. The spirit of this early renascence,
which penetrated every walk of life, was not likely to
overlook the Canon law. The general attitude to suicide and
the suicide legislation of the sixth century were foremost
among the things calculated to jar on an enlightened mind
and to come into conflict with ideas that a new respect for
classical studies had put about. Consequently, throughout
this period one can trace a tendency that tempered popular
severity towards suicides and even succeeded in softening
for a while the earlier legislation.

Though in the first half of the eighth century the Venerable Bede had again affirmed the theory of the self-inflicted
nature of Christ's death on the cross, ideas more favourable
to suicide did not begin to take practical shape until after
800. In A.D. 829 the definitive text of the *Penitentials* was
issued. These now provided that masses should be said for
insane suicides, and prayers for those who committed suicide

through the vexations of the devil. It is most interesting to note the appearance of the now familiar insanity excuse. This ever since has been the subterfuge of the forces of intelligence in their attempts to modify suicide legislation without causing an open breach with popular prejudice.

In 878 the Council of Troyes further officially modified the strictness of sixth-century legislation by admitting certain funeral rites to suicides. Even St. Augustine's writings, for the contrast they presented to the absolute severity of the intervening period, now came to be quoted in support of moderation; and Pope Nicholas I announced that all suicides must be buried—though with the saving popular clause that this was " only lest the omission should be offensive to others ". Even a certain general support was lent to the efforts of the *élite* by events in Spain. There the Muslim persecutions led to a spate of martyrdoms, many of them voluntary, and a certain popular enthusiasm was aroused, similar to that of the early Christian period.

But this relative and guarded leniency towards suicides was not to last. It was not more than a perceptible hesitation on the way that led down to the seventh circle of the inferno. With the break up of Charlemagne's premature civilization the old attitude of absolute condemnation returned. We have, in fact, already watched its reflection and intensification in later canon and secular law. Before turning to its final intellectual and imaginative expression in the two greatest figures of the later Middle Ages, we must see how a desire for death expressed itself in spite of such concerted opposition.

VIII. THE OUTCASTS

It is the fashion to say that there was practically no suicide in the Middle Ages, and that Christianity and feudalism combined to create a world where everyone accepted that state of life to which God and his lord had called him. There were, it is argued, no square pegs in round holes and no influences at work tending to break down the resistances with which people counter a longing for death. Fifty years ago a writer on the subject was unable to find any notable suicides between A.D. 400 and A.D. 1400. In a sense he was right. The individualistic suicide, arising from the mal-adjustment of a highly developed personality, such as we know to-day, was rare enough. Society was carefully integrated, and over long periods comparatively stable. Church and State between them helped to shoulder so many of a man's problems that the individual was not often faced by those questionings and awful decisions which lead to suicide. Problems of "why" and "whither" did not usually crop up for the ordinary person; and, if they did, a solicitous Church had the right answers pat. In a well-knit society where responsibilities, duties, and privileges, were cut and dried, and where the individual found a satisfying extension of his personality in his local community and, beyond, in the universal Church of Christ, there was not much cause or excuse for the suicidal misfit. Within the temporal and spiritual framework a man's problems were perhaps less teasing than at any other time in history.

Outside the framework it was a very different story. The heretic, the Jew, the witch, the excommunicate, were in a terrible solitude. The isolation of life in a modern city is not even comparable with their loneliness. Looking at the logical pattern of medieval times one is apt to miss the rents, the frightening interstices. Your eye is not attuned to the gloominess of the landscape these gaps reveal —the old woman's hovel, the blasted heath, the intellectual hopelessly alone before the circle of inquisitorial faces. Outside the accepted framework there was nothing, absolutely nothing, on which the individual could lean. The old pagan ideas of belief in the self and pride in humanity and the

K

human solution of problems had long before disappeared. Nothing had yet come to replace them. Among all these unfortunates outside the pale, who often had nothing and no one to turn to, the death instinct found an easy discharge. Perhaps among these classes the Middle Ages provide a higher suicide figure than any other period.

The bullying and absolute non-recognition of minorities is one of the salient features of the Middle Ages and the Catholic Church. A study of the causes of suicide at the time brings one into contact with a sadism and a misapplication of ideals that are astounding. Among the heretics we find not only cases of individual suicide brought about by fear and direct persecution, but a general recurrence of the suicide-martyrdom phenomenon, which was so common among the orthodox Christians at an earlier date. At Orleans in the eleventh century an heretical movement was suppressed and its leaders condemned to death. When the rank and file of the unorthodox heard of the sentence they eagerly affirmed their membership of the sect and demanded that they should be burnt with their chiefs. In order to damp their ardour, the pile was actually lighted and they were brought to see it. The smell of smoke and the sight of the burning faggots failed however to dissuade them, so their wish was granted, and large numbers were burnt with their leaders.

The most numerous and famous suicide-martyrs of the Middle Ages were the Albigenses. The ferocity with which this heresy was put down is, of course, a byword. In 1218 alone some five thousand people in Southern France were put to death as heretics. Since the Albigensian heresy was on a high spiritual level, and since the lives of its supporters were far better than those of the average priest, drastic repression was certainly necessary. The measures taken were altogether successful, and thus in the early thirteenth century a body of enlightened doctrine was lost to Europe. The heretics believed in the abolition of marriage and of private property, and tried to detach themselves from the interests of the world even while living in the world; the value of companionship, vegetarianism and the metaphorical explanation of miracles, were further features of the sect. It was for beliefs such as these that hundreds of them sought out death as suicide martyrs. Near Narbonne a hundred and forty *perfecti*, as their spiritual overseers were called, not waiting for their executioners, flung themselves on to a burning pyre. Elsewhere, seventy-four knights, given the choice between death and the recantation of their heresy, chose the former and themselves mounted willingly on to the scaffold. Another story illustrates well how the authorities recognized and made use of this suicidal tendency among the Albigenses. Simon de Montfort, the chief butcher in the suppression, having taken some prisoners, handed them over to the Abbot of Citeaux. The latter, as a good churchman, was most anxious that they should die, but, as a priest, he was most unwilling to condemn them to death himself. He therefore hit on the expedient of offering them the alternatives of punishment, or liberty with recantation, expecting (as he says) that very few would buy their liberty so dearly. He was right. Most of the prisoners leapt with eagerness into the fire which he had prepared.

Another sort of suicide peculiar to the Albigenses stands out from the rest of the voluntary deaths of the period. It was calm, purely religious, and almost ritualistic. After receiving the *consolamentum* (a composite rite which displaced at once baptism, the Eucharist and absolution) it was not unusual for sick people to refuse all further food or even to weaken themselves by bleeding and so to achieve death. This voluntary fast, or *endura*, had as its object their transference to heaven when in a state of guiltlessness and ensured a certain passage into eternal happiness.

Those other perpetual heretics and outcasts, the Jews,

provide the second large source of suicide. England here supplies some charming episodes. The manners of indigent monarchs to their Jewish bankers conform pretty much to pattern, and in our period the protection offered to Jewry by the English kings was payed for in diverse ways. The notoriously ingenious device of extracting the Jews' teeth to ease their pockets is probably apocryphal, but no more drastic than other methods used to aid the exchequer. So long as the Jews remained under such efficient, but painful, protection their case was not too bad. They had little to fear from the people. In the twelfth century, however, the crusades induced a particularly strong and fanatical intolerance; and the country in the early years of Richard Coeur de Lion's reign saw a series of pogroms. These were on more than one occasion forestalled by mass suicides on the part of the unfortunate Jews. At York it appears that as many as five hundred killed each other in this way. It is a grim story. Idle Crusaders and indebted gentry started a nocturnal assault on the Jewish community. The majority, warned in time, fled to the castle, where they were received by the constable. At York, as elsewhere, the authorities were always willing to offer an asylum to Jews; though they would take no measures against their persecutors. The constable, having left the castle on business, returned to find the gates, owing to some error, closed against him. Anger and misunderstanding resulted in the sheriffs giving orders for the assault of the castle. The Jews, in self-protection, took control of the latter, and a full-fledged siege ensued. A fanatical hermit, robed in white, spurred on the besiegers in this minor crusade. When after several days of assault and blockade it seemed inevitable that the Jewish " garrison " must surrender, a courageous rabbi exhorted them not to fall alive into gentile hands. A large majority took this counsel, cutting the throats of their wives and children, firing the building over their heads and finally killing each other. Next day a mere handful surrendered, hoping that they might save their lives by offering to be baptized. The fanaticism of the mob and the strange chivalry of the crusaders refused their offer. They dispatched the remnant in cold blood. A century later in France we find the same sort of thing still happening. Forty Jews seized and thrown into prison on a trumped up charge of poisoning, killed each other to a man, and at Verdun in 1320 more Jewish suicides took place, running into hundreds. It is interesting to notice that these and similar Jewish suicides were all in the tradition described by Josephus in his account of the fall of Jerusalem. The individuals did not take their own lives, but acted as executioners to each other.[1]

Among smaller classes of unfortunates, who outside the social framework were forced into suicide, we must mention witches and the divorced wives of priests. When, in the eleventh century, Hildebrand, to secure the celibacy of his clergy, not only forbade them to marry, but forced them to abandon the women with whom they were already living, the latter (tradition says) in many cases committed suicide. There was no place for them in the careful framework of the Middle Ages. But perhaps the most lost and isolated class of all were the witches. The suicides of these unfortunate and persecuted women are notorious and traditional. They had themselves no hope, and ignorant communities showed them no mercy. It was often preferable to die by their own hands rather than wait for the inevitable day when they would be hauled off to the flames amid general delight. Sprenger, in his *In Malleo Maleficarum*, tells how the witches of North Germany frequently

---

[1] There is no reason to believe that Jewish persecution-suicides have ever ceased. The Spanish Inquisition took its toll when Torquemada drove the Jews and *conversos* into Africa, and cases must have been frequent in Germany since 1931.

made away with themselves, or when they were hauled off
to prison strung themselves up in their cells, or took their
lives in any way they could.   The last witch seems to have
been burnt in Ireland in the nineteenth century : this is the
nearest point in a perspective of many centuries during
which these casual outcasts had literally nowhere to turn but
death.   There is hardly a village or a stretch of country in
the wilder parts of the British Isles which has not still its
ruined witch's hovel or witches' corner.   Such places mark
the spot where a frightened and toothless old hag lived and
tried in vain to combat local prejudice; suicide or the stake
were often the last alternatives that remained to her.

There were, in addition, times when the *cadre* of society
itself temporarily broke up and for a moment the ordinary
man may have felt himself almost as much on his own as the
witch and the heretic.   Such times were the plague years and
the occasions of strange epidemic visitations.   These scourges
were so rude and devastating that they shook even the
stability of the medieval system.   Not only was the horror
and fear of universal death upon them, but people suddenly
found that the habitual *tempo* and customary relationships
of life had broken down.   They were called upon to make
efforts and adjustments for which they felt themselves incapable.   In the seventh century Roger of Wendover reports
something very like an epidemic of suicide arising as the
result of a pestilence which swept the country at that time.
During the Black Death in the fourteenth century the same
sort of thing occurred over a wider area and for a greater
period.   Defoe, in his *Journal of the Plague Year*,
proves that three hundred years later similar suicides were
still common.   " Some," he says, " threw themselves out at
windows or shot themselves, or otherwise made themselves away, and I saw several dismal objects of that kind."
(There were other diseases, of course, like the Dancing
Manias in Germany and Italy in the fifteenth century, which

were often directly suicidal in their development and
symptoms.)

Outside these exceptional categories it is true to say that
suicide was cut down to a minimum in the Middle Ages.
Yet all the same within the normal functioning of society a
desire for death, though repressed, found a certain expression.
It is very significant that this expression was chiefly confined
to the upper and educated class where, as has been pointed
out, both the primitive and economic prejudice against suicide
carried least weight and where the penalties do not seem to
have been enforced. It is interesting to notice that these
personal and individualistic suicides fall under familiar
headings—two are classic types, honour and devotion; one
is mainly a Christian type, chastity. Of the first type Raoul
de Neele, Constable of France, is a romantic fourteenth-
century example. When he was taken at the disastrous
battle of Courtrai, the Flemish burghers wished to spare his
life. But seven hundred pairs of gold spurs, the insignia of
knighthood, were lying on the field, and the Constable said
that he had no wish to live now that "*toute la fleur de
crestienneté*" had died in battle. Throwing himself on his
captors, he compelled them to kill him. The suicide of
Regnault, Comte de Boulogne, in prison after the battle of
Bouvines, comes in the same category; as does also Joan of
Arc's attempt at suicide while in prison at Beaurevoir. She
threw herself from her cell window because, she said, she
preferred to die than fall into the hands of the English. In
her trial this attempted suicide was used against her by the
bishops, who pretended to find in it one more proof of her
susceptibility to the spirit of evil.

At all times suicides for devotion seem particularly noble
and untainted. Perhaps this is because of a vague connection

[1] The only suicide recorded outside these categories between the
fifth and fourteenth centuries seems to be that of Merovius, son of
Chilperic, when ambushed by his father's men in 577.

somewhere in our minds with the fully sanctioned ritualistic wife-suicides of early times, and other civilizations. Such suicides have never ceased altogether, and in our period we find Blanche of Castille wanting to kill herself out of grief for the death of her husband, Louis VIII. What her entourage would not allow her to do, other women achieved.

Lastly, the chastity-suicide continues to occur here and there. For the barbarian invasions of earlier centuries we now get the raids and incursions of the Northmen. In Normandy many women found death the only satisfactory reaction to the coming of the invaders; and we have already seen the steps, perhaps even more courageous, that the Yorkshire nuns took to preserve their chastity.

From the crusades comes a story which proves that, among the upper class at any rate, suicide for the preservation of chastity was not regarded as a particularly odd or immoral act. Margaret, wife of St. Louis (so Joinville reports), fearing to fall into the hands of the Saracens, supplicated the eighty-year-old knight who slept in her chamber during her husband's absence: " *Je vous demant, fist elle, par la foy que vous m'avez baillie que, se le Sarrazin prennent ceste ville, que vous me coupez la teste avant qu'ils me preignent.*" To which the knight answered: " *Soiés certeinne que je le ferai volontiers; car le l'avoie ja bien enpensei, que vous occiroie avant qu'il nous eussent pris.*" Such a reply shows that the suicide-horror, though general, had not penetrated everywhere among the upper class and that a desire for death, though unsanctioned, persisted in finding an outlet throughout the Dark Ages.

IX. THE INFERNO

Abelard, so often a problem to the tenth-century Church, never thought to question the orthodox views on suicide. Perhaps to a person of his vitality the question would have appeared irrelevant. At all events, after the collapse of Charlemagne's civilization, opinion was once more setting too strongly against suicide for even his eloquence to have been effective in its advocacy. Suicides to Saint Bruno in the next century were simply " martyrs for Satan ". Obviously opinion had moved on so far since the days of Saint Augustine that a new and authoritative statement of the position was required. In his *Summa*, Thomas Aquinas supplied it. In this comprehensive work suicide naturally had its allotted place. Given his premises, Aquinas of course treats the question quietly and logically. To begin with, the old pagan pro-suicide arguments are quoted (these serve as mere dummies to be later demolished), followed by Augustine's argument assimilating suicide to murder. Aquinas then goes on to develop his own position, and for three reasons finds that suicide is absolutely wrong. First, it is unnatural. Every man bears an instinctive charity towards himself and should desire to do himself no harm. Suicide, since it is both uncharitable and contrary to the natural laws, is a mortal sin. His second argument harks back to Aristotle. Every man is a member of some community. He is not an individual unit, and his duties and responsibilities touch even his death. Suicide, therefore, is anti-social. Lastly, life is the gift of God; yet, though given, it still remains *His*; it is *His* property. The man, therefore, who takes his own life may be compared to a person who kills someone else's slave. The slave-owner is robbed by the loss of his servant, God by the loss of a life. Suicide is therefore an act against divine property. The sinfulness of suicide is thus restated intellectually. It only remains for Dante to draw his conclusions. Imagination follows the sinners to the underworld.

Dante is precise; there is no trimming in his hell. Justice comes full circle, and to each sin and failure he awards the punishment that seemed merited to a poet of the time.

Below the heretic and the murderer, beyond the Styx and the river of blood, Virgil leads him to the suicides. In a pathless wood whose foliage seemed too dark and dull to be called green, Dante heard wailings on every side. Not believing that he stepped in a forest of dead men or that warped and gnarled trees could have human voices, he put out a hand and plucked a twig from a great thorn. Its trunk cried to him, " Why dost thou rend me? Men we were and now are turned to trees." So Dante found that every tree and bush there in the wood was the soul of a suicide. Pier delle Vigne, once Frederick II's chosen minister, his blood trickling out where the twig had been newly snapped, relates how the spirit that tears itself from its own body, is flung by Minos to the seventh gulf and falling in that wood sprouts where it chances, like a grain of spelt. Shot to a sapling and grown up, the harpies come to feed upon its leaves and bring it pain; and thus it lives out, in the gloomy wood, an endless punishment. So Diogenes Laertes's wise men, stripped of their honours, lost even the shape of gods and mortals. The punishment was ironical. Stoic pride, and the belief in individual action, could have little scope in the limitation of leaves and twigs. These dead could not hope to repeat the self-assertive gesture which ended their lives. The Roman spirit had been circumvented. A thousand years had sadly reduced the men who handled their own destiny and who boasted that, thanks to knife and cup and rope, their honour was inviolable and their life only bad as long as they chose to tolerate it.

A fresh light and liberation were soon due to penetrate the bleeding branches of the wood. Dante's visit marked a nadir in the fortunes of the wise men. Their rescuers were already at hand.

CHAPTER VI

THE RESCUE

I. A STRANGE TEAM

AN odd and unconscious alliance was formed to effect the rescue of the Wise Men—a rescue slow and difficult from the start, and not yet absolute to-day. These classic sages, and indeed sometimes these classic fools, were redeemed from the seventh circle of hell by forces not apparently friendly, and which we may symbolize in the figure of Luther and in the literary and resurrected shade of Seneca.

Any serious modification of the catholic–feudal framework would in the fifteenth and sixteenth centuries have necessarily produced a situation more favourable to suicide even if such a modification brought about no change in anti-suicide opinion. The very fact of disturbing the balance of the Middle Ages in any way, of altering the careful subordination and adjustment of the individual to his social and religious unit, would raise problems likely—in certain people and under certain circumstances—to lead to suicide. That the old framework did in these two centuries receive several severe shocks which changed the face of society is a matter of history. The most severe and disturbing of these shocks is connected with the name of Luther, the representative of orthodox Protestantism.

Periods of disorganization are peculiarly favourable to suicide, and the Reformation, while in essence a period of transition to a fresh integration, appears for our purposes as such a period of disorganization. There is more to it than this, however. Luther represents not only a revolutionary force, shattering the comfortable framework of medievalism and the social shelters behind which the individual had been harbouring for several hundred years; he represents also certain ideas which, besides being revolutionary instruments, tended *in themselves* to promote states of mind likely sometimes to lead to suicide. Briefly these ideas may be summed up in the phrase " personal responsibility ". That trio of teasing, disturbing, and depressing questions which man is sometimes forced to ask himself concerning life—how? why? and to what end?—were sudden re-stated. In the previous thousand years, when some stray voices put such questions, Church and Emperor had their answers ready, which they intended should give full satisfaction or they would know the reason why. Usually it was easy to set the inquirer at rest, because thought itself was in the service of the Church. Nominalists, Rationalists, and Thomists laboured only to reconcile Aristotle and Plato with Christ, and not even these acute and meticulous minds thought to examine the premises on which their intellectual labour rested. With the Reformation and the re-discovery of classic learning things changed; it was now incumbent on everyone to ask the questions which before so few had dared to ask. In one of its aspects Protestantism is the religious outcome of the spirit of rational inquiry. The two chief proposals put forward for the reform of the church by Occam as early as the fourteenth century were a return to the direct study and interpretation of the Bible in its true spirit, and the formation of a representative ecclesiastical council whose authority was to be superior to the arbitrary and prejudiced judgments of any individual Pope. Both proposals are illustrative of the fundamental shift from absolutism and obedience, to personal inquiry and the formation of reasonable personal judgments.

Ideally the Reformation meant two things : first, that man

was to be allowed to apply the test of reason to knowledge; secondly, that a society was to be created where he would be free to apply this test. Of course in practice no such toleration was granted. Zwingli and Calvin were as excellent persecutors as any of their predecessors. Luther, however, is a partial exception. He represents the truer spirit. " It is futile and impossible," he says, " to command, or by force to compel, anyone to believe so, or so." And again : " Everyone should be allowed to believe what he will. If he believes wrongly he will have punishment enough in the eternal fire of hell." And lastly, a key-passage from our point of view : " It is at a man's own risk what he believes, and he must see for himself that he believes rightly."

Once more man was to be troubled by doubts, once more uncertainties had leave to rise and sap the foundations of energy. Life was again superscribed with a question-mark. The beginning of a process had begun which the nineteenth century hardly finished. With insoluble problems to solve, and with the fear of hell awaiting those who found a false solution, with the cast of thought paling over the simple issues of the Middle Ages, certain individuals found suicide the only way to still a beating mind. A rationalism inherent in the new ideas helped to make the step easy : reason once turned on to the problem of life might easily lead in the opposite direction, and the Reformation that was intended to bring Europe closer to God must in the event have indirectly taken many people towards death. For those used to the tight and pleasant framework of the Middle Ages there must have often resulted from the sudden speculative freedom of the Reformation an overwhelming and awful consciousness of isolation, of personal identity and personal problems. Such isolation and consciousness we know to be conducive to suicide.

Calvin was opposed to Luther in every way; with his inquisitorial spirit, with his Paulinism, with his insistence on supernatural salvation rather than on spiritual values, he should have been at home in the ranks of the Catholic Reaction. And yet his very doctrine of predestination was a destructive weapon, and when we imagine its effect on a melancholy and susceptible mind we may well believe that it was an agent tending to provoke suicide.[1] The teasing question of the time " What must I do to be saved? ", did not, of course, arise for the Calvinist. Heaven was not the reward of merit, and salvation was not to be gained by works. He was subjected, however, to doubt and uncertainties of another kind. Was he one of those whom God had already saved, was he among the predestined?[2] If he felt doubtful, not only must the blackest gloom have descended upon him, but a hopeless irresponsibility. No act of his could remedy the situation; he was a " vessel of wrath " and must remain so. Thus damned, no religious hopes and no fear of a worse future could effectively intervene between an impulse to suicide and its execution.

Further, Calvin, by exalting God and removing Him to a plane of inaccessible superiority, tended to minimize and humble man, and so indirectly to reduce the value of the individual human soul, a thing always precious to Catholicism. As we have seen in the Middle Ages the importance of the human soul, and the idea of immortality bound up with this, was a great suicide deterrent and formed the basis of one line of anti-suicide argument.

Even within the Roman and Greek Churches two move-

[1] The suicide-rate in the Calvinistic Swiss cantons has always been exceedingly high.

[2] " Many are called, but few are chosen ". Even the Catholic Church in the Middle Ages was not ever-liberal in its estimate of the numbers of the chosen. The usual figure was 1 in 1000; but Berthold of Regensburg, among the most influential preachers of his time, put it at 1 in 100,000. Burton later attributes much melancholy to the ferocity of preachers, particularly in the Reformed Church, who held out visions of fire and hell to their flocks.

ments may be said to have affected suicide, one indirectly
and the other directly. First the Jesuits by their empiricism
and acceptance of practical issues undermined strict moral
standards. The sinfulness of sin at a particular time and
place became a matter for debate; suicide, the worst sin of
the Middle Ages, inevitably became involved in the general
uncertainty. Partly as a result of the Jesuits and the
casuistical outlook, crimes of violence and immorality
increased in Italy out of all knowledge from 1530–1600. A
typical story that aptly illustrates our theme is that of
Eleana Campireali. Once the mistress of a bandit, she rose
in the world and managed to get herself installed as Abbess
of the Convent of Castro. There, prosecuting her career
with further success, she acquired a bishop for a lover. Unfortunately, the unexpected return of her outlaw put a sudden
end to her plans, and she committed suicide out of shame
and foiled ambition. A general loss of absolute canons and
a doubt as to whether power and virtues resided with Christ
or the devil, led also to a vast increase in witchcraft, which,
as we have seen in the Middle Ages, is so often connected
with suicide. Not only among the people did the practice
spread, but the nephew of a cardinal lost his head in trying
to compass the life of a pope by invoking the devil in his
own palace.

Russia in the following century provides a direct and far
stronger example of the effect of religious teaching on
suicide. It was widely believed about 1666 that the arrival
of the Antichrist was at hand, and a large section of the
uneducated serf population lived either in a state of abysmal
fear or pious exaltation.

> Some of them ceased to till their fields, abandoned their houses,
> and on certain nights of the year expected the sound of the last
> trump in coffins which they took the precaution of closing, lest
> their senses, or what remained of them, should be overpowered by
> the awful vision of the Judgement Day. It would have been well

if the delusion of their disordered intellects had stopped there. Unhappily in many cases it went much further, and suicide, universal suicide, was preached by fervent missionaries as the only means to escape the snares of Antichrist and to pass from the sins and sorrows of this fleeting world to the eternal joys of heaven.[1]

Deaths by fire and starvation were countless, and until the end of the century people continued to forestall the ever-imminent day of judgment with unshaken faith.

We have shifted away and onward from the main current of the Renaissance, and we must hark back to the other influence which, on a different plane from Luther's, helped to achieve the liberation of the Wise Men. From Italy, with the revival of learning, came the shade of Seneca and the resurrection of all those ideas which had made suicide a logical and socially possible act in classical times. The full force of this revival and the awe and enthusiasm which accompanied it are not easily realizable to-day. One must experience a little of the intellectual thirst which had been slowly growing throughout six hundred years to understand Petrarch, ignorant of Greek, kissing the manuscripts of Plato and Homer; and Alfonso of Naples, receiving with a reverence previously accorded only to the relics of saints and martyrs, a shin-bone which purported to derive from the leg of Livy. It was this wild enthusiasm for the persons and ideals of the past that made Mantua strike coins with Virgil's head, and Rienzi style himself amid acclamation *Tribunus Populi Romani*.[2]

Though many of the humanists were admirable Christians, the ideal of Roman civilization inevitably came to be contrasted with Christian Rome. " You follow infinite objects, I follow the finite," said Cosimo de Medici. Among the finite objects which the Renaissance inherited

[1] Frazer, *The Dying God*.

[2] There is an interesting and obvious comparison to be made between this revivalism and many features of Fascist Italy.

RELIGION AND THE MACABRE: ONLY THE DIAMOND
OF FAITH WILL NOT PASS THROUGH THE HOUR-GLASS
OF TIME

(From Imagines Martis, 1555)

from Rome were the self-sufficiency, self-reliance, and reso-lution, of which Cato had provided the best example. The old ideals and the old conceptions of pagan times became common coin again. Once again man was invested with dignity and self-determination; he was again the captain of his body and soul, owing allegiance to nothing but to his own idea of right and to his own nobility. It was for him to determine how his life was lived and to see that he did not fall, or, if he fell, did not remain in any situation unworthy of himself. Pico della Mirandola, whose reputation stood as high as that of any other humanist, re-stated these ideas in the semi-Christian phraseology suitable to the time. He imagines the supreme Maker addressing man :

> " Thou restrained by no narrow bounds, according to thy own free will (in whose power I have placed thee), shalt define thy nature for thyself. . . . Nor have we made thee either heavenly or earthly, mortal or immortal, to the end that thou, being, as it were, thy own free maker and moulder, shouldst fashion thyself in what form may like thee best."

The title of the work in which this passage appears—*Oration on the Dignity of Man*—reveals better than any-thing else the return to classical ideals which had taken place.

This change in outlook was inevitably reflected in the attitude towards suicide. It is true that Petrarch, the earliest considerable humanist, remains opposed to suicide. But his refutation of the arguments in support of it is balanced and without prejudice. The fanatical horror has disappeared. Four of the models chosen by Chaucer in the first five parts of his *Legende of Goode Women*—Cleopatra, Thisbe, Dido, Lucretia—were suicides; and a prominent scholar later dares to refer to Lucreece as a " rare light of chastity ". It is, however, the great Erasmus himself who, in the *Eloge de la Folie*, redeems the lost suicides, calling those who seek their own death in disgust at the nature of life " the next neighbours to wisdom ". Elsewhere he specifically praises

L

the courage of Cato, and his praise is re-echoed by Montaigne for whom Cato was the model chosen by nature to show to what lengths human endurance and constancy could attain.

Rather later in France the Abbé de Saint Cyran, in an effort to bolster up the dignity of kings and to insist on the absolute allegiance owed to them, willingly retreats from the absolute condemnation of suicide which was the Church's official postion. In a work entitled *En Quelle Extremité le sujet pourroit être obligé de conserver la vie du prince aux depens de la sienne*, he admits several contingencies in which a man may kill himself without it being *homicide de soi-même*.

In Montaigne the question of suicide crops up again and again, and though with his natural caution he hedges and covers himself by paying lip-service to the orthodox Christian position, one may see where his real sympathies are situated. Two of the ladies in his chapter entitled *Of Three Good Women*, were suicides. Further, he quotes all the ancients from the Spartan patriots to Hegesias, the orator of death, with evident approval and admiration. "Death", he says, "is not a receipt to one malady alone; Death is a remedy against all evils: It is a most assured haven, never to be feared, and often to be sought." It is here in his pages that we meet again not only the shade of Seneca in reference and argument, but the very resurrected periods of the champion of suicides masquerade as Montaigne's own.

It is in Montaigne that we find something with which we shall have more to do later—the appearance of a shrewd, practical and *bourgeois*, attitude to suicide. In the following quotation it barely peeps through the scaffolding of a typically stoic argument:

All comes to one period, whether man make an end of himself, or whether he endure it; whether he run before his day, or whether

he expect it: whence soever it come, it is even his owne, where
ever the threed be broken, it is all there, it's the end of the web.

Elsewhere a practical view is affirmed more strongly and
throws its weight, as it was always to do later, against
suicide. The opinion which disdains our life, says Montaigne, is ridiculous. This is the only life we have, and we
must make the best of it. We should not set ourselves at
naught, crying for the impossible, or desiring " to be made
of a man an Angell." And what solution is suicide anyway? What can it bring us that is positive? " In vaine doth
he avoid warre, that cannot enjoy peace; and bootlesse doth
he shun paine, that hath no means to feele rest." Two pages
later the practical view assumes its crudest form: the proverb comes into play, and illustrates the maxim that your
luck may change at the very last moment and that people
sometimes evade an apparently inescapable danger. " I have
seen a hundred Hares save themselves even in the Grey-
hounds jawes: *Aliquis carnifici suo superstes fuit.* ' Some
man hath outlived his Hang-man.' "

Montaigne's general attitude to suicide we may take to
be typical of the enlightened opinion of his time. It may be
defined as a re-statement of Stoic ideas, tempered and over-
layed by a moderating Christianity. Both in literature and
court society this mixture can be traced, and Brantome, a
man of the world, in his memoirs reproduces the attitude.
Speaking of a master of arms who committed suicide for
shame at having been twice *touché* by his pupil in a fencing
bout, he says: " *Quelle humeur, quelle résolution et quel
courage d'homme!* " And then immediately, as though
catching himself up, he adds: " *Ce trait ne tient pas du
chrétien.*" The Stoic praise comes first; the Christian modification is an afterthought. Similarly, Madame de Sevigné,
writing of the suicide of Vatel some sixty years later, says
to her daughter: " *On le loua fort, on loua et blâma son
courage.*" The important thing is that the *absolute*

condemnation of suicide has disappeared among the enlightened. Though the primitive suicide-horror is still firmly entrenched among the people, a section of society once more judges suicide from a rational standpoint and inquires sanely into causes, motives, and results.

Of all the suicides of the period perhaps none is so much in the classical tradition, and none has received such praise then and since, as that of Strozzi, the Florentine patriot. Detesting the domination of the Medicis in the free city of Florence, he was privy to the murder of Alexandro de Medici and took the field against Cosimo, his successor. The liberal army, however, was defeated and he was captured. Fearing that he might be put to the torture and in his extremity betray the names of his fellow-patriots, he decided on suicide. First, however, he begged his children to have his dead body removed from Florence to Vienna. If he had not had the happiness to die in a free city he at least prayed that his bones might repose in one after his death, and that his ashes might be in peace beyond a tyrant's territory. The spirit of Cato was certainly abroad. Finally, before stabbing himself, he carved with the self-same dagger this line of Virgil's on the chimney-mantel of the chamber in which he was confined:

Exoriare aliquis nostris ex ossibus ultor.

A quotation, finally, from Sir Thomas More, a great Christian and a great humanist, will illustrate how the light of a reasonable attitude had invaded the forbidden area of suicide. In his *Utopia* he is speaking of pain and illness and of how it may be combated:

> But yf the disease be not onelye uncurable, but also full of continuall payne, and anguishe; then the priestes and the magistrates exhort the man, seinge he is not hable to doo anye dewte of lyffe, and by overlyvinge his owne deathe is noysome and irksome to other, and grevous to himself, that he wyl determine with

himselfe no longer to cheryshe that pestilent and peineful disease. And seinge his lyfe is to him but a tormente that he wyl not be unwillingė to dye, but rather take a good hope to him, and either dispatche himselfe out of that payneful lyffe, as out of a prison, or a racke of tormente, or elles suffer himselfe wyllinglye to be rydde oute of it by other. And in so doinge they tell him he sall doo wysely, seinge by his deathe he shall lose no commoditye but ende his payne.

Here, perhaps for the first time in *Christian* writing, is a serious consideration of euthanasia and an unprejudiced approach to a certain type of suicide.

It remains to consider what were the practical results of this change of opinion on the part of educated society. Officially and legally the change, for a long time, and for reasons which we shall see below, had few repercussions. The lag between *élite* and uninformed opinion, between idea and law, was very large and tended to increase right up to the eighteenth century and in some countries even until the nineteenth. Practically, in the number of actual suicides, what were the effects of these sixteenth-century changes? It is difficult to tell. We have not the " patriot " and " honour " suicides of classic times, easily traceable because they create a stir and involve public issues. On the contrary with the Renaissance, and the growth of psychological complexity which it brought, suicides become more and more personal, in the sense that they spring from occasional and hidden causes and from the subtle interactions and repercussions of things not easily discovered. Estienne, a French writer, complains bitterly of the commonness of suicide, but the general opinion seems to have contradicted him. Certainly no cult of suicide arose between the fifteenth and seventeenth centuries, for several forces were at work to counteract the Stoic doctrines and the example of classic practice. First there was the Christian sentiment, which we have mentioned; but even more important there was the vital *élan* of the Renaissance. Life for the average man was not contracting but expanding; every day there were more possibilities open to him. Symbolically as well as geographically a new world had been discovered. Life for the average man was so rich and so full that the ambition of the great was to retain after death any sort of immortality and share of life here on earth rather than in a future paradise. In Italy, painters, architects, and sculptors were at a premium, and their job was to perpetuate the fame of their patrons; Colleoni ordered that statue of himself which stands in Venice, and Filippino Lippi is seen in his own paintings. In England the poets were the immortalizers. If Elizabeth had not ruled, she would still be enthroned in the *Faerie Queene*, and half of Shakespeare's sonnets are preoccupied with the preservation of an earthly name to his lover. Against such a desire for life, which was eagerly cherished even in the attenuated form of posthumous and artistic memorials, the shade of Seneca, and the oratories of Hegesias, can generally have had no practical virtue. If this pulsing life often seemed intolerable to the point of suicide, it was not classic doctrine that made it so but another more fundamental and more insidious influence whose birth must now be discussed.

II. THE BIRTH OF MELANCHOLY

It has always been too easy to be unhappy, yet in the medieval framework unhappiness was usually occasioned by specific causes. A man was usually able to say just why he found life intolerable at any particular moment. With the Renaissance this ceases to be so. For the first time, at any rate since the Roman Empire, a large number of people are unhappy without knowing why; the birth of melancholy is signalled. The reasons for this are various, but before we try to disentangle them we must distinguish between melancholy and the religious pessimism of the Middle Ages. The fig-tree which Timon grew that he might never want a

branch on which to hang himself is a very different symbol
from the hermit's skull. The first is a symbol of melancholy,
of disgust with the world; the second is a *memento mori*,
a reminder of the briefness of life, a witness to the decay of
the flesh, but also by implication to the indestructibility of
virtue and the immortality of the Christian soul.

The Middle Ages had a great sense of the macabre, and
they were brought up on the *memento mori*. Piety and
morality enrolled the figure of death himself; the poet wrote
of him, and the local painter gave his exact representation on
the walls of the church, where a skeleton led on the *danse
macabre*. Death is, in fact, always grinning over the shoulder
of the medieval man; art, anecdote, preachers, and the
popular consciousness, made his lineaments quite clear.
Looking around them these men were not unaccustomed to
see a grey polished skull below a shock of hair. With the
coming of the Renaissance this preoccupation with death is
intensified: 1485 saw the first edition, with engravings, of
a *Danse Macabre*, and in the same century appeared the
Ars Moriendi—a typical work of its sort, describing the
grim wiles with which the devil tempts the souls of the
dying.

It is to be noticed, however, that there is very little element of sorrow in most of these works: it is not the sweet-
ness of life which death brings to mind but the futility
and inevitable retribution of sin. The emphasis is not upon
the sad shortness of life but upon the awful length of
eternity.

It is just at this moment that a change of spirit can be
detected in the macabre. This change is symbolized in the
difference between the wood-engravings of the *Danse
Macabre* and Durer's *Melancholia*, and it is first clearly
visible in the work of Villon, whose poems gave a new twist
to the tradition of " ghastliness ". There enters now a note
of nostalgia. The emphasis shifts; it is no longer the sinner's

horror of death and eternity which appals, but the touching brevity of life. There is a new insistence on the value of fleeting mortal things. In a single quotation Villon can be seen passing from the negative attitude of the old macabre, explicit in his first four lines, to something different:

> *La mort le fait fremir, pallir*
> *Le nez courber, les vaines tendre,*
> *Le col enfler, la chair mollir,*
> *Joinctes et nerfs croistre et estendre,*
> *' Corps feminin, qui tant es tendre,*
> *Poly, souef, si precieux,*
> *Te fauldra il ces maulx attendre.'* [1]

This new attitude in Villon where melancholy first begins to oust the macabre becomes in time a typical feature of the Renaissance mind and it springs from typical Renaissance influences. Carried on the tide of the sixteenth century this attitude grows complex, leaves hells, skulls and symbols, far behind, and broadens into the comprehensive melancholy of Hamlet. Its causes are various, but first must come the fact that life is acquiring an increasing value; it is more and more desirable and is discovered to have more and more aspects and possibilities. Ideal values move from the next world back to this: they are realizable here and now. But as soon as you situate paradise on earth melancholy begins. This sounds paradoxical, but it is not. If life is valuable, the inability to control or enjoy it is all the more pitiable; if life

---

[1] The sensual element in these last lines unconsciously emphasizes the very close connection between sex and death. In many of Villon's poems the leveller does double work as *mors* and cupid, and his vocabulary of decay has a continuous sexual undertone. There are strange ramifications to follow up here. Incidentally Villon himself contemplated suicide, as he says in his *Grand Testament*:

> *Souvent se n'estoit Dieu qu'il craint,*
> *Il feroit un horrible faict,*
> *Si advient qu'en ce Dieu enfrainct*
> *Et que luy mesmes se deffaict.*

(Anonymous 16th century drawing) *(Photo Giraudon)*

MELANCHOLY

represents really important values and pleasures, and these are unobtainable by any particular individual, his frustration will be correspondingly great. Melancholy arises when life is held to be supremely good (as at the Renaissance), but when its possessor is unable to adjust himself to it. It is the old psychological story : this lack of adjustment leads to repression and then to the jaundiced eye which, to excuse its own failure to obtain pleasure, discolours the world around it. Thus for its own satisfaction it creates a drab picture, flattering itself that there is nothing to be found in a world where itself can find nothing.

The man who could not find happiness in the medieval framework felt after all that he was not missing much; his ideology taught him that the world and its beauty were a delusion, an extensive pasturage for worms. It was paradise that would redress the balance and make the odds all even. But to the man of the Renaissance, that wondrous work, noble in reason, infinite in faculty, whose very proper sphere was the goodly frame of Florence or Elizabethan England, an inability to savour so magnificent a life, to adjust himself to its fleeting and irrecoverable shapes, was a hopeless, tantalizing, and bitter failure for which an eternity of paradise could make no recompense.

One is, of course, generalizing, and to say that there was absolutely no melancholy of the Renaissance type in medieval times is nonsense. Even in the earlier period certain forces produced for certain types of people a situation congenial to melancholy. In Egypt, as we have seen, the melancholy of the monks induced by solitude and their strange lives often led to suicide. They themselves believed that this melancholy which crept upon them, not at night, but in the interminable length of the hot desert noons, was caused by the *daemon meridianus*. It was in itself a sin; and so Dante regarded it who imprisoned the melancholy in the fifth circle of the Inferno. There, half-suffocated with

the wrathful in a muddy bog, their confession came bubbling
to the surface :

> *Fitti nel limo dicon: 'Tristi fummo*
> *nell'aer dolche che dal sol s'allegra,*
> *portando dentro accidioso fummo;*
> *Or ci attristiam nella belletta negra.'*

Chaucer, too, in the *Parson's Tale*, tells how accidia
" makith a man hevy, thoghtful and wrawe ", and how
" the synne of worldly sorrow, such as is cleped *tristitia*,
that sleth, as seith seint Poule ". The emphasis, however,
in nearly all these earlier but post-classic melancholies is
religious. They arise from despair of the grace of God,
and it is as such that they meet with so severe a condemnation.

In the Middle Ages it is really only with the troubadours
and the whole tradition of chivalry that we can detect much
of the different, lingering, and introverted melancholy which
was to become common later. By their insistence on the
supreme value of love and the glorification of the lover-
mistress relationship these people situated a lot of ideal value
in life rather than in the Church. The judgments of the
supreme court of love in Aquitaine usurped some of the
authority and importance which belonged rightly to the
court of heaven. But such usurpations were occasional and
not essential to the period, nor did they touch large numbers
of people. Only with the Renaissance were values really
transferred from heaven to earth; the price of failure and
maladjustment was thus made immediate, tangible, and infinitely more bitter. With so much to grasp, and with the
ever-recurring human inability to grasp it, many people
became addicted to the newly born melancholy.

Another of the agents that participated in the creation of
Renaissance melancholy had also to do with repression, but
with repression of a specific kind : that necessitated by

the antinomy of faith and reason. The fifteenth and sixteenth centuries saw a sudden and intense strengthening of
sincere religious feeling, but on the other hand this was offset
by a new and enthusiastic rationalism. Though these two
forces might form a coalition in an antipapal front, the
success of the Reformation inevitably showed the super-
ficiality of such an alliance. Reason and reformation were
fundamentally opposed and, though an apparent compromise
was often effected, their latent antagonism burst out in
events such as the general persecution of the Anabaptists
who carried principles of reason into the heart of their religion and practice. On the individual plane and in the
psychologies of individual persons this battle of reason and
faith was often waged with an intensity even more bitter.
Faith, entrenched behind the exact interpretation of
the Bible and with all the vigour of the new Christianity at
its disposal, or in the Catholic Church with all the authority
of tradition behind it, was usually successful in stilling
reason. Such successes, however, when not based on recon-
ciliation, are fictitious and costly : the conqueror in the end
has to pay, though payment may come in one of many ways.
The self-justifying harshness and persecution shown by
great and well-meaning men like Calvin were one such payment; in other people it took the form of melancholy. It is
the latter which interests us, and in Luther its genesis and
the whole process of repression is beautifully clear.

In the early days of the Reformation we find Luther well
disposed towards reason. His spirit, his energy, his eagerness for reform, made him recognize it both as a legitimate
fighting weapon and as a light of guidance. Confronted at
the crisis of his career by the Emperor and the assembled
states, he was called upon to retract the beliefs which he had
expressed in writing. In words, which at that solemn
moment must have been well considered, he replied that he
could not do so unless his arguments were refuted by Scrip-

tural text or by *cogent reasons*. A few days later the repetition of this statement still found him linking reason and Scripture in an exalted partnership. The success of the Reformation severed their union. Luther, as so many of his contemporaries, became distrustful of the speed at which things were moving. As a servant, reason was well enough; but as a master it was not to be trusted. The terror in which reason came ultimately to be held by so many of the reformers, and the necessity that they felt for repressing it if they were to save their souls from hell, is only to be understood by reference to their background. Enlightened though they were, the Middle Ages stood close behind them. Melancthon was a caster of horoscopes, and both he and Luther believed implicitly in the multiform monster which was said to have been found in the Tiber in 1496 and " whose physical peculiarities they regarded as indications of the will of God in regard to the papacy ".

In 1522 Luther could still write: " What then is contrary to reason is certainly much more contrary to God. For how should that not be against divine truth which is against reason and human truth? " Reaction, however, was already setting in. Apprehensive of Anabaptism and the other unorthodox beliefs to which he had indirectly given impetus, he forced upon himself a progressive repression of reason with a corresponding insistence on faith. Reason becomes " an ugly Devil's bride " and " God's bitterest enemy ", and finally in the last sermon that he ever preached at Wittenberg, not long before his death, it has sunk to the status of " an accursed whore ". In the presence of reason he says, " all the articles of our Christian faith . . . are sheerly impossible, absurd, false ". So reason now assumes a position of absolute incompatability with Christianity. It stands in direct opposition. Such a deformation of his earlier natural instinct, and such a wrenching of an influence native to the Renaissance, was bound, on Luther, to have psycho-

logical results. Of the countless other people who attempted
a similar violence, many might be able to avoid the conse-
quences; but not he. The sensibility of a fine and enthusiastic nature had to pay the penalty. For years his life
was discoloured by inner conflicts and bouts of typical
melancholy. He writes to Melancthon that " for more than
a week I have tossed about in death and hell : so that, hurt
in all my body, I still tremble in every limb." The storms
and tempests of despair to which he confesses himself liable,
and the hallucinations from which he suffers, bear naturally
enough an altogether Christian tone. They are none the less
true Renaissance melancholy.

Luther's attacks of gloom, though naturally they might
be expected to come under the head of the religious melancholy which has always existed in the Christian Church, have
a fresh emphasis. It was not the fear that he might miss
redemption, and doubt of the infiniteness of God's mercy,
the *homicidia animae* of the Fathers, that troubled Luther.
" The terrible meditation of hell-fire and eternal punishment," says Burton, " much torments a sinful silly soul."
Luther naturally was not such a one. It was the conflict
of the age which tormented him, the first engagement of a
long battle between faith and reason. Burton himself well
realized how this antimony which the Reformation had
brought to the fore was productive of melancholy. When,
as he complained, there were fifty thousand atheists in Paris
alone, could anyone remain secure and unquestioning in
their faith?

Luther's most illustrious rival, the Emperor Charles V,
died in extreme religious melancholy. This eminently
shrewd, practical, and capable king devoted his whole life to
the suppression of reason as it was embedded in the Reformation. He, at any rate, appeared to be secure and unquestioning in his faith. And yet perhaps one can trace in
his final collapse the revenge of a personality whose rational

side had over a period of forty years been consistently repressed in certain spheres. It is tempting to think that his
sudden and terrible eruption of melancholy brought on by
the gout, may have had a certain affinity with Luther's
bouts " of death and hell ". Though in a different camp and
viewing life from a different angle, he was an intelligent man
fundamentally exposed to the same conflict. Robertson, in
his life, tells the story of his extraordinary end at the Spanish
monastery of St. Justus. A few months before his death " an
illiberal and timid superstition depressed his spirit. He had
no relish for amusements of any kind " and after some time

> he resolved to celebrate his obsequies before his death. He ordered
> his tomb to be erected in the chapel of the monastery. His
> domesticks marched thither in funeral procession, with black
> tapers in their hands. He himself followed in his shroud. He
> was laid in his coffin with much solemnity. The service for the
> dead was chanted, and Charles joined in the prayers which were
> offered up for the rest of his soul, mingling his tears with those
> which his attendants shed, as if they had been celebrating a real
> funeral. The ceremony closed with sprinkling holy water on the
> coffin in the usual form, and all the assistants retiring, the doors of
> the chapel were shut. Then Charles rose out of the coffin, and
> withdrew to his apartment, full of the awful sentiments which
> such a singular solemnity was calculated to inspire.

The fears from which he continually suffered in those last
months would appear in a man of his character to have been
caused by the subconscious realization that reason had been
secretly sapping the apparently firm foundations of his faith.
Reason in religious matters, confined for a lifetime in the
subconscious, broke through in his age and weakness. His
extreme melancholy and fearful piety were a last defence;
only in extreme anguish was the fort of orthodoxy held
right up to death.

There were, in addition, causes productive of melancholy,
which, if less acute than the newly emphasized struggle between faith and reason, were more general in their influence.

An increase in thinking which the expansion of the times made necessary was accompanied by an increase in psychological complexity. People became more complicated to meet the more complicated situations with which they had to deal. Instead of the cut-and-dried decisions of the Middle Ages the man in the street found himself faced with a variety of problems and issues. He must stop to think; he must weigh and proceed cautiously. Events imposed " the pale cast of thought " upon him, and in its train came the demons of hesitation and uncertainty. Hesitation walks with gloom; action is its antidote. In the sixteenth century an increase in the uncertainty that waits upon most thought tended strongly to melancholy.

Perhaps nowhere can the melancholy figure be better traced than in literature. Shakespeare, harbouring behind that infinite brain and restless energy the nihilism which Wyndham Lewis pins down in *Lear*,[1] produces Hamlet, Jacques ("melancholy men are witty which Aristotle hath long since maintained ": Burton), and lastly the utter weariness of Prospero, as the final images of melancholy. Among the contemporary types in his *Micro-Cosmographie* Earle draws a figure " vainglorious in the ostentation of his melancholy. His composure of himself is a studied carelessness with his arms across, and a neglected hanging of his head and cloak, and he is as great an enemy to a hatband as Fortune ". But neither this mowing nincompoop, nor agonized Essex before his death, gloomy and irresolute to the verge of madness, are more than sketches beside Hamlet. He is the archetype, and with him we see the inevitable approach of melancholy to suicide.

T. S. Eliot has indicated the appearance of a Senecan sensibility in Elizabethan drama. Roman stoicism is, he

[1] " As flies to wanton boys, are we to the gods;
They kill us for their sport."
One example among many.

rightly says, a development in self-consciousness. The hero in difficulties, confronted with defeat and death, realizes that he stands alone, that only the strength of his own character and his own personality remain between him and annihilation. This realization (and here is the crucial point) far from depressing him is a source of actual consolation. So high is his own opinion of the human character, and thus incidentally of himself, that it sustains him to his death. This is the mixture of vanity and grandeur which makes Othello's last speech a vindication, and his last minutes tolerable to himself. Unlike the medieval Christian, steeped in humility, the Elizabethan stoic dies proudly, never losing his belief in self-determination. Conquered and forced to suicide, Antony remains unbeaten; " I am Antony still," is his last and greatest boast.

With the shade of Seneca suicide returns to literature. It is not surprising that the *Spanish Tragedy* which issues in Elizabethan drama should contain the suicide of two major characters, Hieronymo and Bellimperia. The suicide of Faust, who slays himself both soul and body, is in its double aspect the extreme example of a death to which the Elizabethan tragedians were always sympathetic. Though Hamlet did not willingly cross the bourne, many others did. In eight tragedies Shakespeare gives us no less than fourteen, or possibly fifteen, suicides.

Hamlet's figure is too familiar, and the ground has been gone over too often, for me to try to analyse his melancholy. Perhaps it is because melancholy and suicide are not a philosophic matter that the issues in *Hamlet* are so intangible and mixed. In the soliloquies where Hamlet actually speaks of suicide it is interesting to find that his grounds of argument change and that as the play moves on his restraining motive apparently shifts from the medieval Christian prohibtion to rational argument and simple fear of the unknown. (Not, of course, that either of these deterrents *really* affect his actions. They appear as excuses.) The change is from the complaint in Act I that God had " fixed his canon 'gainst self-slaughter ", to the weighing up of pros and cons in " to be or not to be ". In the latter, divine command gives way to practical considerations, and Hamlet, in his attitude, epitomizes a change that was already spreading over Europe.

The rich and brutal gloom of Webster is less introspective and less typically melancholic in our sense of the word. His mortuary metaphors, his fowl " *coffined* in a baked meat " and his

> Millions . . . now in graves, which at last day
> Like mandrakes shall rise shrieking,

bear a nearer relationship to the macabre of the Middle Ages. For him the pleasures of life are the " good hours of an ague ", and his melancholy does not usually strike the new note, ruminative, cerebral and nostalgic. Ford is more to our purpose. There is something mournful even in the slow, lapsed, and wandering movement of his blank verse:

> For he is like to someone I remember,
> A great while since, a long, long time ago.

This is typically sad, discreet and quiet. Melancholy, like everything else, was becoming private and personal and thus only to be whispered in an undertone.

Cervantes, who died in the same year as Shakespeare, left in *Don Quixote* the perfect companion to Hamlet. He is the comico-melancholic, laughter and tears. Though he does not ask the same imponderable questions " whither? " and " why? " the means he chooses to achieve his ends are, like Hamlet's, so unsuitable, that a vast question-mark is thrown over life and matter. Who, after all, is right? May not windmills be horsemen, and men become sheep? Beside knight and squire rides the melancholy phantom of the time. The ghost of question, the inevitable " is it all worth

M

while?" lurks behind the forlorn hopes that the hero leads. There was, in fact, something ghost-like in " the wound that phantom gave me" of which Don Quixote complained. Hacking on Rosinante through a century, melancholic in spite of all its motion and energy, even the knight's idealism was not proof to contagion by sadness.

We have still to deal with two important literary melancholics, Burton and Donne. The first exhausted the subject of melancholy once and for all; the second produced the first work in support of suicide that we have in English. Burton's great book is divided into three parts: the first treats of the causes and symptoms of melancholy; the second of its cure; and the last, of the melancholies that are associated with love, jealousy, and religion. The width of Burton's treatment, and the eternal ubiquitous melancholy that he reveals, makes one at first hesitate to believe that there was an increase and a modification in kind during his own period and the hundred years that preceded. " The tower of Babel," he says, " never yielded such confusion of tongues, as the chaos of melancholy doth variety of symptoms ". That excess of *atra bile*, which Avicenna considered was the cause of sadness, solitariness, suspicion, and fear, giving men " long, sore, and most corrupt imaginations ", under Burton's patient and contemplative eye widens into a vast black stream seeping through the heart of life and washing even the shores of the New Continent. This very fact is important. If there had not been a different savour of gloom, something freshly melancholic in the air of the seventeenth century, is it likely that Burton would have been pricked to produce such a work? [1]

---

[1] It is significant that he was not the first to feel this impulsion. Some time previously, in 1586, there had appeared *A Treatise of Melancholie*, written by 'Timothy Bright M.D. Shakespeare apparently had read this work and used it in building up his character of Hamlet.

The connection between melancholy and suicide, and particularly Burton's attitude to the latter, are what chiefly interest us. He lived, as he says, " a silent, sedentary, solitary, private life, *mihi et musis* in the University ", and he had himself in spite of his humour a persistent strain of melancholy which he could sometimes only shuffle off by going to listen to the rich abuse exchanged by the bargees on the Isis. He died on the twenty-fifth of January 1639, very near the date on which he had prophesied that his death would occur. Rumour had it that he committed suicide in order to fulfil his own prophecy, as Jerome Cardan, the Italian savant, was reputed to have done sixty years earlier. The students of Christ Church alleged that he had " sent up his soul to heaven thro' a noose about his neck ". Whether or not this was true, the connection between melancholy and suicide had been clear enough to him.

All the infinite varieties of melancholy lead, he says, to self-destruction : " 'tis a common calamity, a fatal end to this disease "; " if there be a hell upon earth, it is to be found in a melancholy man's heart "; he is " that true Prometheus, which is bound to Caucasus : the true Tityus whose bowels are still by a vulture devoured ". Little wonder then if suicide was the escape to which the melancholy turned. " Socrates his hemlock, Lucretia's dagger, Timon's halter, are yet to be had; Cato's knife, and Nero's sword are left behind them, as so many fatal engines, bequeathed to posterity and will be used to the world's end by such distressed souls."

Burton was a parson and a scholar. His judgments on the rightness or wrongness of suicide will therefore be of particular interest as reflecting both the more enlightened scholastic and clerical opinion of his time on this subject. What actually are his views? In practice they do not differ much from those of Montaigne; we find the same conflict between Christianity and classicism, and a similar, though perhaps rather more Christian, compromise. The practical outlook, noted in Montaigne, also makes an incidental appearance: "No man so [i.e. by suicide] voluntarily dies, but *volens nolens* he must die at last, and our life is subject to innumerable casualties; who knows when they may happen?" Having quoted with obvious sympathy the familiar pagan authorities in support of suicide, he remembers his cloth and recovers himself: "these", he suddenly stipulates, "are false pagan positions, profane Stoical paradoxes, wicked examples". He is unable, however, to maintain such an extreme attitude; even the official Christian no longer thinks on these matters as did his medieval counterpart. Circumstances now alter cases. Condemnation is no longer irrational and absolute. "Hard censures of such as offer violence to their own persons . . . are to be mitigated . . . in such as are mad, beside themselves for the time, or found to have been long melancholy." Here are vast loopholes for the countenancing of the act.

Again:

> If a man put desperate hands upon himself by occasion of madness or melancholy, if . . . he doth this not so much out of his will as on account of his disease, we must make the best construction of it, as Turks do, that think all fools and madmen go directly to heaven.

Finally, after quoting the anti-suicide authors and the penalties which had accumulated round the act, he makes a definite break with Church dogma. Ending on a note of tolerance, he questions the eternal damnation of the suicide which had been for so long the central belief of the Church's anti-suicide teaching. He terminates the discussion in the following way, without coming to any definite conclusion:

> Of their goods and bodies we can dispose; but what shall become of their souls, God alone can tell; His mercy may come *inter pontem et fontem, inter gladium et jugulum*, betwixt the bridge

and the brook, the knife and the throat. What may happen to one may happen to another. Who knows how he may be tempted? [1]

Though not published until twenty-five years later Donne's *Biathanatos* must have been written at about the same time as the *Anatomy*. First, the work is important because it links up our subject with the metaphysical poet's love of death and the macabre. Both the suicide which, by a conceit, the lover commits as often as he leaves his mistress ("Deare, I dye as often as from thee I go") and the symbolic term which Donne put to his own life in sitting for his mortuary monument, find rational excuses in the *Biathanatos*. From another angle too the work has an incidental importance, for it points again (as do the *Christian Adviser against Self-Murder* and Sym's work on suicide quoted below) to the prevalent melancholy of the age and comes as a corollary to the *Anatomy*. The latter speaks in abstract of human gloom; the *Biathanatos* is a practical examination of one effect and result of such gloom. We have moved from the general to the particular: Donne is by implication dealing with a contemporary problem—one of the religious, intellectual and social, questions that were in the air of the early seventeenth century.

The *Biathanatos*, written when Donne was a young man, was published by his son, posthumously and against his

---

[1] Not very long after Sir Thomas Browne wrote: "I think no man ever desired life, as I have sometimes death." His melancholy, preserved even in the rhythms of his sentences and the colour of his vocabulary, was of the typical self-protective sort whose widespread arrival has been noticed. It made tolerable the minor scale of Norwich and the succession of fen seasons. Painted in colours such as Thomas Browne's imagination could provide, the unattainable world would have been a torture beyond endurance; but this toning down, this deliberate fogging of landscape, this self-flattering pall of melancholy, made the circle of savants, the buried urns, tolerable and even pleasant.

father's wishes.[1] The strengthening of Donne's religious
convictions, his entry into the Church, and possibly the
knowledge that his manuscript was, on the whole, of no
great literary value, led to its not being published during his
lifetime. The full title of the book indicates its scope and
attitude : " *Biathanatos. A Declaration of that Paradoxe, or
Thesis that Self-homicide is not so Naturally Sinne, that it
may never be otherwise. Wherein the Nature and extent of
all those Lawes, which seeme to be violated by this Act are
diligently surveyed.*" It is divided into three parts, which
are devoted respectively to proving that suicide is not in-
compatible with the laws of nature, of reason, or of God.
Though its interest lies in a variety of anecdote, examples
of which I have quoted elsewhere, its real value is that it
reveals a new attitude. Many of the manœuvres by which
Donne outflanks the religious position are boring, many of
his arguments are quibbles, and many of the points he makes
are now palpably wrong; nevertheless, there is a rational
approach, an attempt to cope with prejudice, that is new in
the post-Augustine history of suicide. Apart from a superficial respect for orthodoxy which has to be maintained, the
moral question is dealt with from a practical angle.
Donne is the first Christian writer on suicide to openly state
the general law that circumstances must alter cases. " No
law can be squared for all events," he says. And again in a
key passage : " No law is so Primary and Simple, . . . but
that Circumstances may alter it; in which Case a private
man is Emperour of himself, *sui juris*. And he, whose
Conscience . . . assures him that the Reason of Self-Preservation ceases in him, may also presume, that the law

[1] Written about 1608, it was published in 1644. Concerning the
manuscript Donne wrote Sir Robert Ker : " Reserve it for me, if I
live, and if I die, I only forbid it the Presse and the Fire : publish it
not, but yet burn it not; and between those, do what you will with
it."

ceases too . . ." Finally, in point of time, Donne's work is the first defence of suicide in English. It is the first occasion on which anyone has come into the open on behalf of the " wise men ".

The *Pelecanicidium*, or *Christian Advertiser against Self-Murder*, published in 1653, was so called since pelicans are reputed to commit suicide. The author, Sir William Denny, referring in his preface to the " late-publisht paradoxes that self-homicide was lawfull ", evidently intended his doggerel poem as a reply to the *Biathanatos*. The final catastrophic couplet runs as follows :

> O Blest the Time, that Christ for all once died!
> Is he our life! Abhorre Self-Homicide!

The arguments throughout are little better than the poetry.

Life's Preservative against Self-Killing, published about fifteen years earlier by John Sym, a clergyman, is interesting and is more valuable in every way. Three manuscript copies of the *Biathanatos* were in circulation when Sym's work appeared, but his particular approach to suicide makes it unlikely that he would have been interested in refuting Donne's meticulous arguments even if he had seen them. His attitude is altogether practical. He seems to have been worried by the increase in suicide and to have set out wholeheartedly to combat it. Self-murder may have been for him " a sin transcendant beyond law and mercy ", but it was also a contemporary problem. His book, as the title explains, sets out to be a preservative against self-murder. He tells when, and how, and why, it must and may be combated. Behind his exhortations one finds an interesting and sensitive mind, and the enchanting style in which he offers advice and arguments is exact and personal.

Man, he says, has a double life, physical and spiritual, and thus " all soules that miscarry are in some sort self-murdered ". This is, however, too abstract a line of thought for him to follow for long, and he proceeds to a purely practical division of suicide into direct and indirect types. Direct suicide we are already familiar with. Though indirect suicide was to be made a lot of later by the Catholic casuists, it cannot be better illustrated than from this early work. *Life's Preservative* tells us that indirect suicide occurs " in *eating* to gluttony, and *drinking* to drunkennesse; using *labour* and *recreations* to surfeiting ". It occurs in duels, or :

> when any doe out of a *bravery*, and gallantry of spirit, goe need-lessly with a charge of money, or of men's persons, or errands; *either* in the night, through a place haunted and beset with mur-derous robbers; *or*, at any time through knowne *ambushments*, and strong *troupes* of enemies.

Or again, it is indirect self-murder " when *self-conceited*, wilfull, *foole-hardy men* will fight against their *enemies*, upon desperate *disadvantages*; and imminent perill of death ". To plead " guilty ", even if your hands are dripping with innocent blood, comes under the same head. And lastly, of course, are included among indirect suicides the commission of mortal sin and the keeping of company with accursed persons.

When every type of suicide has been enumerated, dis-cussed, and damned, John Sym proceeds to methods of prevention. He has the psychologist's eye for the living individual rather than the divine's vision of a future con-flagration. When men have " ghastly looks, wilde frights and flaights, nestling and restlesse behaviour, a mindless-nesse and close dumpishnesse, both in company and in good imployments; a distracted countenance and carriage; speaking and talking to, and with themselves, in their solitary places and dumps ", then is the moment for care and the time to circumvent the devil. The melancholy man must take practical measures and be chiefly cautious

> in forbearing lawfull use of weapons, or knives.

shunning to go upon lawfull calling into solitary retired places; over waters, bridges, upon battlements of houses; or neere steepe downe places . . .

shunning to be alone, or in dark places.

Such are among the specific prescriptions that Sym lays down for the new melancholia. These, with sobriety, an honest occupation, and the Church's comfort, will keep suicide at arm's length, and wean Hamlet from his gloomy moods.

III. KINGS AND COLONIES

It is characteristic that Sir Thomas More, the advocate of utopian suicide, should have died at the command of a king.[1] Throughout the Middle Ages philosophy and scholarship were the eager servants of religious authority. To whatever school you belonged you were first and foremost an avowed supporter of the Church and of pious kings who were the chief weapons in her temporal armoury. The work of the schoolmen merely achieved the union of philosophy and theology. They consistently worked to reconcile Aristotle to Christ. Christianity was the fixed absolute, the gate through which the ancients must squeeze their philosophies or be rejected. An inverse process, the turning of a direct philosophical light on to Christianity itself, was unthinkable.

With the Renaissance there came a change. An examination of premises, whether Christian or pagan, brought learning into open conflict with authority and broke up their old alliance. The Reformation and the decline in the universal power of the Church brought about a second change. The kings, whether those of the Catholic reaction or of the

---

[1] Madame de Stael calls More himself a suicide, in the sense that the voluntary martyrs were suicides. The King wished to spare his life; and every opportunity was used to induce him to withdraw the statement of his opinions.

Protestant party, took upon themselves, both directly and by a supervision of Church policy, the imposition of that uniformity of ideas and straitjacket of orthodoxy which had before been directed solely from Rome. Thus the old anti-suicide policy was now prosecuted by the kings on religious and economic grounds. Suicide and the tolerance of suicide is an insult to the authoritarian; More's death is in this way symbolic. In England such a scholar and philosopher might earlier have been burned by the Church; in the sixteenth century he was beheaded by a king.

It is perhaps equally significant that Spenser, writing for a queen as the official laureate and poet of reaction, should have attacked suicide. The visit of the Red Cross Knight to the cave of Despair is one of the most enchanting passages in the *Faerie Queene*. Despair cunningly tempts him to suicide, saying that he daily wanders farther from his goal. Despatch is easy;

> What if some little pain the passage have,
>   That makes frail flesh to fear the bitter wave;
> Is not short pain well borne, that brings long ease,
>   And lays the soul to sleep in quiet grave?

To which the Red Cross Knight replies with the orthodox argument, which has so often been lifted from the *Phaedo*:

> The term of life is limited,
> Ne may a man prolong, nor shorten, it:
> The soldier may not move from watchful sted,
> Nor leave his stand until his captain bed.

Despair counters this, saying that he who

> . . . points the sentinel his room,
> Doth license him depart at sound of morning droom.

Finally, seizing his opportunity, he presses a dagger upon the Red Cross Knight:

He to him raught a dagger sharp and keen,
And gave it him in hand : his hand did quake
And tremble like a leaf of aspen green,
And troubled blood through his pale face was seen
To come and go with tidings from the heart,
As it a running messenger had been—
At last, resolved to work his final smart,
He lifted up his hand. . . .

Una, however, intervened in time, and Despair, robbed of his victim, picked a halter and hanged himself.

But death he could not work himself thereby;
For thousand times he so himself had drest.

The opposition to suicide of the kings, and of the new authoritarianism which they represented, accounts for the fact that a tolerance for suicide among the *élite* had so little effect on law and official opinion until well into the eighteenth century. We have seen how educated opinion from the Renaissance until the time of Burton swung steadily away from the medieval condemnation of suicide. This movement continued and gathered force in the last half of the seventeenth century. Tolerance grew; though society in the France of Louis XIV and in Restoration England were forced to remember that suicide was a temporal crime they no longer believed it an inexpiable sin. Suicide and the Church had parted company. Diarists and writers in both countries share this new complaisance, but it is in the drama that it shows most clearly.

In England the tragedy of blood had died. Dramatic convention no longer imposed on the poet a plot in which the stage of the last act resembled a morgue. In the old plot suicide as often as not was forced on the characters willy-nilly; their own daggers merely forestalled vengeance or justice. The new drama might, therefore, have been expected to show no interest in suicide. Such was not the case. The two foremost tragedians of the period, Otway and Dryden, each build their best play round suicide. Otway was an intimate friend of Falkland's; the heir of that Lord Falkland whose touching suicide was one of the memorable deaths of the civil war.[1]   In his *Venice Preserv'd* Jaffier stabs his friend Pier to spare him the pain of execution, and with the words "And this is well, too," turns the dagger upon himself.   Jaffier, a free man and pardoned by the senate, was in no danger.   The point to notice is that his suicide is voluntary; as an expiation for the betrayal of his friend, it is calculated to gain the audience's sympathy.   His suicide comes as proof of his moral integrity, and in the last act makes him the hero, not the villain, of the play.   This use of suicide as a supreme sacrifice that is able to reconcile a character to the audience, as we shall see, was being exploited contemporaneously by Racine.

The story of Antony and Cleopatra necessarily involves the treatment of suicide; it is not the theme, but Dryden's handling of it which makes his *All for Love* important in the present context.   His general attitude is one of praise, pity and admiration.   Of Antony's death he makes Cleopatra say "thou alone wert worthy so to triumph", the implication being that suicide is the only fit and dignified end for so great a man.   The last line of the play seals the praise: "No

---

[1] Respected of all who knew him, poet, philosopher, and finally Charles' Secretary of State, Falkland was horrified at the futility of the Civil War.   Being unable to envisage any solution, "the calamity and destruction which the country did and must endure, took his sleep from him".   At the siege of Gloucester the words "Peace! Peace!" were always on his lips, and in the following September (1642) he went to voluntary death at the battle of Newbury.   His end was in the high Roman tradition.   Having told his friends that he would be "out of it ere night", he put on clean linen and dressed himself with care.   Later, mounting his charger, he rode at a hedge of Roundhead pikes and muskets. With supreme patriotism he preferred to die rather than to continue fighting against his own countrymen.

lovers lived so great, or *died so well*." But there is more
than this. In Cleopatra's suicide we see the emergence of a
principle, almost a rule, which was well established on the
continent: that a mistress should not outlive her lover, or
vice-versa. Survival, the unwillingness to commit suicide,
brings the quality of love and the nobility of the lover into
suspicion. Suicides such as Cleopatra's were becoming
almost a duty. "Let dull Octavia," she says, "survive to
mourn him dead"; the inference is that for a lover of her
quality, and for the heroine of the play, there remained a
nobler role.

"It seems unjust to me", says Dryden in his preface to
All for Love "that the French should prescribe here, until
they have conquered". Where dramatic conventions of
suicide were concerned it was, however, impossible not to
take lessons from the Continent. Corneille and Racine, reflecting a new tolerance for suicide, had already established
the types of self-destruction proper to the classic stage.

First we have that convention of which we have just
spoken: the suicide of a lover. This type was capable,
in the French dramatist's hands, of subtle complication. Thus, Atalide, the heroine of *Bajazet*, who kills herself on hearing of her lover's death, combines this type of
devotional suicide with a second category: suicide for
remorse or expiation. While railing on the cruel destiny
which has condemned her to survive her lover, she yet
realizes that she is the true cause of his death. After
apostrophizing him in these words:

> "*Il faut, par un prompt sacrifice,*
>   *Que ma fidèle main te venge et me punisse*",

she commits suicide and the necessary atonement is made. In
Phèdre such an atonement suicide appears in a simple form;
Phèdre, by her suicide, far from adding horror to an anti-
pathetic character, rehabilates herself to some extent in the

eyes of the audience. Self-destruction has become an action that lends a person dignity, and vouches at any rate for the good quality either of their villainy or love. Lastly, that invaluable piece of ventriloquial machinery, the confidante, whether maid or mess-companion, was not expected to survive the object of its hero-worship. Cépise, in *Andromache*, learning that her mistress is going to take her life, burst out with the words,

" *Ah, ne prétendez pas que je puisse survivre* ",

and Osmin, in *Bajazet*, cries to Acomat with robot devotion,

Si vous mourez, je meurs.

To what extent did this new attitude penetrate into practical spheres? And did it influence legislation? Let us first look at France. As to the canonical law there was no breath or question of a reform. Though in practice the well-to-do were usually able to obtain a decent burial, officially the Church still set itself sternly against suicide, and among the lower classes the suicide was deprived of burial. Fillucious, in his contemporary *Moralium Quaestionum*, deals with the subject by question and answer. Some of his points are worth quoting, as they show how little the orthodox Church had shifted in its ideas on the subject:

1. *Question.* Is suicide under any circumstances permissible?
Answer. Never, without the express order of God; Samson and Eleazar either acted on such divine command, or *ex ignorantia inculpata.*

2. *Question.* May one commit suicide to save one's chastisy?
Answer. No; the women who did so also acted *ex ignorantia inculpata.*

3. *Question.* May a guilty man condemned to death drink the poison which is to be his means of execution? Or, if he is condemned to die of starvation, may he refuse any nourishment that comes his way?

Answer. He may not drink the poison; he may only open his mouth so that it can be poured in. He may, however, refuse food.[1]

Richelieu said that it was worse to desire one's own death than that of another, and most of the Jansenists would have agreed with him. In their reaction against the trimming of the Jesuits they threw their weight strongly against suicide, and even Pascal upbraided Montaigne for his over-liberal views on the subject.

As regards civil law—mutilation of the corpse, and confiscation of property—we find a similar situation. The change in public opinion is reflected in an intermittent non-application of penalties where the rich are concerned, but there is no change in actual law. For the poor, penalties are usually applied; for the criminal suicide, always. In 1670 when public opinion might have been expected to set about achieving some reform, the Criminal Ordinances impose new and reactionary legislation. In these measures the kingly authoritarianism, an inheritor, as we have seen, of the old suicide antagonism, makes itself felt. In the first place, suicide is now assimilated, not to mere murder, but to high treason and heresy; secondly, if the corpse of the

[1] This distinction smacks of the intricacies worked out by the more precise Catholic casuists. We have seen that Sym divided suicides into direct and indirect; the casuists made a further sub-division into positive and negative suicides. Thus, according to Suarez, if you are involved in a shipwreck there is no sin in sacrificing your life for others by omitting to take a place on a crowded raft (negative suicide). However, once safely on the raft, it would be sinful to slide off and give up your place to a fellow-castaway (positive suicide). Special circumstances here constitute the innocence of negative suicide; similarly the secrecy of the confessional can make even positive suicide blameless. For instance, if a priest has learnt in confession that a chalice is poisoned, he must nevertheless drink it, if his abstention would inevitably betray the fact that he had learnt of the poison in the confessional.

suicide is not to be found, a sentence of defamation may be brought in against his *memory*; lastly, the reasonable distinction between accused and innocent suicides is allowed to lapse.

Here is, indeed, a drastic attempt to put the clock back; it was, as it turned out, a most unfortunate attempt. The new legislation, it seems, was unpopular from the start and never wholly enforced; in fact, the authorities often decently buried suicides, particularly those that occurred in prison, without attempting a trial which they feared might arouse resentment. We find the authorities informing the King's prosecutor and judge that if they really wished to make inquiries into a certain suicide would they please " *concerter le temps et la manière* ", so as to avoid making any stir. Lastly, the Ordinance of 1670, by holding up a natural process of readjustment, drew the incensed attention of cultivated society to the question of suicide. The measure was, in a sense, a declaration of war, and the challenge was willingly accepted by the philosophers and reformers of the coming century. It was, to say the least of it, a false move to remind the age of Voltaire that an orphan, or a husband crazed by the loss of his wife, if convicted of suicide, might be legally dragged through the streets by the feet, face down, and thrown into the common sewer.

In England in the last half of the seventeenth century, though the situation was not altogether parallel, there was a similar divergence between enlightened opinion and the letter of the law. The solvent of reason, however, met less opposition; for kingship was poorly entrenched and only too glad of a Hobbes to point out the bonds of self-interest which bound the individual to authority. Though this philosopher might state that by the laws of nature " we are forbidden to do anything destructive to our life ", society was sceptical. It generally refused to regard suicide, at any rate among people of any substance, as either very sinful or very criminal. As in France, the law officially paid no attention to this change, and the statute books remained unaltered. It must be remembered that since the reformation of Henry VIII canon law had been assimilated to the civil law. The three penalties—refusal of burial, desecration of the corpse, and confiscation of property—were therefore officially imposed by the same civil court. Now what happened was that the sentence against the corpse was simply not carried out; with the increased humanity of the later seventeenth century, the practice of desecration and burial at the cross-roads lapsed (it was not officially abolished until 1823). As regards the denial of Christian burial a certain latitude and discretion were also used. There remained only the question of confiscation. Here circumstances, the character of the suicide and the possession or lack of influential friends, were usually decisive. As time went on the crown became more and more lenient, and ever more prepared to waive its rights in favour of the suicide's family and dependants.

The actual state of affairs can be admirably illustrated from a series of letters in Pepys's *Journal* where we find him intervening on behalf of his cousin, the wife of an unfortunate suicide.

Jan. 21st, 1667

Up, and while at the office comes news from Kate Joyce that if I would see her husband alive, I must come presently. The story is that it seems on Thursday last he went sober and quiet out of doors in the morning to Islington, and behind one of the inns, the White Lion, did fling himself into a pond, was spied by a poor woman and got out by some people binding hay in a barn there, and set on his head[1] and got to life, and known by a

---

[1] " The absurd practice of holding up drowning men by the heels when taken out of water, occasioned the loss of many lives. The object was to *let the water run out*! "—BRIGHT.

N

woman coming that way; and so his wife and friends sent for. He confessed his doing the thing, being led by the Devil; and do declare his reason to be, his trouble that he found in having forgot to serve God as he ought, since he come to this new employment:[1] and I believe that, and the sense of his great loss by the fire, did bring him to it, and so everybody concludes. He stayed there all night, and come home by coach the next morning, and there grew sick, and worse and worse to this day. I stayed awhile among the friends that were there, and they being now in fear that the goods and estate would be seized on, though he lived all this while, because of his endeavouring to drown himself, my cozen did endeavour to remove what she could of plate out of the house, and desired me to take my flagons; which I was glad of, and did take them away with me in great fear all the way of being seized; though there was no reason for it, he not being dead, but yet so fearful I was. So home, and there eat my dinner, and busy all the afternoon, and troubled at this business. In the evening with Sir D. Gawden, to Guild Hall, to advise with the Towne-Clerke about the practice of the city and nation in this case; and he thinks that it cannot be found self-murder; but if it be, it will fall, all the estate, to the King. So we parted, and I to my cozen's again; where I no sooner come but news was brought down from his chamber that he was departed. So, at their entreaty, I presently took coach to Whitehall, and there find Sir W. Coventry; and he carried me to the King, the Duke of York being with him, and there told him my story which I had told him: and the King, without more ado, granted that, if it was found, the estate should be to the widow and children. I presently to each Secretary's office, and there left caveats, and so away back again to my cozen's, leaving a chimney on fire at White Hall, in the King's closet, but no danger. And so, when I come thither, I find her all in sorrow, but she and the rest mightily pleased with my doing this for them; and, indeed, it was a very great courtesy, for people are looking out for the estate, and the coroner will be sent to, and a jury called to examine his death. This being well done to my and their great joy, I home, and there to my office, and to supper and to bed.

[1] He kept the *Three Stags* tavern at Holborn Conduit.

Jan. 22nd, 1667

Stole away after dinner to my cozen Kate's, and there find the Crowner's jury sitting, but they could not end it, but put off the business to Shrove Tuesday next, and so do give way to the burying of him, and that is all; but they all incline to find it a natural death, though there are mighty busy people to have it go otherwise, thinking to get his estate, but are mistaken.

Jan. 30th, 1667

When come home, I find Kate Joyce hath been there, with sad news that her house stands not in the King's liberty, but the Dean of St. Paul's; and so, if her estate be forfeited, it will not be in the King's power to do her any good. So I took coach and to her, and there found her in trouble, as I cannot blame her. But I do believe that this arises from somebody that hath a mind to frighten her into a composition for her estate, which I advise her against; and, indeed, I do desire heartily to be able to do her service, she being methinks, a piece of care I ought to take upon me for our father's and friend's sake, she being left alone, and no friend so near as me, or so able to help her.

Feb. 4th, 1667

After dinner I abroad by coach to Kate Joyce's, where the jury did sit where they did before, about her husband's death, and their verdict put off for fourteen days longer, at the suit of somebody, under pretence of the King; but it is only to get money out of her to compound the matter. But the truth is, something they will make out of Stillingfleete's sermon, which may trouble us, he declaring, like of fool, in his pulpit, that he did confess that his losses in the world did make him do what he did.

The result of Pepys's efforts on behalf of his cousin we are never told; but as there are no further entries, it is reasonable to guess that the affair was satisfactorily settled. There are several points about these extracts that throw an intimate light on the contemporary attitude to suicide and are therefore worth noticing. First of all Pepys himself as we should have expected in so practical a man, shows no sign of horror or prejudice in relation to the act of suicide. He treats this death without moral comment, much as he would have treated any other. Secondly, the coroner's jury " give way to the burying " of the man, though he is still suspected of suicide. This penalty evidently is no longer of the first importance. The money is the thing. Confiscation of the estate is the penalty that makes the coroner's court interested in obtaining a verdict of suicide. In this context there are two or three points to notice. First the King seems willing enough to forgo his prerogative; and we may guess incidentally that such confiscations were not generally popular. Secondly, the estates of suicides did not always devolve upon the King, but in certain districts seem to have been the perquisite of a spiritual or temporal Lord; in this case perhaps the Dean of Saint Paul's. Thirdly, the unscrupulous seem to have had a finger in such pies. They attempt to get a verdict of suicide and the enforcement of confiscation, in which case the property would be sold by auction and they would buy it up for a song. Alternatively, trading on the chance that suicide would not be proved, or confiscation not enforced, they play on the fears of the suicide's family and try to get them to compound for their estate at a low figure. Lastly, both the character of the dead man and his reason for committing suicide are taken into account. It apparently weighed severely against Joyce that his action was said to have been occasioned by monetary difficulties rather than by some more respectable reason such as prolonged melancholy or ill-health. This discrimination is a most important point with reference to the general attitude towards suicide, as it indicates a drift away from absolute condemnation based on horror and superstition, and an approach to a reasoned attitude where each case is judged on its own merits.

This, it is interesting to know, was not the only occasion on which Pepys intervened to save the property of a friend who had committed suicide. In the caveats of the Record

Office for 1667 the following entry appears : " That no grant pass of the estate of Francis Gurney of Maldon in Essex, who drowned himself in his own well on Tuesday night ye 12th of this instant August, at the desire of Samuel Pepys, Esquire, August 20th, 1667."

As we have seen, authority in all its forms, whether Catholic or Protestant, opposed suicide and the loosening-up of anti-suicide prejudice. Yet paradoxically this same authority contributed, in at any rate one sphere, to the creation of actual suicides. The new colonial expansion under national flags, whether stimulated by royal economy or by commercialism, brought to the natives in all parts of the world a fresh acquaintance with death, and often an unjust and ineluctable oppression that made it better to be dead than alive. In different centuries and at places far removed —in the American plains, in the East Indies, in Mexico— colonial development, or economic exploitation of non-white races, has usually been the cause of much suicide. Probably at no place and period in the world's history has suicide been so common as in Central America and the West Indies under Spanish rule in the sixteenth and seventeenth centuries. Though sentimentalism is apt to exaggerate, Columbus probably discovered in Hispaniola a people as innocent, sociable, and gentle, as could be found anywhere. Within a couple of hundred years many of these islands were left desolate and deserted—a depopulation due as much to mass suicide as to the deaths directly caused by the astonishing cruelty of the Spaniards. Cortez and Pisarro massacred, De Soto burnt his guides, and Vasco Nunnez threw living natives to his bloodhounds; such things were a significant prelude to the long and dreary tale of Spanish oppression. But though the spirit of the natives could be broken, it could not be tamed. There remained one exit and release which had ceased to be bitter in the face of such suffering. Countless numbers chose this way out. Suicide was no sin to these people, and self-destruction did not bar the entry to their paradise. A typical story is that of certain Yucatans who were forced to labour in the Spanish gold-mines in a country that they had once owned. The appalling conditions under which they worked at last forced their old king-chieftain to call together his fellow-slaves.

> My worthy companions and friends [he said], why desire we to live any longer under so cruel a servitude? Let us now go unto the perpetual seat of our ancestors, for we shall there have rest from these intolerable cares and grievances which we endure under the subjection of the unthankful. Go ye before, I will presently follow you. Having so spoken, he held out whole handfuls of those leaves which take away life, prepared for the purpose, and giving everyone part thereof, being kindled to suck up the fume.[1]

The worst was yet to follow. Such deaths represented a severe loss to the Spaniards in the form of slave labour. The conquerors, therefore, devised an expedient by which they might deter the natives. "The Spaniards, by some counterfeiting, made them think that they also would kill themselves and follow them with the same severity into the next life." To dissuade your victims from suicide with the threat that you will follow them into the next world seems to be the last refinement of cruelty. That such trickery should have been at all effective is a terrible comment on the fear with which the Spaniards were regarded.

When Negro slaves, imported from Africa by the English, replaced the original inhabitants, they were not much more fortunate. An eighteenth-century number of the *Spectator* tells of Negro suicides in St. Christopher owing to mistreatment by whites; but the more usual reason for suicide was a longing to return in the life after death to their native Africa. The English traders, with a sound business sense and an almost unexampled lack of taste, used to cut off the hands

---

[1] Froude, *England's Forgotten Worthies*.

of such suicides to deter others from following so expensive an example. The natives believed that if the body was buried maimed it would proceed without hands into the next life.

Meanwhile, Portugal was expanding, perhaps less wantonly, but none the less effectively in the East. Montaigne tells the story of one of the suicides that were the price the natives paid for commercial penetration. In its splendour and sense of the dramatic it is truly Renaissance, an end that one might expect to have found and applauded in Italy and not in the East Indies. Ninachetuen, a petty king in Malacca, having divined the Portuguese viceroy's intention to depose him without cause, resolved as follows :

> First, he caused an high scaffold to be set up, somewhat longer than broad, underpropped with pillars, all gorgeously hanged with rich tapestrie, strewed with flowers and adorned with precious perfumes. Then, having put on a sumptuous long robe of cloth of gold, richly beset with store of precious stones of inestimable worth, he came out of the palace into the street, and by certaine steps ascended the scaffold, in one of the corners whereof was a pile of aromaticall wood set afire. All the people of the citie were flocked together to see what the meaning of such unaccustomed preparation might tend unto. Ninachetuen, with an undaunted, bold, yet seeming discontented countenance, declared the manifold obligations which the Portugal nation was endebted unto him for, expostulated how faithfully and truly he had dealt in his charge.

Then, saying that honour was dearer to him than life, and that though he could not oppose the foreigners' injuries he could at least remove himself from them, he threw himself into the fire which had been so carefully and daintily prepared.

The British Empire, and particularly our early history in India, would certainly yield many similar stories of native suicide. The subject is worth research, and results would throw a curious light on colonial expansion. Probably it would be possible to find a connection between many such native suicides and phenomena like the disappearances of Oceanic tribes. The extermination of the natives of Tasmania, however, and the change of population in places like Tahiti (reduced by three-fourths in the forty years that followed the death of Captain Cook) have to do with race suicide and will be dealt with later.

IV. GOD WITH THE GO-GETTERS

It is in the seventeenth century that there emerges unashamedly a set of new ideas which were to have a profound and stimulating effect on suicide figures, a set of new ideas which were to raise poverty suicides from a comparatively humble position to one of importance. " It is an error to believe that the rich consider you as their equal." So runs a Chinese proverb which is painfully true to-day. In medieval times, however, this was true only in a very qualified sense. Poverty carried no moral stigma : you were not bad, or stupid, or undesirable, simply because you were poor. In the capaciousness of an all-comprehensive Church, and at his particular post within the feudal hierarchy (that state of life to which God had called him), the poor man could feel a certain equality and sense of fellowship with the richest. He was acknowledged to be a part of the whole. Property involved duties first and foremost; it was primarily a trust rather than a source of income. Poverty on the other hand had acquired, from religious associations, a certain mystical importance and glamour. Neither was it divorced from power; St. Francis, the beggar, had founded an order, and even in worldly monasteries (whose abbots ranked as feudal lords) it was, in theory, not the individual but the house to whom the wealth belonged.

For these reasons poverty rarely seemed a sufficient cause

for suicide. It is possible that one exaggerates its rarity in
the days before the coming of the Puritans and capital. The
poor suicide is always the unnoticed suicide. Our statistics
begin late in the eighteenth century, and it is only with the
appearance of the statistician's prying and unbiased eye that
the humble death is noticed and rightly valued. Once we
come to columns of figures the tables are turned; Jones now
obscures Cato.

With the rise of commercialism and the breakdown of the
medieval framework there came a drastic change in the
attitude of society towards the poor. Social relationships
came to be regarded by purely economic standards; the sense
of responsibility towards one's fellow-men disappeared,
leaving in its place an energetic but ruthless individualism.
Every man was for himself and the devil might take the
hindermost. Then, as now, the hindermost were inevitably
the poor.

This change was rationalized, excused, and given
a further impetus, by the teachings of Puritanism. As
Tawney says, " the moral self-sufficiency of the Puritan
nerved his will, but it corroded his sense of social solidarity.
For if each individual's destiny hangs on a private transaction between himself and his Maker, what room is left for
human intervention? " In fact, the poor may starve. There
was more to it than this, however. The Puritan, not wishing to realize that distress has primarily economic causes
which should be put right, preferred to attribute it to moral
deficiencies. God, he said, rewarded the good with prosperity and meted out poverty to the evil. Thus, economic
failure was the mark of sin, and it grew harder for a camel
to negotiate the eye of a needle than for a poor man to enter
the Puritan heaven. God Himself became a business man,
and economic self-interest the first of his commandments.
Practical success is the corollary of spiritual salvation; and
conversely the Puritan " sees in the poverty of those who

fall by the way not a misfortune to be pitied and relieved, but a moral failing to be condemned ".

Such teaching provided sage reasons for leaving behind the old ideas of " just price ", and Calvin himself raised the age-long ban on usury. Since the pursuit of wealth was a duty towards God and society, the floodgates of competition could be thrown wide. God would see that it was the evil who drowned.

Such a change in the attitude of society towards the poor did not pass unnoticed or without opposition. *Radix malorum est cupiditas* had been a favourite maxim of Chaucer's, and much of the best element in the country tried to stem the new economic ideas both by legislation and precept.

In the century before the establishment of the commonwealth, distress had been growing owing to economic causes, but there was much opposition to the new temper of callousness and business irresponsibility. The Elizabethan Poor Law was envisaged only as a supplement to religious charity and the social duty to one's neighbour; many hospitals, almshouses, and so on, were built in the period; and, lastly, some stand was made against enclosure, and Parliament passed acts against depopulation.

The new spirit was unfortunately linked to the fortunes of the winning party. It conquered, and even the Restoration could not shake it. When the old tradition was beginning to break, Latimer gave vent to opinions that were rarely to be heard again in England until the time of the early socialists. " The poor man," he declaimed from his pulpit, " hath title to the rich man's goods; so that the rich man ought to let the poor man have part of his riches to help and comfort him withal."

The results of the new attitude brought about by the union of Puritanism and Commercialism were sad enough for the poor. The doctrine that poverty should not be pam-

pered left them without relief. Not only were they now
unpitied, but they were actually branded and vilified.
Bishop Berkeley proposed that beggars should " be seized
and made slaves to the public for a term of years "; others
suggested the galleys. Work was the only thing that was
good for them, and that in quantity. Work was an end in
itself. " Those that are prodigal of their time despise their
own souls," says a contemporary writer. Seventeenth-
century England had, in fact, brought forth the capitalist
ethos complete, if still in embryonic shape. The eighteenth
century was to see it well grown. As for the poor outcasts
excluded by moral failure from God's economic grace, their
lot was grim. Numerous writings during the Puritan rule
call attention to their sad condition, but unfortunately such
appeals remained unheard. The poor, now both socially and
morally outcast, suffered as they had never done before. It
is not surprising that many turned to suicide and that
poverty, directly or indirectly, soon became an important
cause of self-destruction.

However, even with a moral stigma added to an unpleasant economic situation, it was change of fortune, the
decline from prosperity to poverty, rather than poverty
itself, which must have accounted for most " poverty "
suicides. Any situation is bearable if one has never known a
better; but for the failure, the man beggared overnight, the
new status of poverty, where contempt and damnation were
added to penury, must often have been the last straw. Death
was preferable to the life of the outcast.[1]

---

[1] The period 1770–1830 is that covered by the first statistic that
I can find. In four thousand male suicides in London just under
one in every four was due to poverty.

CHAPTER VII

MORAL VICTORY

I. THE " AYES "

WITH the eighteenth century the history of suicide enters a new phase. Opposition both to the suicide prejudice and suicide penalties comes into the open; it is no longer furtive, roundabout, or doubtful. The apologists burn their boats and launch a direct and reasoned attack.

As one would expect, it is in France that the philosophic opposition is most determined and enlists the greatest names. One can distinguish two distinct pro-suicide attitudes. First, there is the reasonable and practical attitude of Voltaire. Though he himself was temperamentally disinclined to any sort of self-destruction, he realized that at times it must be defendable. Circumstances, not dogmas, must direct our judgment: each case must be examined on its own merits, and in the abstract it is impossible to attribute either praise or blame. While admitting the possibility of its social and moral validity, he never ceases to regard it as abnormal, and draws attention to the physical and inherited nature of suicidal tendencies. His practical attitude, in fact, corresponds better than that of any of his contemporaries with the outlook of the averagely intelligent man in the twentieth century. " *Chacun*," he says, " *a ses raisons dans sa conduite*," and it is by the value and nature of these reasons that action must be judged. He has no patience with suicide cults or romantic endings, and he twits the heavy melancholics. The young girls, he says, who hang and drown themselves for love should not be so precipitate; change is as common in love as in business. This practical and half-joking tone reappears constantly. " Certainly," he says, referring to a Senecan dictum, " a man has a right to leave his mansion when he is sick of it, but most people prefer to sleep in a bad lodging than under the open sky."

Again, writing to Madame du Deffand about a suicide, he says : " *C'est un parti que je ne prendrai pas, du moins sitôt, par la raison que je me suis fait des rentes viagères sur deux souverains et que je serais inconsolable si ma mort enrichissait deux têtes couronées.*" One could hardly move further than this from the old suicide horror.

D'Holbach represents the other type of suicide support, unconditional and absolute. His attitude is extreme and provides a sharp contrast to Voltaire. " *La mort,*" he says, " *est la remède unique du dèsespoir.*" In his *Système de la Nature*, which was publicly burned by parliament, he supports not a particular case, but the general theory—in fact, he is explicit in defying the whole anti-suicide tradition. His outlook is naturally based on his atheist and materialist philosophy, and the two chief arguments which he puts forward to prove the legitimacy of suicide fall within this framework.

These arguments, which will be treated more fully in a consideration of Hume's ideas on suicide, we can indicate here. First, suicide is not contrary to the law of nature. The unhappy man for whom existence is unsupportable, by taking his own life " *accomplit un arrêt de la nature, qui veut qu'il n'exist plus; qu'enfin cette nature a travaillé pendant des milliers d'années a former dans le sein de la terre le fer qui doit trancher ses jours* ". Secondly, suicide is not anti-social. The individual's contract with society is based on mutual benefit. If society can give him nothing, if it cannot make even life tolerable, the suicide has every right to consider the contract void and to cut himself off. Besides, of what use can a really unhappy man be to society? Since there is no future retribution, no punishment or well-deserved recompense, an unfortunate man cannot be unwise to pocket his losses and close up shop. Let the unhappy lover, he says, the outcast, and the old deserted parent, fly from a world which is for them only a desert.

The contrasted attitudes of d'Holbach and Voltaire we can supplement with a third. It is the attitude of men like Rousseau, and perhaps Montesquieu, who were temperamentally favourable to suicide, and expressed this sympathy in a semi-rationalized, indirect, and literary form. In the eighteenth century none of the more serious contributions to the discussion of suicide caused as much stir as two letters by these authors, one in the *Lettres Persanes*, the other in the *Nouvelle Heloise*.

Though Rousseau has been wrongly accused of committing suicide, he was very familiar with the subject, and when living with Hume at Wotton must have talked of it with that out-and-out apologist. The famous twenty-first letter in the *Nouvelle Heloise*, containing an extensive apology for suicide, goes from a young man, Saint Preux, disappointed by life and love, to his intimate friend, Lord Edward. The tone, as one would expect, is highly idealistic; there is none of the practical scepticism of Voltaire, nothing of d'Holbach's atheism. The unhappy writer begins by avowing his honesty and desire to find the truth. Is suicide a crime? " *Je hais,*" he says, " *le crime encore plus que la vie; j'adore l'être éternal.*" He then goes on to develop arguments by which he proves to his own satisfaction that suicide is not a crime and is compatible with his love of the eternal being. First of all, suicide, he finds, is not against the law of nature: " *Chercher son bien et fuir son mal en ce qui n'offense point autrui, c'est le droit de la nature* ". Thus, it is up to us to leave life when it seems to be no longer good, but evil. God did not give us life that we should suffer it in an eternal quietism. He gave us liberty to do good, conscience to wish for it, and reason to choose it. He wrote in our hearts: "*Fais ce qui t'est salutaire et n'est nuisible à personne.*" Precisely because God has given us life we must do with it what we think best. Reason tells us that a sad life must be remedied as much as a diseased body. "*Pourquoi serait-il permis de se guérir de la goutte, et non de la vie?*"

He next turns to refute the argument, used by Plato, that life is like military service and that a man should not desert his post. A semi-quibble serves his purpose. If it is illegal for you to leave life, how is it that you leave a town where life has placed you, but where your affairs do not prosper, for another town where you hope you may do better? The third point which Saint Preux makes is altogether new and was directed at the theologians. Those, he says, who maintain that suicide removes us from the providence of God are altogether wrong. By suicide we do not destroy our existence, but only our body. God is in touch with our soul and by death we move closer to Him; "*si je croyais que la mort pût me soustraire à sa puissance, je ne voudrais plus mourir*".

The sophists who use semi-philosophical arguments to condemn suicide next claim his attention. Life, such people say, cannot ever be an ill. What nonsense, retorts Saint Preux. In this world the only difference between the good man and the evil is that one suffers and does his best, and the other suffers and does his worst. No, even here in life, sages prove that the imitation of death is the best thing.

What does the sage do, but "*se concentrer, pour ainsi dire, au fond de son âme, et s'efforcer d'être mort durant sa vie*"? "*Le seul moyen qu'ait trouvé la raison pour nous soustraire aux maux de l'humanite n'est-il pas de nous détacher des objets terrestres et de tout ce qu'il y a de mortel en nous, de nous recueiller au dedans de nous-mêmes, de nous élever aux sublimes contemplations?*" [1]

However, these sophists, continues Saint Preux, not content with having life always desirable, perform a sudden *volte face*. Life becomes elsewhere an evil which we are reproached for not enduring, and from which it is cowardly to run away. Surely only a madman endures what he can well escape. Were Cato, Cassius, and Brutus, cowards? He who does not know how to relieve an unhappy life by a prompt death, resembles a man who allows his wound to gangrene rather than call in a surgeon.

Finally, Saint Preux admits that "*des devoirs envers autrui ne permettent pas a tout homme de disposer de lui-même*". But he himself is in no such position. Neither a father nor a magistrate, he has no ties, no family, and not even a friend except "Mylord Edouard". Since the scriptures have no word to say against suicide, he can, with a free mind, "render to God the death which He imposes upon us through the voice of reason, and peacefully return to His bosom the soul for which He calls".

"*Jeune homme, un aveugle transport t'égare*," begins Lord Edward in his reply. However, his condemnation of Saint Preux's suicidal intentions, though downright, lacks force and argument; the Englishman even shows a sneaking liking for the high Roman suicides of the past. There is, in fact, no doubt that Rousseau's sympathies lie with Saint Preux; the reply is a conventional sop to orthodox opinion. A letter to Voltaire bears out this supposition. The wise man, Rousseau wrote to Voltaire, will sometimes lawfully give up his life without murmurings or despair, when nature and ill-fortune give a distinct order to depart. During his own lifetime it does not seem to have been doubted that

---

[1] This is an interesting quotation, linking up as it does, with the tendency of religion to retract from life into quietude and Nirvana, and to approach the inorganic. (See Chapter X.)

Rousseau was favourable to suicide. People came to connect him firmly with all those moods of idealistic despair which the literature at the end of the eighteenth century began to portray. A sombre and strange testimony to his influence was found in the will of a child-suicide thirteen years old, who left a piece of paper at his death on which appeared the words:

Je légue mon coeur à Rousseau, mon corps à la terre.

Montesquieu devotes one of his *Lettres Persanes* to the subject of suicide. Usbek, writing from Paris to a friend in Smyrna, ridicules the barbarity of European law, and continues with a defence of suicide. "*La vie m'a été donnée comme une faveur; je puis donc la rendre lorsqu'elle ne l'est plus*": when a gift ceases to give pleasure, why should I not part with it? As for society, is it fair that the prince should wish me to remain his subject when I receive no benefit from the association? The bargain is unjust. Lastly, my death, he says, cannot trouble the order of providence, or disturb the balance and beauty of the world. The separation of my body from my soul merely creates a fresh disposition no less natural and no less dependent on the laws of the universe than the present combination. As an ear of corn, or a blade of grass, will my body be any less a work of nature? Will my soul, unencumbered with a mortal fame, grow any less sublime?

Diderot and d'Alembert occupy a doubtful position between the two camps, uncertain whether to condemn or support. The latter, while tolerant of individual suicides, opposes it in general on social grounds.

It is interesting to notice the change in emphasis which this opposition implies. The selfishness of suicide from the point of view of the survivors, which is indeed the true and valid criticism applicable to most suicides, is beginning to come to the fore. As far as the suicide and his Maker are

o

concerned it is a matter for the individual, and the intelligent critic is ceasing to worry. The social results, and the sorrow that suicide may inflict, these, on the contrary, begin to engross attention.

Diderot has a long article on suicide in the *Encyclopedie* of 1765. He starts off: "*Pour ce qui regarde la moralité de cette action, il faut dire qu'elle est absolument contre la loi de la nature.*" Not only is it against the instinct of self-preservation, but it transgresses the law of God, and disregards society. Even a soldier, it appears, may not kill himself to avoid falling into the hands of the enemy. This seems a condemnation absolute enough; however, having taken up this position, he spends the major portion of his article in hedging away from it. He gives a sympathetic and detailed account of Donne's *Biathanatos*, refers to the lapse of certain suicide legislation, and finally says that suicide cannot be called criminal if a man is insane or "*tombé dans une noire mélancholie*". The latter is a loophole through which a large percentage of suicides may slip away without dishonour. It seems almost as if, divining the indignation that was to be aroused by the pro-suicide sentiments of the *Système de la Nature*, his initial condemnation was a matter of policy, a tactical move to cover himself on a matter about which there is no reason to think that he felt very strongly.

Before summarizing the pro-suicide arguments of the eighteenth century in the attitude of the English philosopher, Hume, there are two other writers who must be mentioned for their contemporary influence. John Robeck, a Swedish philosopher, is one of those rare writers whose practice conformed to his theory. Having written a work entitled "*Exercitatio philosophica de morte voluntarii,*" in which he maintained that a philosophic disdain of life should go so far as to embrace death, he himself decided on suicide. If his soul was mortal, he argued, suicide could do it little harm; it would be annihilated anyway. If, on the other hand, it was immortal, suicide by freeing it rendered it the greatest service. In 1735 he distributed all his property and, buying a small boat, rowed out on to the Weser, where he was at that time living. His body was washed up later on the banks. His death and writing made some stir, and there is a reference to him in *Candide*. The passage is worth quoting for two reasons: first, it shows Voltaire more favourable to suicide, regardless of its practical implications, than he appears in the *Dictionnaire Philosophique*; secondly, if we take the number of suicides mentioned in the passage as based on Voltaire's own experience (which to a certain extent we are justified in doing), they give us some idea of the frequency of suicide in the world in which he moved. *La Vieille*, daughter of Urban X, is telling her astounding misadventures to Candide and Cunégonde. " Only a love of life, that still persisted, kept me from suicide," she says.

> *Cette faiblesse ridicule est peut-être un de nos penchants les plus funestes; car y a-t-il rien de plus sot que de vouloir porter continuellement un fardeau qu'on peut toujours jeter par terre; d'avoir son être en horreur, et de tenir à son être, enfin de caresser le serpent qui nous devore, jusqu' à ce qu'il nous ait mangé le coeur?*

In her time she had seen

> *un nombre prodigieux de personnes qui avaient leur existence en exécration; mais je n'en ai vu que douze qui aient mis volontairement fin à leur misère, trois nègres, quatre Anglais, quatre Genevois, et un professeur Allemand nommé Robek.*

In England at the end of the seventeenth century the death of Charles Pope Blount, and the events which followed, caused a stir as great as that produced by Robeck's death on the Continent. Charles Pope Blount, who had been the friend of Dryden, on his death in 1693 left behind an un-published work entitled the *Oracles of Reason*. The cause of his death was suicide, though Pope, in his role as the "wasp of Twickenham", says he only pretended to stab himself to cause a stir. To his horror he found too late that he had inflicted a mortal wound. The *Oracles of Reason* with their rational eighteenth-century flavour were given point and " news-value " by the suicide, and Gildon of the *Dunciad* undertook to give them to the world. When they appeared it was found that Gildon, in a long preface, had made the author's death an excuse for an open defence of suicide. The coffee-houses hummed and the *Oracles of Reason* developed into a minor scandal.

The eighteenth-century apologists all use more or less the same arguments in support of suicide, and doubtless they were influenced by each other's writings for there is an extraordinary similarity even in the use of phrase and metaphor. For our purposes Edward Hume, the only English advocate of first-rate importance, may be allowed to sum up these arguments from a rather extreme angle.[1] If suicide, he says, is to be regarded as criminal, it must be proved to be a transgression of our duty either towards God, our neighbour, or ourselves.

To the first Hume devotes the larger part of his essay. His God approximates roughly to the embodiment of scientific law. To govern the animal world He has endowed all living creatures with bodily and mental powers; with senses, passions, appetites, memory, and judgment, by which they are impelled or regulated in that course of life to which they are destined. Thus, all events may be pronounced the action of the Almighty; they all proceed from those powers with which He has endowed His creatures. A house, says Hume, which falls by its own weight, is not brought to ruin by His providence any more than one destroyed by

[1] Owing to ecclesiastical opposition, only a few privately circulated copies of the rare first edition of Hume's essay, *On Suicide*, were sold. A second edition was issued from the relative safety of Basle.

the hands of men. When the passions play, when the judgment dictates, when the limbs obey, it is all the operation of God. The lives of men are dependent on the general laws of matter and motion; and men, like animals, must therefore rely on their own skill and prudence for their conduct in the world. Man may as lawfully employ the power, which has been given him, to destroy himself as to bring about any other modification in matter. His life is of no more importance to the universe than that of an oyster. If the disposal of human life were reserved to the Almighty almost any action would become an encroachment on His privilege. "If [he says] I turn aside a stone which is falling on my head, I disturb the course of nature and I invade the peculiar province of the Almighty by lengthening out my life beyond the period, which, by the general laws of matter and motion, He has assigned it." There is no being, he says, which possesses any power or faculty, that it does not receive from its Creator; "when I fall on my own sword, therefore, I receive my death equally at the hands of the Deity as if it had proceeded from a lion, a precipice, or a fever". Quoting Seneca he says, let us thank God that no one can be compelled to live.

Agamus Deo gratias, quod nemo in vita teneri potest.

That suicide cannot be a crime against ourselves seems so obvious to Hume that he only devotes a few lines to the subject.

> That suicide may often be consistent with interest and our duty to ourselves, no one can question, who allows that age, sickness, or misfortune, may render life a burden, and make it worse even than annihilation. I believe that no man ever threw away his life while it was worth keeping. . . . Both prudence and courage should engage us to rid ourselves at once of existence when it becomes a burden.

Hume's considerations whether suicide is a breach of duty towards " our neighbour and society " though longer than his examination of the personal problem, can be as easily summarized. " A man who retires from life does no harm to society; he only ceases to do good; which, if it is an injury, is of the lowest kind." All our obligations to do good to society, says Hume, imply something reciprocal. So long as I receive a benefit from society, it is up to me to promote its interests; but when I withdrew myself altogether from society, I am no longer bound. It is not incumbent on me to prolong a miserable existence on account of some frivolous advantage which the public may obtain from my life. And suppose my life, as so often happens when a man is without health, power, or authority, is not an advantage, but a positive burden to society? " In such cases my resignation of life must not only be innocent but laudable."

So far we may perhaps agree with Hume, but it will be noticed that in a way he has shirked his last problem. In his arguments he refers to the relationship of the individual to society, but not to his neighbour, as he had promised. It is this last relationship which ultimately makes it impossible to generalize about suicide. The parent, the friend, or the un-provided child left behind, these are the real deterrents for the person with suicidal wishes and the real stumbling-block for the philosopher who wants to establish the absolute innocence of the act. These are the circumstances which alter cases.

II. THE " NOES "

Apart from Madame de Stael the writers of the anti-suicide camp can boast no great names.[1] None the less, Jean Dumas in 1773 went into the subject in greater detail than anyone had done since Donne and his *Traité du Suicide* reached four hundred pages. However, it gives us practi-

---

[1] Kant touched on this subject. Suicide, he said, was an insult to humanity in oneself.

cally no new ideas, and is inclined to go over the old medieval ground, only at great length. Of its seven chapters the first is devoted to restating the familiar idea that we are God's chattels, and thus suicide is theft. The second chapter chides Voltaire for his pessimism and points out that ills and miseries are no excuse for suicide, being native to our state and a burden natural to carry; the third chapter returns to the argument that suicide is opposed to the instinct of self-preservation and thus against the law of nature; the fifth claims that it is anti-social. The other chapters are devoted to the discussion of its history in classical times and to a refutation of Rousseau, Montesquieu, and other supporters. His replies to the latter are on the whole unsatisfactory and often based on scriptural authority; he is more interested in the " *erreur de leurs principes* " than in the " *faux de leurs raisonments* ", and the *Système de la Nature*, is from the outset " *ce livre abominable* ". In general one feels that he is twisting reason to support the religious premises from which he starts and which seem to be the basis of his aversion to suicide.

Two points are interesting in Dumas, as they illustrate a change typical of the century. The unreasoning horror of suicide has weakened and at times seems almost to have disappeared. We find him saying that since we cannot tell how our luck may change for the better " *il est de la prudence de se decider pour la vie* " : this reveals a quiet and reasonable attitude hardly possible before the eighteenth century. The word *prudence* itself links up with the other point of interest : the steady growth of the practical point of view which was first detected in Montaigne and rediscovered in Voltaire. " Think again, you may not be as badly off as you imagine " : such is the advice now coming into fashion.

Mérian, who, ten years earlier, had published a *Mémoire sur le Suicide*, had made much of such sound advice. We cannot anticipate, he says, how the good and evil will be mixed in our lives, therefore suicide must always be premature. Mérian, however, is chiefly important for being the first writer on suicide to move away from the confusion of the moral issue. Though flatly opposed to all but patriotic suicide, self-destruction does not appear to him primarily as a crime, but as a disease. Suicide is a mental malady, and all suicides are in some degree deranged or they could not so run counter to the law of nature. Voltaire had touched on the hereditary character of the suicidal instinct, but Mérian presents in a recognizable form the medical theory of suicide which was to become so familiar in the nineteenth century.

Formey's approach to suicide is yet another sign of the changing times. In his *Melanges Philosophiques* he devotes some thirty pages to its condemnation; but he expressly discards more than one of the old religious arguments, probably as being out of date and subject to more than one interpretation. He prefers to base his attack on the incompatibility between suicide and natural law.

In England the attack on suicide opens with the century. 1700 sees the publication of *An Essay Concerning Self-Murther* by a clergyman named Adams which, as its title-page states, is a direct, though belated, reply to Donne's *Biathanatos*. It is also significantly enough addressed to those others, " of which there are many in this age ", who undertake to defend the lawfulness of suicide. The arguments run on general lines that are familiar to us: in Adams's own words, " Human Life is *God's own Propriety*, 'tis entrusted to man only for a certain End [elsewhere stated as " the following of Reason by Virtue "], and therefore he has no . . . Liberty to destroy it ". The keenness of Adams's attack betrays him into curious statements. It is, for instance, better, should one be thrown adrift in a small boat, to cast lots and eat one's shipmates than to face with suicidal obstinacy the alternative of certain death by starvation. Elsewhere his argument leads him to a pleasing but unexpectedly pacifist conclusion: "No man has *naturally* any right to *destroy himself* for his Country, *designedly* and positively; but to *hazard his life* only."

The next writer publicly to condemn the suicides was Hutcheson, an early utilitarian and the teacher of Adam Smith. Writing fifty years later he altogether condemns suicide in his *System of Moral Philosophy*. Not only, he claims, must society employ force to punish suicide and to deter an action so prejudicial to his interests, but also it is the duty of every individual to exercise his influence to the same end. It is, however, left to Hey, a fellow of Magdalene, Cambridge, who won a university prize with his *Dissertation on Suicide*, to uphold the orthodox position as Dumas had done in France. In practice, Hey adds no fresh arguments to those which Dumas had already advanced. But it is significant that, writing twelve years after the *Traité du Suicide*, his tone is milder and his appeals to reason are more convincing. Also, not altogether to one's surprise, he devotes a fifth of his whole work to the *Imprudence* of suicide.

Less orthodox than Hey's work, but far more interesting and complete is the Rev. Charles Moore's *Full Inquiry into the Subject of Suicide*. Not published until 1790, this shows a leniency and an absence of absolute condemnation which is not found in any of the earlier anti-suicide writers of the century. In recognizing that circumstances alter cases, he overcomes the instinctive and primitive horror in the act. We cannot tell for certain, he says, that any particular suicide is damned. "As the motives which lead to suicide may be very dissimilar, there arises from hence a great variation, as well as disproportion in the measure of guilt." Thus, stricture must vary with each case, and suicide, he believes, may even be forgivable when due to errors of philosophical judgment.

Beyond this Moore makes no concessions. The old arguments that suicide is against nature, God, society, and even the individual's own interests (since it may deprive him of paradise), are produced without fresh variation. On the other hand he was apparently a good classical scholar and a person of wide reading, with the result that he collected much information not to be found in other books on the subject.

The eighteenth century which tackled the most various subjects in verse, saw also the publication of an anonymous poem, entitled *Suicide*. In precise decasyllabic lines a libertine invokes suicide, "sweet cure for all the ills of life"; but he is inevitably rebuked by a sage, who in typically eighteenth-century vein, tells him to turn back to nature in whose bosom he will find virtue and happiness. The chief interest of the poem is the contrast it provides with *Pelecanicidium*, the anti-suicide poem written over a hundred years earlier. In the eighteenth-century verse the tone and arguments throughout are no longer religious, but moral, and they pretend to a basis of reason rather than of faith.

Blair, in his gloomy poem, *The Grave*, also devotes a couple of pages to an attack on suicide, reproducing in verse arguments with which we are familiar. For instance, he writes:

> Shall Nature, swerving from her earliest Dictate
> Self-Preservation, fall by her own Act?
> Forbid it Heaven! Let not upon Disgust
> The shameless Hand be foully crimson' o'er
> With Blood of its own Lord.

Of the poets, however, it is Young who is most, and most interestingly, preoccupied with suicide.

No writer has expressed the fascination of the grave at such length and in such detail as Young in his *Night Thoughts*. Its nine books are a panegyric on death. For him dying was more real than living, and the rites and obsequies of death more significant than the details of daily life. Death was positive, almost creative, the wonderful and

necessary corollary of living rather than a meaningless *néant*.
He rediscovered and loved that balance between life and
death, which civilization is always doing its best to upset
or obscure. The sudden and consecutive deaths of a wife, a
step-daughter, and a son-in-law, led him to the cemetery,
which in spirit he never left. Not only did his "dreams
infest the grave", but his actual pleasure was in walking
among the tombs. A token brought from there, a polished
skull, sat on his study mantelpiece. "How populous," he
cries, "how vital is the grave." He loved it as though it
had been a person and when the night came he devoted himself to it in the silence of his study. Essentially death in
Young loses the last vestiges of the macabre. It becomes a
living thing and puts flesh almost upon dead bones.

Here one might have thought to find the wholehearted
and passionate apologist for suicide. However, this love of
death, and lovingly nurtured melancholy, was subordinate to
one thing—his Christianity. As a clergyman Young had to
bring his illicit despairs, and yearnings for the grave, within
a Christian framework. They had to be interpreted as a
longing to cast off the body, to cut free from the vanity
of life, and to appear in God's presence. The grave had to
become the gate of paradise; then as a whited sepulchre it
could be a respectable object of interest and contemplation.
Similarly his Christian outlook rendered suicide, the most
conscious approach to the grave that he so loved, absolutely
sinful. The violence of his attack upon it probably reflects
to some extent the strength of a natural and suppressed
sympathy towards it.

In a lengthy passage he claims that he will

> "detect the cause
> Of *self-assault*, expose the monster's birth,
> And bid *abhorrence* hiss it round the world."

The prevalence of the crime in England, he says, cannot
be excused on the usual climatic grounds:

> " Blame not thy clime, nor chide the distant sun;
> The sun is innocent, thy clime absolv'd;
> *Immoral* climes kind nature never made."

The real cause of suicide is always the " beggarly vile appetites " of man. It is a moral question. The suicide is the evil-liver, and

> " A sensual unreflecting life, is big
> With monstrous births, and *Suicide* to crown
> The black infernal brood."

Suicide remains, even for Young, the worst of sins. Finally, in an almost *surréaliste* passage, typical of much in the *Night Thoughts*, he returns to his love of death and his belief in its regenerating powers. If suicides would only think on death, they would never seek it. Only that man is saved, who will

> " impress,
> Indelible, *death's* image on his heart."

With Madame de Stael's *Reflexions sur le Suicide* we are into the nineteenth century. Its tone, however, is late eighteenth century, and the fact that it was written in refutation of an early essay, *Sur l'influence des Passions* (1796), which supported suicide, allows us to treat of it here. It is an essay of a very different calibre from most of the anti-suicide works we have quoted; parts of it might still serve as a model plea against the individual's right to commit suicide. By an odd paradox it was the influence of sorrow which prompted her to set down her change of view. She says in her dedicatory letter, " *J'ai écrit ces réflexions sur le suicide dans un moment où le malheur me faisoit éprouver le besoin de me fortifier par le secours de la méditation.*"

The reflexions are divided into three parts. In the first Madame de Stael begins by opening up a new line of argument. What, she asks, is the influence of suffering on the human spirit? " *Il ne suffit pas de croire avec les stoiciens*

*que la douleur n'est point un mal; il faut être convaincu
qu'elle est un bien.*" For Madame de Stael this conviction
is easy, since pain " serves to regenerate the soul ".

> *La necessité rafraîchit . . . Il n'y a point de doute que nous ne
> sortions sensiblement meilleurs de l'épreuve de l'adversité, quand
> nous nous y soumettons avec une fermeté douce. Les plus grands
> qualités de l'âme ne se developpent que par la souffrance . . .*

To escape from pain is thus to escape from something that
may by its action make you better and greater. Such an
escape is, in fact, a refusal to realize the possibilities of your
nature.[1] In her second section Madame de Stael goes over
very familiar ground : " What are the scriptural prohibitions
of suicide? " Even here, however, she strikes a new note.
She is less occupied with trying to stretch inappropriate texts
to cover the subject, than with interpreting what she thinks
is the attitude of the Christian spirit. For the doubtful
relevance of the sixth commandment, she replaces the text
" Blessed be those that weep, for they shall be comforted ".
That God never deserts the true believer is the burden of her
consolation. In the blackest hour anyone may receive perfect comfort. The audacious and magnificent justification
which Louis XVI, as he climbed the scaffold, received from
the lips of a priest, and the dictation of an angel, *Fils de
Saint Louis montez au Ciel!* may be heard by anyone in
his extremity. We shall not be deserted, therefore we
have no right to commit suicide and to perpetrate an act
" which more than any other seems formally to remove us
from the protection of God ".

Madame de Stael's third section sets out to prove that
suicide is not consonant with the moral dignity of man.
Here again we have a line of approach not explored since
classical times. But the author makes much less of this
section than she might; there is no coherent thread of reason
that links the whole thing together, and hardly an argument

[1] Cf. Plotinus, page 73.

of importance is put forward. A good distinction is nevertheless made between institutional and patriotic suicide, and purely personal suicide. Life, she says, may be sacrificed in two ways, " *ou parce qu'on donne au devoir la préférence sur elle, ou parce qu'on donne aux passions cette préférence* ". Institutional and patriotic suicides belong to the first type; purely personal suicides to the second. On the other hand, this section is full of observations on national characteristics and individual deaths which show shrewd psychological insight. Some of these will be referred to later.[1]

In spite of this battery of anti-suicide pens, it was in fact unrepealed laws which remained chief among the " noes " during the greater part of the eighteenth century. In England our period produces no written change or modification in the old medieval statutes. On paper the situation remains unaltered, and savage legislation is still the official expression of the suicide prejudice. In France the story is different. At first it seems that, in a last desperate effort to regularize the situation and to work a law that was becoming unworkable, the code was actually strengthened. A Royal edict of 1712 empowers judges to institute an inquiry in cases of doubtful death and to call in medical evidence; they are empowered to do this, since parents and others, in order to evade the suicide laws, hush up the cause of death and secure premature burials. In 1736 another edict to meet the same abuse orders that in cases of doubtful death no burial is to be permitted without licence from the authorities.

[1] Madame de Stael quotes at length a very fine and moving letter from Lady Jane Grey to Doctor Aylmer (afterwards Bishop of London), explaining why she must refuse some poison which he had conveyed to her in prison. I can find no trace of the actual letter, and there is no reference to the incident in contemporary histories or in Strype's *Annals and Life of Aylmer*. The whole thing seems to be a forgery, produced by someone interested in discrediting suicide.

THE DESECRATION OF THE CORPSE

(*from Delisle de Sales "Philosophie de la Nature"*)

The peak of severity is reached with this law, and in the following year comes the first measure of leniency: in 1737 appeal by the family and heirs is made obligatory and thus the chance of an error of justice is considerably lessened. By 1770 official opinion appears to have moved very fast; it is announced that in future the body of a suspected suicide shall be buried and that legal action shall only be taken against his memory. The degradation of the corpse is in fact abolished. With the coming of the Revolution the confiscation of property and the defamation of the suicide's memory also disappear, for the whole complex structure of the old law is swept away at one stroke. In the new penal code of 1791 suicide is not even mentioned. In France the law has ceased to be interested. For a brief period during the terror a measure is in force to prevent a loss of property to the Republic through the suicide of aristocratic suspects. The old Roman law is revived, whereby the suicide of persons arrested on a capital charge is punishable with the confiscation of their property. As the fury of the revolution dies down even this measure disappears.

There remain only the penalties of the Canon law, and these too the revolution robs of their sting. A movement of de-Christianization, parallel to that which took place in Russia after the Communist revolution, makes many people completely indifferent to the Church's attitude. Proud of a newly acquired atheism, citizens even prefer a purely civil burial. At the same time the law actually limits the Church's power. No priest may appear in public with his vestments; the tricolour must deck the coffin on its last journey to the cemetery; and once arrived at the place of burial, no good republican may be denied his plot of ground. The cemeteries have become the general resting-place of the citizens, and the Church cannot refuse access to anyone. The state thus removes the suicide from the power, both of the canon and the civil law.

In both France and England, however, practice anticipated respectively the changes of the revolution, and the incomplete liberal legislation of the nineteenth century. The tone of public opinion and the findings of courts and juries often did not support the official outlook. Thus it remains to trace the attitude of educated eighteenth-century opinion towards suicide penalties and to try and find out how often the letter of the law was actually imposed. D'Holbach, Montesquieu, and Voltaire are, as we should expect, strongly opposed to the existing suicide legislation. Montesquieu, writing in 1721, says, "*Les lois sont furieuses en Europe contre ceux qui se tuent eux-mêmes: . . . ils sont traînés indignement par les rues; on les note d'infamie; on confisque leurs biens.*" Voltaire attacks the law all round. Confiscation of the suicide's property is for him "brigandage". He appends an ironic note on the use to which such confiscations were usually put. To console the child of the dead man he says, "*On donne son bien au Roi qui en accorde presque toujours la moitié a la première fille d'Opéra qui le fait demander par un de ses amants; l'autre moitié appartient de droit à Messieurs les Fermiers généraux.*"

Delisle de Sales includes a section on suicide in his *Philosophie de la Nature*, and though suicide remains in his eyes "*un larcin fait à la société et un attentat contre la nature*", he is strongly against the existing penalties which only create fresh misery for the innocent. In a sub-section, entitled *Memorandum Addressed to the Legislators by the Widow of a Citizen Punished for the Crime of Suicide*, he reproduces an engraving of the corpse of a suicide being dragged through the streets. The wife of the dead man stands there with her children, and it is she who makes a bitter appeal to the legislators for justice. No indignity, she says, has been spared to her own innocence or to her husband's corpse: "*On a traversé son cadavre d'un pieu, on l'a traîné sur la claye dans les rues de la capitale, et on a refusé à ses lambeaux sanglants les honneurs funèbres qu'on accorde aux morts que pour soulager la douleur des amis qui leur survivent.*" Liberal opinion seems pretty much unanimous in its condemnation of such suicide penalties.

Madame de Stael in her work against suicide never even mentions punishments. Presumably by 1811 reprisals against a corpse seemed to her hopelessly out of date. It is not so with her earlier eighteenth-century allies. Adams, Hutcheson, Hey, and Moore, all demand penalties. But it is noticeable that the last two, while insisting that " some certain mode of treating the body of the deceased be invariably observed, and some marks of ignominy be affixed to his memory ", counsel the abolition of confiscation. Confiscation, Hey says, by dissatisfying a number of heirs, upsets the quiet course of society which depends upon inheritance.[1] Implicit in his reasoning may be detected the appearance of the capitalist idea that it is more serious to touch property than person. Dumas is more extreme. He upholds the old French procedure and insists on the liberty of each state to make what suicide laws it likes. Man is a social being and every one of his actions may therefore be punished by society.

To which opinion, it may well be asked, did the experts adhere? Did the jurists, the people who knew the ground intimately, follow Voltaire or Dumas? Blackstone, while supporting punishments, thought that those against the corpse had no real foundation in English law. Beccaria, the great Italian publicist, in his *Traité des Délits et des Peines*, gives a more liberal judgment. Both punishments to the corpse, and confiscations, are quite out of place. The first should be abolished because they are as futile as beating a statue, and are useless as deterrents. A man who has overcome the instinct of self-preservation will not be restrained

[1] Cf. " Men more quickly forget the death of their father than the loss of their property ".—MACHIAVELLI.

P

by the fear of posthumous ignominy. Confiscations should equally be done away with, because of the injustices they inflict on a man's heirs and family. Only God, he concludes, can punish suicide. In France the jurists are inclined to support the orthodox and traditional attitude until the middle of the eighteenth century. Soon after a change appears; a new school of legal theory comes to the fore whose most eminent supporter is Brissot. Bayet discovers that out of fourteen legal works which devote space to suicide twelve are opposed to the existing law. Only two make concessions to repressive legislation. The jurists have in fact followed the lead of the rational philosophers.

Lastly, there are signs that even among the French populace the law is not regarded with favour. Twice within two years in the department of the Tarn there are public demonstrations. Once armed men force a prison and seize the body of a suicide; on another occasion a crowd tries to stop the execution of a sentence against the corpse and many demonstrators are arrested. Such spontaneous manifestations have their own significance and show which way the wind was blowing.

To discover how far the suicide laws were actually enforced during the eighteenth century is more difficult. Only a careful and interminable examination of court registers and records would get at the real truth.[1] It is none the less possible to form a rough estimate by reference to certain of the contemporary writers whom we have already quoted, and to isolated figures and allusions. As a general rule it is true to say that the divergence between practice and theory, already operative in the seventeenth century, grew steadily wider. Indignities to the body or memory of

---

[1] It would be a lengthy business. For instance, in England the coroners' courts, which would provide most material, are unfortunately not "courts of record". Information would have to be obtained all over the country by direct access to innumerable archives.

a suicide after 1770 must have been rare both in England and France. Horace Walpole, in 1788, writing of suicide to to Hannah More, refers to " the absurd stake and high-way *of our ancestors* ". Application of the law was, in fact, the exception rather than the rule. The evasion was made possible by two things. First, by the unwillingness of civil and religious authorities to insist on their prerogative; secondly, by the sophistry of bringing in a verdict of insanity.

It is significant that Hume, writing sometime after 1742, makes no mention in his essay of the suicide laws. Presumably their application in England was already lenient enough to escape his censure. Adams and Hey bear out this sup-position. Both find juries culpable in their evasion of the law, and Hey complains rather bitterly of " the verdict of self-murder being so rarely brought in by a jury ". Black-stone was of the same mind. Coroners' juries, he insisted, strained the excuse of insanity too far. Adams wrote that it is " a general supposition that *everyone* who kills himself is *non-compos* ", and Hey further states that, " In our own nation the confiscation of property is frequently avoided by a verdict of lunacy." The words *confiscation of property* are particularly revealing; it would seem that by 1785, the date at which he is writing, reprisals against the corpse had al-ready fallen quite out of use in England. Confiscation of property was the only punishment which remained for the jury to evade.

In 1667, it will be remembered, permission was readily given to bury Pepys's friend, Joyce; but the law would not forgo its right to try and enforce the confiscation of his goods. A hundred years later, however, it appears that the law of confiscation was differently regarded and its general applicability to suicide was doubted. Umfreville in 1761 states in his *Lex Coronatoria*, a summary of the law and procedure of coroners' courts, that confiscation of a suicide's property should only take place if the accused had been charged with a capital crime before his suicide. This, of course, constitutes a reversion to Roman law. " When a man killeth himself," Umfreville adds, "upon any impatience or infirmity of body or sickness, the civil law does not punish it at all." Thus it seems that by 1760 penalties, not only against the corpse, but against property, had largely fallen out of use.

As to the actual leniency of coroners in this period, we happen to have some interesting and conclusive figures collected by Moore. Between 1770-1788 the coroners for the County of Kent sat on the bodies of about thirty-two suicides per year. For all these suicides, roughly 580, there were only fifteen verdicts of *felo de se* returned. Though it would be interesting to know the actual penalty imposed in these fifteen cases, the important fact emerges that public opinion was opposed to punishment and that the average eighteenth-century suicide could count upon his jury. The wealthy Clive and the poverty-stricken Chatterton could both find their way into the grave without confiscations or more humiliation than they had experienced living.

In France the situation is a little more difficult to envisage. Diderot, writing in the *Encyclopedie* in 1765, says:

> La justice ordonne que le cadavre sera trainé sur une claie, pendu par les piés, et ensuite conduit à la voirie. . . . On pronçait autrefois la confiscation de biens, mais . . . suivant la nouvelle jurisprudence cette peine n'a plus lieu.

This reads as though the old corporal punishments were still being inflicted and as if confiscations had been abolished. But what is *la nouvelle jurisprudence?* In point of fact there had been, before 1765, no new jurisprudence alleviating the suicide laws. Diderot was apparently under a misapprehension, and we learn elsewhere from Voltaire that confiscations *were* in force at this period.

Voltaire, writing in 1770 of a suicide pact which caused

some stir at the time, says : " *La justice n'a fait nulle infamie dans cette affaire, cela est rare.*" How rare indeed were the occasions when the law did not take its own course? How often were confiscation, and the degradation of the corpse[1] and memory, carried out? Possibly Voltaire, in his crusade against injustice, aggravates their frequency. It is true that as late as 1768 a corpse was dragged through the streets of Toulouse with a knife attached to the guilty hand which had perpetrated the suicide. It is also true that trials took place in the old seignorial courts and there was no sympathetic jury to bring in a verdict of insanity. On the other hand Bayet has gone into the archives of certain departments and districts (ten in all) and has produced figures which seem to show that the penalties for suicide were rarely enforced. *Procès-verbaux* on the bodies of probable suicides abound, but very seldom do these seem to have been followed by criminal proceedings. Between 1700 and 1760 he finds only fifteen successful actions taken against the corpse or the memory of suicides. Between 1760 and 1789 only three actions appear. During the same periods there are hundreds of charges of murder. It thus seems probable that a very small percentage of suicides were brought to trial. This leniency on the part of the law finds striking witness in a passage by a certain Mercier, whose *Tableau de Paris* appeared in 1782.

> *La police* [he says], *a pris soin de dérober au public la connaissance des suicides. Quand quelqu'un s'est homicidé, un commissaire vient sans robe, dresse un procès-verbal sans le moindre éclat et oblige le curé de la paroisse d'enterrer le mort sans bruit. On ne traîne plus sur la claie ceux qui des lois ineptes poursuivaient après leur trépas. . . . Plusieurs suicidés ont adopté la coutume d'écrire préalablement une lettre au lieutenant de police afin d'éviter toute difficulté après leur décès. Ou récompense cette attention en leur donnant la sépulture.*

[1] It will be remembered that after 1770 degradation of the corpse was officially abolished in France.

One can hardly ask for more complete testimony, not only
to the non-working of the suicide laws, but to their deliberate
evasion by the law officers themselves. At the beginning of
the century the suicide may have been proceeded against
fairly often; but there is no reasonable doubt that by 1789
the law was a dead letter and that the revolution freed the
suicide from purely theoretical penalties.

In Geneva, indignities to the corpse were officially
abolished in 1770, owing to the stir in public opinion caused
by a miscarriage of justice when the body of an innocent
man was dragged through the streets. As for confiscation of
property, an inhabitant of Geneva, writing before 1790,
speaks of its abolition " many years " earlier. The denial of
Christian burial was the only penalty that remained for the
suicide.

III. THE PUPPETS AND THE PUBLIC

So much for the philosophers and the jurists, the law and
the gaps in the law. There remain the individuals and the
public—the people who executed their dance of death pulled
by strings of love or poverty, pain or fear; and the audience
who watched them.

Though suicide was never a fashion and never developed
the strong intellectual and social sanctions of the Roman
period, yet as the century proceeded a certain fairly general
tolerance developed for love suicides, or suicides with a philosophic flavour. At all events, though its applause may often
have been desultory, the audience never hissed. A certain
sympathy had developed among the general public. This
was in part offset by the emergence of a new anti-suicide
force, which for convenience' sake one might call the suburban spirit. Though it was not until the nineteenth century
that this spirit gained its great victories, it makes its appearance hand in hand with eighteenth-century nonconformity
right under the nose of Voltaire. It was fostered in the

chapel and thrived in the first middle-class drawing-rooms. Its apprehensive but determined voice is heard in the moralizing of the century. Suicide, like anything else which is odd, out of the ordinary, unlike the fate of the next person, is dangerous. Only the aristocrat can be unusual; for Amelia, or Richard, suicide is unforgivably vulgar. It is a thing to be hidden, no longer for fear of the law and a primitive horror, but because it will cause a stir. There will in fact be " talk ", and this the suburban spirit fears above all other things. When Richardson in *Clarissa Harlowe* speaks of suicide as the most " dreadful " of deaths the adjective already bears the stamp of the new spirit. One almost hears the flutter of fans and the whispers: " Yes, my dear, too dreadful, it's the *third* in the family . . . but you know, they always have been rather *queer*." We already smell the Victorian Sunday and touch the fringe of that vastly respectable world whose daughters received piano lessons. In France, as one might expect, the eighteenth-century form of this snobbery is less virulent and retains a certain polish and grace; it flaunts something of aristocratic affectation. A certain Denisle, writing upon honour, says:

> La corde est un genre de mort dont l'infamie est si bien décidée qu'un homme qui le choisirait dans le désespoir, à moins qu'il ne fût de la lie du peuple, serait irrémissablement dés-honoré parmi les honnêtes gens. Il faut le poison, le fer ou le feu. L'eau est encore un désespoir roturier.[1]

Hanging and drowning acquired their peculiar taint from early religious superstitions (see page 39), but the peculiarly social twist which is here given to the whole subject is new and significant.

The Calas affair, which caused such a to-do in the middle of the century, might well be quoted as a dire example of

[1] A similar prejudice finds expression in a number of the *Con-noisseur*, where it appears that " the man of fashion always dies by a pistol ".

the force of the social prejudice of which we have been speaking. The story is briefly this. Marc Antoine Calas was the melancholy son of John Calas, an aged merchant of Toulouse, a man of great probity and a Protestant. The young man experienced difficulties with his law studies and hanged himself in his father's shop. The parents finding him, removed the cord from the body, and attempted to hide the cause of his death. It was an unfortunate move. When the boy's death became known it was said that his father had murdered him to prevent him from reverting to Catholicism. A wave of religious fanaticism swept the town; the body was seized and the old man thrown into prison. Finally, after an inadequate trial, he was condemned by the Parliament of Toulouse and broken on the wheel.

He died protesting his innocence, and Voltaire took up his cause. Four years later, in 1765, a re-trial unravelled the true facts. The decision of the parliament was reversed and the memory of John Calas vindicated. In the re-examination of the evidence it appeared that the parents had concealed the cause of death through shame and a dread of the talk and notoriety that the affair would provoke. No property was involved, and punishments against the corpse were, as we have seen, rarely enforced at this period. It was a cruel, poetic justice, that this typically Protestant caution, and fear of the unusual, should have resulted in such a Catholic vengeance.

It is the eighteenth century which first brings to the fore those considerations of nationality which have since become a preoccupation with writers on suicide. A remark of Voltaire's shows that suicide at any rate in England and France was not too hardly regarded: " *A Rome* " he says, " . . . *cela passe pour ferocité barbare, à Paris pour folie, à Londres pour grandeur d'âme.*" It was a false but generally accepted belief at this time that the English were particularly prone to suicide. Blair wrote:

(Chodowiecki 18th century engraving)

MONK SAVING A SUICIDE

Self-Murther! name it not: Our Island's Shame!
That makes her the Reproach of neighbouring States.

Montaigne seems to be the first person to notice an English *penchant* for suicide, and he attributes it to the climate. Montesquieu, in the *Esprit des Lois*, says that the English " *se tuent dans le sein même du bonheur* ", and he puts it down to a " *defaut de filtration de suc nerveux* "; Dumas again revives the climate idea and Delisle de Sales habitually calls suicide " *Anglomane* ". Writing to Sophie Volland, Diderot says of the English, " *l'ennui les saisit au milieu des délices, et les conduit dans la Tamise, à moins qu'ils ne préfèrent de prendre le bout d'un pistolet entre leurs dents* ".

Voltaire says " *les Anglais quittent la vie fièrement quand il leur en prend fantaisie* ", and he quotes several English suicides of note, among them William Temple's son, Secretary of State for War; Lord Scarborough; and the romantic Philip Mordaunt, cousin of the Earl of Peterborough. He also makes special reference to the *spleen* of the inhabitants of Great Britain. This aspect of melancholy seems to have exercised the English themselves. A certain Green produced a long, eighteenth-century poem in octosyllabic couplets, entitled *Spleen*, in which he deals with its treatment and cure, and Cheyne's *English Malady* (1733), turns out to be no more than spleen in disguise. Our moist climate, together with other factors, have, Cheyne says, " brought forth a class and set of distempers with atrocious and frightful symptoms, scarce known to our ancestors, and never rising to such fatal heights, nor afflicting such numbers in any other known nation."

It is, however, Madame de Stael's reflexions on national suicides which are the most interesting. England, she says, is the country where the greatest number of suicides are committed. This she attributes, not to the climate—"*car le ciel de la liberté m'a toujours paru le plus pur de tous* "—

but to more likely reasons. "*Le caractère Anglais* [she says] *en général est très-actif et même très-impétueux*": those who think the English cold have allowed themselves to be deceived by a reserved manner.

But she discovers a second more cogent reason which links up with the rise of the suburban spirit, *la grande terreur du blâme*: "*Une autre cause rend aussi les suicides plus fréquents en Angleterre, c'est l'extrême importance que l'on y attache à l'opinion publique: dès que la réputation d'un homme est altérée, la vie lui devient insupportable.*" Madame de Stael's remarks on France provide a just and illuminating contrast to this English picture. There, suicide is attributable "*ni à la mélancholie du caractère, ni à l'exaltation des idées*" but, as one would expect, to "*malheurs positifs*". What a light this throws on the shrewd, reasonable, ever-practical Frenchman.

It is usual to pay little attention to the eighteenth-century accusations levelled at England in the matter of suicide, but Moore, writing in 1788, says: "Scarce a publication of the day in town or country, but what . . . shocks our senses with these self-murderous proceedings". The first figures we have—they can hardly be graced with the name of statistics—support this statement, and show a very high rate for London. It seems more than probable that the London of Vauxhall, of salons, duels, trollops, poverty, and wagers, was rich in suicides. It was just this London which the visiting Frenchman would see, and if we substitute London for England, his strictures may well have been true. Figures, as we shall discover, would bear him out in such an accusation.

Did suicides, however, irrespective of nationality, actually increase during the eighteenth century? At first sight one is apt to think the increase in suicide was large. This probably is because records become more and more frequent; we are almost "within memory", and thus suicides appear on all sides. Saint-Simon records them for posterity, and Walpole for his friends. In practice it is not the frequency of suicide but the frequency of records that makes us discover so large a relative increase. A small increase undoubtedly set in with the arrival of rationalistic ideas; this was undoubtedly maintained and further increased throughout the century, gaining added impulsion from the non-enforcement of criminal legislation, and from the favourable veering of both philosophic and general opinion. So much one can say with certainty. The few figures that are to be found are most unreliable and vary considerably. On the one hand there is obvious exaggeration in the three hundred suicides which were said to have taken place in Versailles alone in 1793, as a result of the Revolution; on the other hand, there is Voltaire's modest assertion that, in 1764, you could have actually counted more than fifty suicides in Paris. Both Mercier and Dumas quote an anonymous author who says that there were 147 suicides in Paris in 1769. For 1782 Mercier gives 150. This may be taken as an approximate figure for the recorded suicides of Paris, and works out at about 21.4 per 100,000 taking the population at 700,000. Thirty years later, when the rates everywhere had fallen, owing to the Napoleonic wars, London (Westminster) had 16 suicides per 100,000. Such an estimate may be compared with one or two other English figures. The *London Medical and Surgical Journal* gave the number of yearly suicides in London between 1770 and 1830 as about 120; another source (Falret) gave the number as high as 225 per annum for 1794–1823. A list of London suicides given by Winslow, and dating back to 1690, is interesting, though of uncertain provenance. It must refer to the City of Westminster.

One wonders whether the high figures from 1720 to 1740 have any connection with the mid-century wave of speculation and the South Sea Bubble.

1690–1700	24 suicides per annum		
1700–1710	28 ,,	,,	,,
1710–1720	30 ,,	,,	,,
1720–1730	48 ,,	,,	,,
1730–1740	50 ,,	,,	,,
1740–1750	42 ,,	,,	,,
1750–1760	36 ,,	,,	,,
1760–1770	35 ,,	,,	,,
1770–1780	34 ,,	,,	,,
1780–1790	22 ,,	,,	,,
1790–1800	27 ,,	,,	,,
1800–1810	34 ,,	,,	,,

The sharp drop registered at the end of the century is found elsewhere, and must have been partly due to international affairs. It is important to notice that the systematic collection of suicide figures[1] had hardly begun at this time, with the result that the rise in nineteenth-century suicides, observed when Europe quietened down after 1820, appeared to observers to be absolute and unprecedented.

It is possible to argue—working, it is true, from early and scanty estimates—that a higher rate prevailed in London and Paris at certain times in the eighteenth century than in the nineteenth century, in spite of the apparent rise usually recorded. To-day, with a population of several millions, London produces about six to seven hundred suicides each year (593 in 1935). This works out at a lower rate per hundred thousand than several eighteenth-century estimates. Either the earlier figures are exaggerated, or it may be that the eighteenth century really produced, in the London of John Cleland and the Paris of Rétif de la Bretonne, a higher suicide rate than was to be found in Victorian England or post-revolutionary France. If this is indeed the case, the steady increase of suicides since the nadir of the Napoleonic wars is not so fearful as one might suppose.

[1] The first name associated with this is Cromaziano in 1788.

Paris and London may have already seen and survived the growth and decline of as high a rate as they know to-day.

As to the types of suicide in vogue, Voltaire complains that people have lost the grand manner of the antique heroes. "*Nous nous tuons aussi nous autres*" he says, "*mais c'est quand nous avons perdu notre argent, ou dans l'excès très-rare d'une folle passion pour un object qui n'en vaut pas la peine.*" Sometimes, he says, people also commit suicide on account of disease, but that, he adds, shows great weakness. Such suicide seems, anyway, to have been fairly rare, and Madame de Stael speaks of its infrequency. Dishonour and financial ruin are, she says, the two commonest motives of her time. The latter motive, linked with poverty, came into prominence, as we have seen, in the seventeenth century; Madame de Stael regards it as being of first importance at the end of the eighteenth. "*Les revers de la fortune* [she says] *telle que la société est combinée, causent une peine très vive, et qui se multiplie sous milles formes diverses.*" Helvetius, writing in 1781, speaks of "*nombreux suicides dans la Capitale*" resulting largely from the perilous state of the public *finances*. Poverty and financial ruin, in fact, exact a toll everywhere from Chatterton to Richard Smith.

The death of Richard Smith and his wife in 1732 probably attracted as much attention as any other suicides of the century. Voltaire and Diderot comment upon their death, and Smollett mentions them in his *History of England*. Richard Smith, a bookbinder, had got into financial difficulties, and with his wife and small daughter, two years old, was imprisoned for debt. Upon reflection, husband and wife came to the conclusion that life in absolute poverty had nothing to offer them, and they decided to commit suicide. After killing their child in the cradle beside them, they hung themselves. A very English note was left for their landlord, recommending to his protection a cat and an old dog. What, however, is of interest is the long letter which they addressed to the public. Its insistence on the hopelessness of poverty, its mixture of the rational and the religious, and its general tone are all very typical of the period. The letter caused much discussion; it runs as follows:

These actions, considered in all their circumstances, being somewhat uncommon, it may not be improper to give some account of the cause; and that it was inveterate hatred we conceived against poverty and rags, evils that through a train of unlucky accidents were become inevitable. For we appeal to all that ever knew us, whether we were idle or extravagant, whether or no we have not taken as much pains to get our living as our neighbours, although not attended with the same success. We apprehend the taking of our child's life away to be a circumstance for which we shall be generally condemned; but for our own parts we are perfectly easy on that head. We are satisfied it is less cruelty to take the child with us, even supposing a state of annihilation as some dream of, than to leave her friendless in the world, exposed to ignorance and misery. Now in order to obviate some censures which may proceed either from ignorance or malice, we think it proper to inform the world, that we firmly believe the existence of an Almighty God; that this belief of ours is not an implicit faith, but deduced from the nature and reason of things. We believe the existence of an Almighty Being from the consideration of his wonderful works, from those innumerable celestial and glorious bodies, and from their wonderful order and harmony. We have also spent some time in viewing those wonders which are to be seen in the minute part of the world, and that with great pleasure and satisfaction. From all which particulars we are satisfied that such amazing things could not possibly be without a first mover—without the existence of an Almighty Being. And as we know the wonderful God to be Almighty, so we cannot help believing that he is also good—not implacable, not like such wretches as men are, not taking delight in the misery of his creatures; for which reason we resign up our breath to him without any terrible apprehensions, submitting ourselves to those ways which in his goodness he shall please to appoint after death. We also believe in the existence of unbodied natures, and think we have reason for that belief, although we do not pretend to know their way of subsisting. We are not ignorant of those laws made *in terrorem*, but leave the disposal of our bodies to the wisdom of the coroner and his jury, the thing being indifferent to us where our bodies are laid. From hence it will appear how little anxious we are about " hic jacet " . . .

(Signed) RICHARD SMITH
BRIDGET SMITH

It is possible indirectly to link up with poverty another type of suicide to which attention has not yet been drawn, the scholastic suicide. Marlowe in his *Hero and Leander* gives mythological evidence why " to this day is every scholar poor "; and Burton devotes a section of the *Anatomy* to discussing the question of scholars' melancholy. *Grammaticus non est felix*. " They live," he says, " a sedentary, solitary life, *sibi et musis*, free from bodily exercise, and those ordinary disports which other men use." Such habits, combined with overmuch study, are a sufficient cause for melancholy. To this scholastic spleen the venom and vituperation of eighteenth-century arguments and antagonisms gave a new aggravation. The uncertainty of patronage, the length of his labours, and the prospect of Grub Street, if he were unsuccessful, might well daunt the lamp-enslaved grammarian. The memory of Servius, the great commentator of Virgil, who thirteen hundred years before had taken his own life in the reign of Honorius, was an excuse and an example when the melancholy fit descended. For the successful Wharton, the triumphant Bentley, there was no danger. It was their unsuccessful opponents who went under. Dr. Sike, the Hebraist of Trinity College, hung himself by his sash in his rooms in 1712, and not long after Kuster, another Trinity don, was also reported to have killed himself. Richard Johnson, Bentley's Horatian antagonist, drowned himself in Nottingham meadows nine years later, and in 1737 Eustace Budgell, the friend and protégé of Addison, translator of Theophrastus, half-scholar, half Grub Street journalist, and inmate of the *Dunciad*, threw himself into the Thames. He left behind him a significant slip of paper on which appeared the words, *What Cato did and Addison approved cannot be wrong.*

It was, nevertheless, Creech's death in the first year of the century that made the greatest mark. Voltaire says that he wrote in the margin of the manuscript of his translation and commentary of Lucretius, " N.B. I must remember to hang myself when I have finished my commentary "; Voltaire's supposition is that he wished to end his life by suicide in imitation of the classical author whom he so much admired. Whether this is true or not, he subsequently engaged on a translation of Horace, and for nearly twenty years he did not commit the suicide which he appears to have intended. His death was eventually occasioned by a combination of troubles which stimulated his naturally melancholic bent. The jury brought in a verdict of insanity.

In France much the same type of suicide must have been occurring as Madame de Stael speaks of literary suicides, and Dumas says that the man of letters of his time was " *l'homme le plus réfléchissant et par conséquant le plus malheureux* ".

The peculiar melancholy, whose birth we noticed at the Renaissance, takes in our period a new romantic and Rousseauistic tinge; it is imbued with a " *sentimentalité maladive* ", of which Madame de Stael speaks. Its existence probably promoted the general indulgence towards love-suicide, and in literature it joined hands again with the macabre to produce the " grave " poetry and prose of which Young's *Night Thoughts*, Blair's *Grave*, and Harvey's *Meditations Among the Tombs*, are the best English examples. Translated into action it lends to many of the suicides of the time a self-conscious, narcissistic flavour. Its influence may be traced in the most famous love-suicide of the century.

A certain Faldoni, a gallant and beautiful young man, falls

in love with a virtuous and equally beautiful young lady in Lyons. Her parents will not consent to the marriage and the young man is in despair. To aggravate matters he now bursts a blood-vessel fencing, and the doctors tell him that he cannot recover. His mistress conveys a message to him and a clandestine meeting is arranged in an empty chapel. She arrives with two pistols, and two daggers in case the former should fail. Having embraced melodramatically on the altar steps, they prepare to die. To the trigger of each pistol a rose-coloured ribbon is fixed. At a given moment each lover pulls the ribbon attached to the other's pistol, and they both fall together. The emotional repercussions of the affair are tremendous. The "lovers of Lyons", as they come to be called, inspire a laudatory epitaph from Rousseau, a history, a novel, and some imaginary letters. The law does nothing. The love-suicide has by this time established its right to exist. A jingle which dates back at least to the eighteenth century, playfully posits suicide as an answer to the everlasting problem of love and poverty :

> Gai, gai, marions-nous—
> Mettons-nous dans la misère;
> Gai, gai, marions-nous—
> Mettons-nous la corde au cou.

In spite of Voltaire's complaints at the bourgeois character of contemporary suicide there are plenty of signs that the " noble " suicide—for honour or for country—was often admired, and sometimes practised. The success of Addison's Cato was enormous; and Pope wrote to one of his friends that " Cato was not so much the wonder of Rome in his days, as he is of Britain in ours ". In France the liberal attitude of the seventeenth-century stage towards noble suicide continues; there are plays on Lucreece, Brutus, Cassius, and at least two on Cato.

In England the most talked of suicide for honour was the noble but slightly ridiculous end of Lord Scarborough.

Q

Throughout his life he had proved himself to be a scrupulously upright man. On one occasion he was accused in the
House of Lords of supporting the king's party merely
because of his position as Master of the Horse. To vindi-
cate his good faith he gave up his office on the spot, saying,
" My Lords, to prove to you that my opinion is independent
of my place, I resign it this moment." Later in life he
found himself in a more difficult position; having already
promised marriage to one lady, he fell in love with
another. Being unwilling to imperil his honour, or sacrifice
his affections, suicide seemed to him the only possible
and dignified way out of the dilemma; he therefore killed
himself.

In France suicides for honour, patriotism, and party, became very common with the idealism of the Revolution.
Before passing to a consideration of that period, it is worth
referring to two interesting stories where ideas of honour are
indirectly involved. The first concerns a certain French
gentleman who had fought seventeen successful duels. After
some time the images of the rivals whom he had dispatched
in these " affairs of honour " began to haunt him night and
day. To calm his harassed spirit he buried himself in a
Trappist monastery. However, even this retreat was to be
denied of him, for with the coming of the revolution the
monastery was broken up. He was again forced into the
world, still dogged by the seventeen faithful images of his
murdered rivals. Their company now proved to be too
much for him and he took his own life. In a very intimate
sense his death was the result of honour.

The other interesting story in this connection concerns an
appeal made by Napoleon to his soldiers' sense of honour
and dignity. At Saint Cloud the death by suicide of two of
his grenadiers within a few days of each other, apparently
made him apprehensive of an epidemic. The following
notice was issued as an " order of the day ".

St. Cloud. 22 Floreal, *an X:*

The grenadier Groblin has committed suicide, from a disappointment in love. He was, in other respects, a worthy man.
This is the second event of the kind that has happened in this
corps within a month. The First Consul directs that it shall be
notified in the order of the day of the guard, that a soldier ought
to know how to overcome the grief and melancholy of his passions;
that there is as much true courage in bearing mental affliction
manfully as in remaining unmoved under the fire of a battery.
To abandon oneself to grief without resisting, and to kill oneself
in order to escape from it, is like abandoning the field of battle
before being conquered.

(Signed) Napoleon
Bessieres

Added point is given to this notice by the fact that Bonaparte
is reported by his faithful Montholon to have tried to commit suicide himself. After the retreat from Moscow he is
said to have always carried a preparation of opium with him,
and to have used it soon after the death of Josephine when
worried by his misfortunes and reverses. Unluckily the dose
was not fatal; he was discovered and easily persuaded to take
the necessary antidotes.

As far as our subject is concerned, the Revolution and the
early years of the Republic create an almost watertight compartment separated from the rest of the century. Different
forces were at work and they produced special results. The
attitude of the public tells us a lot: wholly absorbed in
passionate enterprises, they had little time to react to suicide.
They neither glorify nor condemn it; they meet it with an
almost unparalleled apathy. Writers, too, have practically
nothing to say on the subject. When Dufriche-Valazé stabs
himself before the Convention the press hardly pauses to
comment on it and the official records merely note that
" *Cet évènement excita un petit movement dans la
salle* ".

A similar lack of interest marks the suicides of Condorcet,

Roland, and Clavières—all men of importance. The world was full of breathless events, and political suicides had grown too common. A single ironic story will illustrate their frequency. Madame Augnié, who had been personally attached to Marie Antoinette, fully expected to suffer under the tyranny of Robespierre. When at last the guards appeared before her house to convey her to prison, she flung herself from the balcony and was taken up dead. As her corpse was being carried to burial, the bearers had to stand aside to make room for a tumbril that was passing on its way to the guillotine. It contained her enemy Robespierre on his way to the scaffold, suffering agony from a wound in the jaw which he was popularly believed to have inflicted upon himself.

The one type of self-destruction which does seem to have evoked enthusiasm was the patriotic suicide of defeated republican soldiers in the old Roman tradition. General Beaurepaire's self-inflicted death after his defeat at Verdun is the most famous. His action is cited amid general praise; a street is named after him; and he is accorded a burial in the Panthéon. His inscription reads as follows: *Il aima mieux se donner la mort que de capituler avec les tyrans.* Beaurepaire's death sets a fashion: several generals in a similar position follow his example; captains scuttle their ships; and officers blow themselves up in their last redoubt.

The suicides, however, which are most touching and the most typical of this period are the suicides of indignant royalists faced with the revolution and the suicides of the revolutionary minority in the Vendée. Particularly among the royalist suicides, we meet again the same symptoms and the same psychology as in the period of the Christian martyrs. The parallel is clearer than one might suppose: there is the same self-denunciation, the same refusal to put up a defence, and often the same unwillingness on the part of judges to inflict the death penalty. A certain Voillemier

writes to the revolutionary tribunal at Chaumont: " I
denounce Charles Voillemier as an out-and-out Aristocrat,
who wishes only for the restoration of the monarchy. I hope
that you will do justice on me immediately. 7 June 1794,
the fifth year of brigandage." Elsewhere a young girl is had
up before a tribunal for insulting the cockade, the president
wishes to save her, but in their presence she tramples the
cockade underfoot. The son of an aristocrat is led out to the
fusilade with his father; the soldiers take pity on him and
wish to spare his youth, but he cries " Long live the King! "
until they are compelled to shoot him. This cry " *Vive le
Roi* ", ringing out in public squares, in tribunals, from the
lips of ladies and of harlots, is the contemporary equivalent
of the old avowal of Christianity. More rarely the cry
" *Vive le Republique!* " has the same significance. Not all
the political suicides, of course, have this dramatic self-
denunciatory character. Many royalists commit suicide in
prison, and Paris kills himself after writing :

> *Ce n'est que par la mort qu'on peut fuir l'infamie*
> *Qu'imprima sur nos fronts le sang de notre roi.*

The examination of eighteenth-century suicide should
finish on a philosophic note, since the great figures of the
century were its philosophers. Adam Lux, idealist and
revolutionary, arrived in Paris to represent his native town
of Mayence. But indignant at the turn the revolution was
taking under Marat in 1793, and horrified to see it betraying
those very ideals of liberty and justice for which it had been
created, he determined to sacrifice his life for his principles.
He hoped that by a conspicuous and altruistic death he
might open the eyes of the Convention to their brutality and
egoism, and redirect the revolution into ideal channels. He
planned to place himself at the bar of the Convention when
it was in full session, and to address the assembly as follows :
" Since the second of June my life has been distasteful. Shall

I, the disciple of Jean-Jacques-Rousseau, be ignoble enough
to watch without protest the doings of such men as your-
selves? Shall I see without protest the oppression of liberty
and virtue, the triumph of vice? Never!" At this point
he intended to place a pistol to his temple and shoot himself. Only the arguments of his friends dissuaded him. But
the spirit of the philosophers was strong in the last twenty
years of the century, and soon after he contrived another
method of openly testifying to his ideals. When Marat's
death was announced he publicly proclaimed his admiration
for Charlotte Corday and cried that he would die for her.
On his arrest and sentence he went with the greatest pride
to the guillotine, only asking that he might be buried beside
his master, with the epitaph: " *Ci-gît Adam Lux, élève de
Jean-Jacques-Rousseau* ".

CHAPTER VIII

MR. BLOOM'S FATHER

I. ON THE WAY TO THE FUNERAL

" The worst of all," Mr. Power said, " is the man who takes his own life."

Martin Cunningham drew out his watch briskly, coughed, and put it back.

" The greatest disgrace to have in the family," Mr. Power added.

" Temporary insanity, of course," Martin Cunningham said decisively. " We must take a charitable view of it."

THIS scrap of conversation from Joyce's *Ulysses* takes place in a cab on the way to a funeral. Silent among the speakers is Mr. Bloom, whose father committed suicide. Martin Cunningham, aware of this, tries to change the topic and excuse the act.

For us this passage is significant and well worth a detailed examination. Let us begin with Mr. Power's second observation on suicide: *the greatest disgrace to have in the family*. Most characteristic is the use of the word *disgrace*. Before the nineteenth century [1] *crime* or *sin* would have been the term employed. Sometime after Waterloo, however, a change takes place; the comforts of Victorianism overlay the primitive horror of suicide and blunt the precise dogmatic teaching of the Church: it is no longer the thing in itself

---

[1] The nineteenth century for our purposes may be considered to last until 1914.

that creates the scare, so much as what other people will think of it. Thus *disgrace*. Again, how odd, but how typical of the period, to bring in the family. In earlier times when confiscation was put into effect, the family had indeed been involved, but in a straightforward pecuniary fashion. With the nineteenth century it begins to suffer quite differently : for loss of fortune is substituted the scourge of gossip. In other periods the suicide was responsible to the Church or to society; in the nineteenth century he was, typically enough, responsible to the family. This body knew an apotheosis of power in the latter half of the century; the family council usurped the authority of medieval Church synods, of guild gatherings, and of the judgments of " good society " passed in eighteenth-century salons. The family, however, had to defend its own position against that of other families, rather in the same way that one early Church council would struggle to maintain the validity of its canons against those of a council with similar authority in another part of the Empire. Nothing lowered the prestige of a family as much as the " talk " that a suicide involved. It broke the façade presented to the world; the suicide therefore was primarily culpable in relation to his family. He indeed created a *disgrace in the family*, for suicide, instead of chiefly bringing on a soul the wrath of God and the law, now brought to the ears of the family the twitter of malicious tongues. In another sense also the family became involved (as we shall see) through medical theories of suicide and heredity, which forced down its shares on the marriage market.

The strong attitude of families, and thus both of upper middle-class and *bourgeois* society, towards suicide represents simply a strengthening and solidification of that suburban spirit whose growth was glimpsed in the eighteenth century at the time of the Nonconformist revival. Its absolute force may be universally traced in the modesty of its methods, in the whisper, the meaning glance, and in

Martin Cunningham's discreet cough. These are its weapons and it needs no others.

Its effects, moreover, on the flavour of suicide, as distinguished from the simple attitude of people towards suicide, were corruptive and poisoning. Suicide went out of sight; it saw the light neither for praise nor punishment. It became secretive, and when the motives for suicide became unknown all possibility of a rational judgment disappeared. Again, mistaking the greater for the lesser ill, the family sheltered behind insanity, and all the strange and unpleasant associations of madness drew closer to self-destruction. Finally, when suicide did not go out of sight, it went below stairs. Behind the façade of the well-to-do family it was always possible to rig up a shooting accident, a heart attack, an overdose of sleeping-draught. In the kitchen, however, the scullery-maid was found hung; the labourer drowned himself in the pond. The musty odour of backstairs, and more recently the whiff of gas in rented rooms, infect the whole subject. One misses, until well into the twentieth century (when note the appearance of the aeroplane) the gentleman's sword and the philosopher's decision. Such impressions are sentimental and snobbish, but they correspond to certain real changes caused by a conspiracy of concealment and the family policy of forcing suicide underground.

Seeing that the family and society looked so askance at suicide in the nineteenth century, it may be asked where they obtained a reasoned basis for this attitude. The answer is that no sanction was obtained or asked. Without a desire to examine premises or arguments, the average man condemned suicide, stating, without preamble like Mr. Power: *the worst is the man who takes his own life.* No important figure rose to denounce suicide, and no new argument was forged to demonstrate its wickedness or inexpediency. In the other camp, Reason continued to argue and demonstrate, though with a marked loss of enthusiasm. There was, in fact, little left to prove; the major anti-suicide positions had been turned in the previous century. The anti-suicide prejudice was left without any justification except feeling and the support which could be derived from the acceptance of non-rational Christian dogma. None the less the prejudice flourished for many decades and still flourishes to no small extent—nourished chiefly on emotion.

It is curious that this should have been possible at a time when science was forging ahead and a rational outlook was beginning to control people's attitude to the physical world. That ideas about morals and behaviour made little attempt to keep pace was probably due to fear, and not least to fear of political changes. Opinion, remembering the French Revolution, retreated for half a century from the moral positions of the eighteenth-century philosophers; attitudes to suicide were naturally involved in this general movement. It has been ingeniously suggested that this halt in the rationalization of moral and ethical ideas—a halt even called by those who, like Huxley, in other spheres worked on rational principles—was due to the fear of having eventually to submit rooted sexual prejudices to reason. Rather than do this, people shelved the whole question of applied morality. Old standards were taken on trust and reform was taboo. Thus the suicide suffered because fear would not apply the light of reason to the strong emotions that surrounded sex.

Mr. Power, as we have seen, did not demand a logical justification for his feelings about suicide. Neither did philosophers and essayists suggest that he should pause and think. Though by no means silent on the subject, in the nineteenth century they rarely occupied themselves with a fresh presentation of the moral arguments. The ground had been gone over so often by their predecessors.

The Church maintained its attitude of absolute

condemnation, but its methods showed a change of emphasis. Scholastic argument, proving suicide to be a sin, was abandoned; in its place was substituted insistence on the punishments which the suicide will receive. Colton, more famous as a fisherman than as a divine, who himself committed suicide in 1832, wrote " the act of suicide renounces earth to forfeit heaven ". The same sentiment is echoed at greater length and with less delicacy in a didactic poem, Le Suicide, published anonymously in Paris in the middle of the century: though your troubles may seem interminable here, think, the writer says, how much unpleasanter they will be, and how much longer they will last, in hell.

Auguste Comte, who maintained that one of the great glories of Catholicism was to have denounced so unequivocally the anti-social practice of suicide, serves to exemplify the tacit alliance which is always apt to exist between the Church and the philosophers and essayists who attack suicide. Of the latter only two in the course of the nineteenth century wrote enough on our subject to deserve consideration. The first, Leopardi—here it is as the author of the Dialogues not as poet that he is in question [1]—stood alone and would have been the last person to approve of Catholic penalties; the second, Gurnhill, is principally important for his attempt to preserve the old condemnation of suicide in the new religious framework of a vague, "enlightened" nineteenth-century Christianity.

Leopardi, who was always interested in suicide, treats the question of its morality in an imaginary dialogue between Porphyry and Plotinus. As a sidelight on the attitude towards

---

[1] Characteristically enough Leopardi, as a poet, shows no opposition to suicide, and conforms to the general poetic attitude of the nineteenth century (see page 274). In his poem Bruto Minore he praises the courage of the Roman who, " smiling at death, drives the painful steel into his side ", and he sympathizes with the animal world, where no man-made laws stand between life and death.

suicide among intelligent people in the early nineteenth century, the dialogue is most interesting; as reasoned argument it is without value. The dialogue begins on a fairly quiet tone, but as Plotinus replies to Porphyry's defence of suicide, the tempo changes, emotion breaks through. Suicide is " an atrocious and inhuman act . . . an exhibition of the most sordid and inconsiderate self-love, such as the world cannot parallel ". One recognizes the almost hysterical phrases, the sweeping condemnations of fear and prejudice which are so familiar in the history of the subject.

The dialogue chiefly runs in very familiar channels. Two points will be enough to show the weak texture of the argument, in what is perhaps the most considerable moral attack on suicide, ostensibly based on reason, that the nineteenth century produced. Plotinus begins by claiming that suicide is opposed to nature: " a moment's reflection must show you," he says, " that voluntary and unnecessary self-slaughter is palpably opposed to nature ". By introducing the word *unnecessary* Leopardi fights from the start against a shadow. The most ardent supporters of suicide would usually condemn it when unnecessary. As soon as one speaks practically and not mystically about the morals of suicide, the essence of the problem is to discover just this—when is suicide *necessary* and what constitutes this *necessity*. (In practice *necessitas*—though Plato gave it a more limited application—may be established when a suicide and its ramifications promote a balance of happiness. At all events such a suicide cannot be condemned as *unnecessary*.)

Battling against a shadow Leopardi finally arrives at the following sentiment: " Let us not refuse to submit to that portion of the sufferings of our race which destiny has appointed to us." As a mystical conviction this may be well enough, but as practical counsel it is short-sighted. Submission to human suffering leaves malaria marshes undrained and cancers uncured. It is indeed the most suicidal of all reactions to life. The quietist may practise it regardless, but the opponent of suicide has no right to produce it as a rational argument against self-destruction.

Gurnhill's *Morals of Suicide*, written at the very end of the century, adopts a rather different approach to the moral question than that of any writer we have yet met. Written by a clergyman this book uses few of the orthodox canonical arguments and such as it adopts it changes, soaking them in the milk of an Anglican kindness. *Christian Therapeutics*, the title of one of the chapters, gives an idea of its would-be practical, preventative nature. Inclined to be flabby in texture, and sweeping in its statements, the book produces no argument against suicide valid for non-Christians. This does not prevent it being full of obvious and very true things about the value of temperance, hard work, and faith, as antidotes to the suicidal impulse. Though it may not have been necessary to write a book to prove this, the *Morals of Suicide* is of special interest as being probably the only work in which " broad-minded " Protestant Christianity approaches the problem of suicide. A confusion of issues and a woolliness, that one is apt to find in modern Christianity as soon as one moves out of the Catholic Church, are evident enough. But what is significant is that the old prejudices survive behind the self-deception of an over-frank manner. Much mention of love, and of allowances for the unfortunate brother, bring one in the last part of the work suddenly face to face with a demand for punishment. The author in 1899 can still regret that a verdict of *felo de se* is not more often returned by the courts, and he would like to see unsuccessful suicides doing the two years' hard labour which the law has a right to impose on them.

Midway between those who condemn and those who support suicide come the nineteenth-century essayists. These more intimate and often over-confidential descendants of Addison, though arbiters of taste rather than of belief, touched on every subject, or rather made use of every subject as a peg for style or sensibility. Thus Leigh Hunt discusses in a superior and bantering vein the frequency of suicide among butlers, which he attributes to sedentary habits in the pantry, horse-racing, and worthless shares. It is noticeable that the thing itself receives neither support nor defence; it is a mere handle for his humour, and this in itself shows an absence of prejudice perhaps hardly possible in earlier centuries. De Quincey, who was more interested in his subjects for their own sake, has a section on suicide in his essay on *Casuistry*, and an essay *On Suicide*. He, too, shows an admirable lack of emotion, and concerns himself less with the morals of self-destruction than with the task of detaching the martyr and the idealist from the ranks of the suicides. Though he is unwilling to " diminish by one hair's weight the reasons against suicide " he supports Donne in distinguishing self-homicide from self-murder. Not every man who kills himself, says De Quincey, is *felo de se* : " whenever a paramount interest of human nature is at stake, a suicide which maintains that interest is self-homicide, but for a personal interest it becomes self-murder ". Specifically he exonerates from suicide both the woman who kills herself to save her chastity, and the man who takes his life to avoid corporal punishment, not from personal fear but regarding it as a degradation of the human species in general to which no man should be submitted. The latter is a particular extension of the right to suicide which we have not met before, and De Quincey in a curious passage supports it because he finds that corporal punishment is a man's particular *sexual* degradation and corresponds to the forcible loss of chastity which it is permissible for a woman to avoid by suicide.

From De Quincey it is only a step to the recognition of a general right to commit suicide, a recognition which certain sections of nineteenth-century society were inclined to grant for fortuitous reasons. Periods, such as the birth of the

Third Republic in France, were by their very anti-clericalism and their claim to a monopoly of reasonableness and common sense in politics, driven into a kinder view of suicide. Yet such sympathy was usually inarticulate and the active defence of suicide on moral and philosophic grounds was left for a century to the scattered pens of three or four individuals.

The most outspoken defence of suicide and the most effective attack on anti-suicide prejudice came not unexpectedly from Schopenhauer. Not only is there " nothing in the world to which every man has a more unassailable title than to his own life and person ", but " it will generally be found that as soon as the terrors of life reach the point at which they outweigh the terrors of death, a man will put an end to his life ". Yet it is not as simple as this. The terrors of death are strangely resistant : " They stand like a sentinel at the gate leading out of this world . . . [and] perhaps there is no man alive who would not have already put an end to his life, if this end had been of a purely negative character, a sudden stoppage of existence ". It was the attitude of the clergy that particularly irritated Schopenhauer. Failing to discover any condemnation of suicide in the Bible, they turned, he said, to " philosophical grounds of their own invention, . . insipidities, . . [and] the nonsensical remark that suicide is *wrong* ". He does not linger over their " weak sophisms that can be easily refuted ", but refers the reader to Hume. He chooses himself rather to explore the psychological causes of the churchman's antagonism. Its secret reason he discovers in the fact that " the voluntary surrender of life is a bad compliment for him who said that *all things were very good* ". The Church, seeing in suicide a reflection on Christianity, is forced to denounce it.

For Schopenhauer himself there is only one valid moral objection to suicide. The attainment of moral freedom, which is the individual's highest aim, can only be achieved by a denial of the " will to live ". Suicide, however, is an emphatic assertion of this will. To destroy oneself is not to destroy one's " will to live ", since the man who commits suicide has not outgrown the desire for life; on the contrary he merely wishes with great bitterness and violence that life were different. He is goaded by an image of happiness, and he thinks that by dying he will approach at any rate relatively closer to it. Thus in the last analysis, Schopenhauer finds that the desire for death is as much an assertion of the " will to live " as the desire for life. Both are a perturbation of the soul, a divergence from the goal of philosophic detachment. Yet if suicide in this sense appears wrong to Schopenhauer, it is no more wrong than the whole of life as most people know it. The suicide, if not elevated to the meditative company of the elect, is yet admitted on equal terms, and with a certain flourish of introduction, to the general society of his striving fellow-men.

Senancour's support of suicide is more sentimental, and he might with justice be included among those writers to be dealt with later, in whom *le mal du siècle* developed a romantic tolerance, if not an idealization, of suicide. However, since he makes a show of replying to anti-suicide argument, he has a right to be classed among the philosophers and essayists. In practice his arguments are as weak as those he wishes to refute. How can his suicide, he says, remove him from God, since his soul will always be with its Maker? And on what rests the absurd pretension that man in society has no right to renounce the liberty of life? If suicide is a crime, by what authority do these sophists who forbid man to approach death, try to persuade him to mount the scaffold or follow the wars? The whole anti-suicide philosophy, he concludes, is a mere expedient " to make us bear our servile misery in the false belief that it is necessary ".

Outside creative literature there is no other important vindication of the morality of suicide by argument until the last quarter of the century, when a certain Bonser published in pamphlet form an essay entitled *The Right to Die*. The author is wise enough not to weaken his arguments by claiming that such a right is absolute; it is a right based on circumstances, and will sometimes be present and sometimes not. Such an attitude makes his position unassailable, since it is easy enough to prove that at certain times and under certain conditions to retire from life is the better, wiser, and more moral course. Not every suicide is selfish, he says, and the sick man who takes his life to lighten the burden that his existence lays on his friends is altruistic to the point of heroism.

Though Bonser's defence of suicide is dependent on circumstances, his opposition to state interference is unconditional. There are rights which the individual does not alienate to society, and which therefore cannot be taken from him : among these is the ultimate liberty which consists in the right to die. The state's opposition to suicide in cases of illness seems to him particularly unfair and he makes a point of demanding the legalization of suicide as a remedy for painful and incurable disease. To-day it seems hardly necessary to argue that the forcible retention of the cancer patient in his torture is undesirable, but in the eighteen-eighties, outside the safety of imaginative literature, this frank return to a classic position was not orthodox or usual.

One other point is of interest. The conception of the sacredness of property and of life had been growing steadily stronger throughout the century. Bonser, possibly realizing that a confusion of ideas on this subject might contribute arguments against suicide, makes, for the first time in reference to suicide, the obvious distinction between the *social* sacredness of life and its *natural* valuelessness. In nature nothing is cheaper than life. Only in a social sense, and in the same way as property, is life sacred, or, to be more precise, inviolable by others. People, therefore, have no right

R

to demand that others should suffer because life is sacred. Its sanctity is social and has a significance for others only; it is irrelevant when a man comes to take his *own* life.

Beyond the limits of the nineteenth century both the antagonists and defenders of suicide grow silent. In our time educated opinion has tacitly granted a conditional right to die. Interest has shifted from the moral aspect and has been replaced by a close questioning of the causation of suicide. It is the statisticians and not the moralists who now argue. Further, the interpretation of the suicide laws, which grows progressively more lenient, make it improbable that the moral question will attract attention for some time. When only the rare and obscure individual suffers legal injustices, it is difficult to arouse effective protest. In recent years I can only trace two writings on the morals of suicide: an inconsiderable American pamphlet, *Is Suicide Justifiable?* and an *Essay on Suicide*, by G. R. Malkani, published in 1924. As regards the state and the individual Malkani believes that the latter's obligations are only valid while life remains worth living within the state. A second point is of interest here as it apparently marks the first infiltration of the modern sociological theory about the causation of suicide (see Chapter X) into ethical writing: Malkani says, far from having the right to punish suicide, the state is responsible and culpable for producing the sort of conditions that lead to a suicidal mentality. As far as the personal aspect of suicide goes, Malkani would only condemn it when against the best interest of the individual. He asserts with every right that suicide, to realize ideals and values, represents something at least as valuable as the self-preservative instinct and the will to live.

The essay ends with an unexpected and penetrating observation, so simple that former writers on the subject seem to have overlooked it. Actually it goes to the heart of the question and throws a tragic ray of light on the last

deception of the man who is about to die. Suicide is
definitely not a means of achieving what life has failed to
give; and yet the suicide always envisages a new and less
painful condition. He projects his personality *beyond* the
event in order to make the event appear desirable.[1] Thus,
even suicide is the result of an effort of the imagination.

Throughout the latter half of the nineteenth century, perhaps almost as much as to-day, it was not these philosophers
and essayists, occupied with the moral problem, who were
important among writers on suicide. The period saw the
rise of an altogether different type of suicide literature
embodying the medical (and sometimes the statistical)
approach. The number of these writers was legion, and
among them were to be found Winslow and Westcott in
England, and on the Continent such names as Esquirol,
Lisle, Brierre de Boismont, Legoyt, and Moreau de Tours.
Though a few of these works were religious in flavour and
unbending in their attitude towards suicide, the majority
adopted a tone of very qualified reproach. So far as we are
here concerned the latter writers had a double but contra-
dictory influence on contemporary opinion. It is in them
that we find stated the reasonable belief that each suicide
must be judged on its own merits. For the first time
intelligent opinion seems to grasp the fact that it is the
circumstances under which a suicide is committed which
must determine whether the act is good or bad, wise or
foolish. This idea, however, did not penetrate to the popular
consciousness or ease the case of the suicide; for the time
being its repercussions were limited. It was otherwise with
the more purely medical conclusions at which many of these
writers arrived.

[1] This would not be true, of course, if a suicide's attitude could be
altogether negative and death appear only as oblivion. Given the
nature of desire, such an attitude must be impossible; *some* idea of
pleasure will be associated even with a state of rest.

Broadly speaking, they believed that suicide was the result of simple physiological causes, and usually a sign of madness. So convinced were they of the relation between insanity and suicide, and so eager to find pathological proof of this relationship, that they formulated the most preposterous theories. Thus Gall claimed that suicide occurred in people with thick craniums, and Cabanis asserted that it was due to an excess of phosphorus in the brain. Such speculation was given the widest currency and had an undoubted and unfortunate effect on public opinion. *Temporary insanity*, as we have seen, was a phrase that came naturally to the lips of Martin Cunningham. All the superstitious fear of the queer and the mad attached itself to suicide; the instinctive withdrawal of the sane from the tainted extended itself to cases of the calmest and most rational suicide. Finally, these new medical ideas hardened family prejudice against suicide: a suicide in the family became tantamount to insanity in the family, a stigma not confined to one member, but attaching jointly to the whole group and its descendants. Further, medical writers elaborated theories of suicidal-heredity, as though it were an actual physical defect which could be handed on from one generation to another (rather than a possible tendency for certain individuals to react in a similar way to exceptional situations). This fallacy made families hush up suicide with even more determination, hoping that the closely guarded secret would not damage their children's chances of making a " good " marriage.

There were, outside the classes to whom reference has been made, two or three writers such as Garrisson, Etangs, and Geiger, who concerned themselves neither with the medical nor moral aspect of suicide, but with some particular facet of its history, such as suicide in politics or law. To these, one should be grateful as their detached examination of facts at any rate created an atmosphere unfavourable to prejudiced emotion and tended to clear the air.

Oddly enough it would seem at first sight that the law in nineteenth-century England was better disposed to suicides than the people. Yet it must be remembered that a suicide was buried at a cross-roads in 1823 and that the law could hardly have grown *more* severe: progress was only possible in one direction. Even so, it took sixty years to bring the laws of suicide anywhere near the reasonable position adopted in 1789 by French legislation. Whether this change would have taken place spontaneously, at the time that it did, is extremely doubtful. For once fortune favoured the suicide; the *felo de se* became involved in the general movement for legal reform and benefited by that series of changes initiated by Sir Samuel Romilly, himself a suicide.

The first change in the suicide laws which had remained naturally unaltered for centuries came in 1823, when George III's parliament decided that suicides should no longer bear the trampling of traffic at every cross-roads, but should be granted an honest burial. Decency, however, still forbade that they should be buried by daylight. They were to be interred in the " suicides' corner " of the cemetery without religious rites between nine and twelve midnight. In 1870 came the general abolition of forfeitures for penal offences, which, among the rest, perforce did away with confiscations for *felo de se*. Thus the suicide fortuitously benefited. The crown, however, had long ceased to exercise its nominal right of seizure, and in one particular only did the act of 1870 make any practical difference: the bodies of unclaimed and destitute suicides no longer went, as they had apparently done during the previous fifty years (Lecky), to the schools of anatomy for dissection. In 1879 and 1882 came further concessions. Suicide ceased to be legally considered as homicide, and the maximum sentence for attempted suicide was reduced to two years. In addition suicides were granted the right of burial at normal hours and not merely after dark, while the question of religious rites was left to the discretion of ministers. On the other hand, the abetting of suicide was made punishable by penal servitude for life.

Thus, at the end of the century the law, while still considering a suicide as *felo de se*, did not penalize either his property or his corpse, and only punished three things—attempted suicide, the abetting of suicide, and constructive murder. The last is a curious legal doctrine to which reference has not yet been made. The doctrine is as follows: anyone committing a felony and, while so doing, causing the death of another person, even without intending it, is none the less guilty of constructive murder. In practice this means that anyone who, in committing suicide, happens inadvertently to kill someone else, is a murderer in the eyes of the law.

Though improved, the position of suicide was obviously still unsatisfactory. It remains to trace how the courts in our time have dealt with these anachronisms. The stigma of *felo de se*, as the papers tell us every day, is commonly avoided by a verdict of temporary insanity. In London in 1935, out of 593 suicides, coroners' juries only brought in two verdicts of *felo de se*. This has an added advantage in that it often permits the dependants of a genuine suicide to get the premiums and benefits due to them from insurance companies. On the other hand it means that every suicide to-day is still a criminal or a madman. A ridiculous position which only a reform of the law can remedy.

The act which makes abetting a suicide a penal offence does very little harm, except in the instance of suicide pacts, as cases are very rarely brought into court.[1] It is, in practice, a safeguard against unscrupulous people who might try to bring about the suicide of relations or friends for personal

[1] Complicity is not an offence in France or Italy, but it remains so in China, Chile, and certain of the Swiss cantons and United States of America.

reasons. The ideal modification of this law would be to make complicity in a suicide only indictable where malice or personal interest could be proved, as is the case to-day in Japan.

The law dealing with attempted suicide is more irrational and more unjust. Yet, as administered to-day, it causes less hardship than might be expected. The courts, exercising their discretion, make very few charges and seem to be showing an ever-increasing clemency. Thus, in the County of London in 1933 there were recorded 653 unsuccessful attempts at suicide, but at the Assizes and Quarter Sessions there were only eight trials and only three prison sentences were imposed. None the less, it seems a monstrous procedure to inflict further suffering on even a single individual who has already found life so unbearable, his chances of happiness so slender, that he has been willing to face pain and death in order to cease living. That those for whom life is altogether bitter, should be subjected to further bitterness and degradation seems perverse legislation. Reform on this point is really very necessary.

Where suicide is concerned, the law of constructive murder—rarely applicable at the best of times—appears to be falling into abeyance, though the question was raised afresh by a recent London suicide. The circumstances of the latter were curious. In August 1937, a woman jumped from the parapet of a roof near New Oxford Street and succeeded in committing suicide. She had, however, overlooked the danger her action might cause to people in the street, and a young man below, who was struck by her falling body, died of the injuries he received. The coroner, after returning a verdict of " Suicide while of unsound mind ", went on to say that the doctrine of constructive murder " has been falling into abeyance of late years, and it is not construed so strictly as it used to be. . . . The woman never intended to hurt anybody but herself . . . [and] to record a verdict of murder in these circumstances against this woman would be very hard and improper."[1]

So much for the reform of the suicide laws and their position in England to-day. In France the situation in the nineteenth century was rather different, and it is exceedingly interesting to see how the fluctuations of French politics affected the attitude towards suicide legislation. Whenever reaction came into power there was a tendency to try and override the liberal legislation of the code Napoleon, and conversely when ideals of liberty and democratic government dominated, the rights of the suicide were again scrupulously respected. The new code that was the product of the Revolution ignored suicide : the state did not occupy itself with the man who took his own life. More than this, the state soon after charged the civil authorities with the duty of burying a suicide, should the Church refuse. The latter, possibly infected with the fervour of the time, did not resent the new status of suicide as much as one would have expected. For a time bishops seem even to have fallen in with the attitude of civil authority and to have exerted their influence on priests to make them accord funeral rites to suicides. Thus at Toulouse the archbishop relieved of his duties a priest who refused to bury a suicide.

With the restoration of Louis XVIII came the turn in the tide. The Church rediscovered scruples about the burial of those who had killed themselves, and by 1820, propelled by steady Catholic pressure, people were beginning to demand legal penalties against suicides. In 1836 a prefectorial circular instructed local mayors not to exert pressure on the clergy in the matter of the burial of suicides, and a decade later the Minister of Justice himself was supporting the clerical attitude. In the army Marshal Soult, an admirable general, but hardly a valuable person in other respects, gave concrete form to the renascent anti-suicide prejudice by ordering that

[1] *Evening Standard*, August 3, 1937.

funeral honours were not to be accorded to soldiers who took their own lives.

After Napoleon III's *coup d'état* the position of the suicide became more and more difficult. Not only was he refused Christian burial, but the authorities began to frown on civil interments. Soldiers and government officials were not encouraged to attend them, and in one department they were only authorized to take place in the very early morning. Thus the alternative funeral, allowed to the suicide whom the priest would not bury, grew to be a mark of ignominy and dishonour, and was carried out in the most slipshod fashion. In 1869 it appears that the corpse of a labourer who had killed himself was actually pushed to the cemetery in a wheelbarrow.

The antagonism of Church and Government served both to intensify popular prejudice and drive suicide underground. After 1830, when the suicide of the Prince de Condé was reported as assassination in the Press, secrecy and misrepresentation began to develop in the same way as they had already done in England. Stimulated by fear, the family turned in vindictive anger against the suicide in its midst.

With 1870 there came the inevitable change. The swing back to liberal and democratic ideals, the revulsion from a government that had oppressed Michelet and Renan, and chained a free Press, was reflected in the attitude to suicide. In proportion as the Church lost ground the position of the suicide improved, both practically and in the eyes of society. The *morale laique* of the Republic was unwilling to tolerate that its citizens should be subjected to indignities on what were apparently religious grounds. In the eighteen-eighties the government forbade discrimination against anyone in the matter of burial, and finally insisted on the application of proper honours, whether in religious or civil funerals.

II. POLITICIANS AND ROMANTICS

Joyce's loquacious mourners, bowling along to their funeral, could not discuss suicide with the freedom that they would have liked. Mr. Bloom's feelings were involved. With the nineteenth century the canvas grows overcrowded. The self-destroyed are our fathers and sons; if not these, they will include a girl in Paris who took poison, the friend who, longing for death, went to fight in Spain. It is not merely that our closeness to the event shows up the obscure and local tragedy which history does not record, or that yearly fewer suicides slip through the statistician's net; for a hundred years other causes have been at work increasing not only the apparent, but the real number of suicides.

As the nineteenth century progressed the old religious and social groupings, the strongest bulwarks against suicide, lost effectiveness. On the one hand, there was a weakening of the idea of responsibility to God and of the feeling of cohesion between the members of a given congregation; on the other hand, there was a weakening of the bonds of society based upon responsibility to one's neighbour and of the familiar personal contacts and mutual interdependences which had formed the cement of village and guild life. More and more individuals were left to shift spiritually and emotionally for themselves and to face on their own the problems of living.[1] Along every plane, capitalism, by its insistence on purely material values and its cold monetary standards of measurement, accelerated this process. If, as Mercier wrote at the end of the eighteenth century, innumerable suicides were due to the inability to gain a living, how much more was this true when capitalism got properly under

[1] Much of the best poetry of people like Clough and Arnold had its origin in the sense of loss and bewilderment that the new isolation brought. Arnold wrote: " We mortal millions live *alone* ". The italics are his.

way? Speculation and simply the increasing use of stocks and shares plunged people overnight into undeserved and unexpected poverty. As the system grew more complicated and less resilient, cycles of depression with their attendant unemployment grew more severe. No section of society altogether escaped, and in our time, after the American crash of 1929, papers reported almost daily the fall of ruined magnates from twenty stories. Even more important than these economic dangers was the disintegrating force of capitalism on social life: while making people more and more interdependent economically, it isolated them socially. The larger cities grew, the more solitary became their citizens, who found to their bewilderment that the fellowships of faith, responsibility, and group life, were disappearing overnight.

Suicides due also to the more consciously irresponsible methods of capitalism cannot be altogether overlooked. The squeezing of the wage-earner produced its own suicides. In 1856 eight hundred Chinese workmen who had been persuaded to come to England found themselves at the mercy of their contractors. The *Moniteur Universel* at the time said, probably with some bias and exaggeration that they "committed suicide by hundreds". At all events it appears that a mere remnant—two hundred, the paper says—survived to be shipped to Jamaica.

Why Bloom's father committed suicide is not recorded, but it was probably for one of those domestic and personal reasons, questions of jealousy, penury, anger, and prestige, which always operate regardless of time and place. Though such causes do not change it is possible in nearly every century to pick out types of suicide which seem characteristic, either because of their unusual frequency, or because they fit in with events and special attitudes to life typical of the period in which they occur. This is particularly true in the nineteenth century, which gives its own colour to certain suicides, in the same way as it modifies the faces of many of its public men or even changes the character of the landscape before which its painters set up their canvases.

To speak first of two types of suicide which, though not uncommon in certain periods, are noticeable by their very absence in the nineteenth-century scene—the suicide of reason and the suicide of religion. The former is perhaps always considered rarer than it is. Its calm and studied nature create little stir, and it is apt to avoid detection as suicide; similarly the most common and most understandable motive for these reasoned suicides is the colourless and un-sensational pressure of disease or old age. If we discount the appeals to reason which in the suicides of art and litera-ture simply try to rationalize, as we shall see, the romantic desire for death, suicides of reason appear to be few and far between in the nineteenth century. Rarer than in the previous epoch, they do not, however, disappear, and Richard Smith has his modern prototypes, most eminent among whom are certainly the Laforgues. This talented French writer and socialist, together with his wife, the daughter of Karl Marx, committed suicide in 1911. His death strikes the clear and rational note of the Stoic period. In a written statement he points out that he has gone to meet death, " before pitiless old age (which is taking from me one by one the pleasures and joys of existence, and depriving me of my physical and intellectual strength), paralyses my energy, breaks my life, and makes me a burden to myself and others. Years ago I promised myself not to live beyond seventy."

Religious suicide, as one would expect, continued to decrease throughout the nineteenth century. The masochistic impulse, which is often at the bottom of this sort of suicide, continued to find expression in the martyr psychology of the missionary movement. Those who went blissfully to the cooking pots of cannibal tribes maintained an immemorial tradition. There were, also, real outbreaks of religious suicide in Russia and Brazil. The latter occurring in the eighteen nineties was both in its size and violence more typical of an earlier date. The story is impressive. Antonio Conselheiro, a man of genius and belief, arose as a prophet and mystical reformer. Though his righteous life and disruptive teachings drew the attention and persecution of the Brazilian Government, Conselheiro found in the Jagunço tribes of the interior ardent and determined believers. Retreating into their fastnesses the mystic ruled as prophet and king over a devoted following. Wherever he placed his headquarters that town became a holy city and preparations for resistance went on side by side with prayer and fasting. One Government expedition after another was defeated with heavy loss, and in the end the full force of the Brazilian army was mustered to suppress the prophet and his defenders. Even so, the task was by no means easy. The position of the prophet's capital, the climate, the difficulty of getting supplies, made the Government anxious to come to terms. Time and again, however, its proposals were turned down. As they saw their numbers dwindle, themselves surrounded, and their walls a series of breaches, the religious ardour of the Jagunços only grew stronger. Famine came to join them, the prophet died, and at last their powder gave out. Even then a mere remnant would not accept the proffered peace. Arrogant of their right to die, they fought on with swords and knives. The Government had no alternative : since they would not take peace, the reluctant soldiers were compelled to engage them to the very last man. The holy city only fell when there were no defenders left.

If religious and reasoned suicides grew generally rare, they were replaced by an increase in other more contemporary types of self-destruction. The nineteenth century saw a momentous change in the attitude of the average man towards politics. Whereas previously politics had been the privileged and practical business of a few, and had usually captured only the interest of a minority, with the growth of democratic ideas the man in the street became heavily involved. Previously politics had been a matter of practice, they now became to some extent a matter of theory and automatically involved the more extreme loyalties and hatreds that attach to abstract ideas. In addition, those who could only grasp the most elementary abstract conceptions, found in the artificial solidification of peoples into nations, and the growth of nineteenth-century nationalism, an all-too-easy peg on which to hang irresponsible prejudices and enthusiasms. People who had previously minded their own business now allowed their passions to be aroused by the map of Europe. The defeat of George III's army at Saratoga did not drive the London burghers to suicide : for the English, territories not beliefs were involved. It was a very different thing when Marat betrayed liberty, or the allies entered Paris. The growth of feelings of responsibility towards the people probably also had its effect, for some time, on politicians themselves. Their failure began to involve more than their personal career, and Castlereagh's distraught suicide appears in a certain light as an acknowledgment of responsibility and an expiation of conscience. The increase of political suicide was not unnoticed at the time, and in 1860 Des Etangs traced its history in France from the Revolution to the establishment of the Second Republic. England, spared the political upheavals of France, did not suffer in the same way, but one thing is true for both countries : the spread of general political ideas, in all their violence, to the mass of the people, created loyalties, beliefs, and expectations, whose disappointment persistently created a type of disillusion and unhappiness not widely experienced before, and likely to lead to suicide.

The first traces of this political suicide appeared in France with the Revolution. To get a clear idea of its full force it will be worth while to move back into the eighteenth century and take up our station at the Hôtel de Ville in Paris where Robespierre, with a group of faithful followers —among them his young brother, Lebas, Saint-Just, and Couthon—was in tragic consultation on the 9th of Thermidor 1794. A handful of men under Bourdon, who forced their way into the Hôtel de Ville expecting easily to arrest the dictators of yesterday, did not count on their mental exaltation. The men who imagined they were guiding France towards the Supreme Being were not likely to yield to their enemies. The intrepid Lebas, absolutely devoted to the cause of Maximilien Robespierre, drew a pistol and shot himself. The younger Robespierre threw himself out of a window, but did not succeed in killing himself. Couthon, the curious paralytic, wished to die like Cato. But, though armed with a dagger, he found his hand in this crisis as disobedient as his legs habitually were, and in the last resort he too threw himself out onto the street below. The elder Robespierre, when the commotion of the soldiers' entry had subsided, was led off with a bullet wound in the jaw, whose exact history will probably never be known. At the time one school of opinion put it down to accident, another to attempted murder, and a third to unsuccessful suicide.

These men were not cowards, and those of them that reached the scaffold gave remarkable testimonies of courage. Neither were they professional politicians in the old sense of the word. They were men interested not in partitioning territories, but in the victory of certain ideas. With their own success was bound up not merely their personal safety, but their beliefs and their ideology. The despair and determination that made them suicides sprang from the latter. Throughout the nineteenth century the danger of similar suicides was imminent whenever general political conceptions took precedence of fact and swept off their feet men who, in the eighteenth century, would have been content to leave government to experts or rogues.

Though those who doubt the sincerity of Robespierre and his followers might put a different interpretation on these suicides, other less eminent suicides in the Revolution, in the Empire, and in the restorations that followed, admit of no double meaning. They are suicides that result purely and simply from political sorrow or disillusion at the defeat or failure of an idealized cause. Thus a Hungarian prisoner committed suicide in Paris on hearing of the subjection of his country by Napoleon.[1]

Even more altruistic was the attempted suicide of Williams Johnson, a friend of Paine's. A person of intense idealism, he had come to Paris to see the face of liberty at close but reverent quarters. His arrival, coinciding with Marat's rise to power, plunged him into a turmoil of blood, egotism, and anarchy. Horrified by the sinister twist that had been given to the revolution, and disillusioned to find that liberty and justice could not be bought even at the price of innumerable lives, he tried to kill himself. With the author of *The Age of Reason* he left a note saying that he had come to France to rejoice at the birth of liberty, a liberty that Marat had now killed. Since the anarchy of France was worse even than the despotism of England he preferred to die. He was not going to assist at the triumph of madness and inhumanity over talent and virtue.

The Restoration continued this tradition of political suicide. The shame of foreign invasion, the extinction of liberty, and the idealistic adoration that was still felt for Napoleon, led many officers of the *grande armée* to commit suicide. The colonel who cut his throat because, as the contemporary police statement says, he was "unable to

---

[1] One may not include the Englishman who cut his throat on hearing a rumour that the Emperor had been victorious at Waterloo. His business, not his faith, was involved.

forget his Emperor ", typifies the political disillusion of the time.

It is in the stories of Gracchus and Camille Babeuf, reminiscent of the Decii in Rome, that altruistic political suicide touches its most striking note. Gracchus Babeuf, almost the last of the true revolutionaries, condemned to death for conspiring against what he believed to be the tyranny of the Directory, stabbed himself in front of his judges. Before he died he committed to the keeping of the French people, whom he so well trusted, his two sons, Emile and Camille. Nearly twenty years later the latter showed the persistence of his father's uncompromising spirit. Identifying himself with the welfare of his country, he suffered also with its reverses; the day that the victorious allies entered Paris, Camille Babeuf threw himself from the top of the column in the Place Vendôme.[1]

About the middle of the century, or rather earlier, a change occurs; socialism invades the political scene, and the ideas of Owen and Saint-Simon divert much of the energy and idealism which would otherwise have run into the old political channels. The appearance of new social theories was, however, premature. The objective situation offered these utopian socialists no chance of success, and reaction followed a short-lived popularity. Saint-Simon himself, sensing the inevitable failure of his scheme in France, tried to blow out his brains, and Des Etangs discovers that the workmen, who had been shown their plight but were as yet offered no means of remedying it, in their disillusion also

[1] Suicides with a political background, but usually with a practical aim, are common again in our own time. Repression has created a new book of martyrs who have testified to various faiths in Russia, Italy, Germany, Austria, and Spain. The German workman who jumped from a third-story window rather than betray the names of his fellow socialists when under torture, and Lauro di Bonis, flying to Rome and certain death with an aeroplane full of pamphlets, are types of a persisting heroism.

S

turned to suicide. The hopes of 1848, followed by the subsequent reaction, further darkened the social horizon. To
the gloom was added uncertainty; the number of reformers
and their varying panaceas only confused a class uneducated
and unaccustomed to abstract thought. The situation did
not brighten until Marx's over-simplification created a rallying point in dialectical materialism, and, more important, the
formation of semi-effective labour parties held out hopes of
redress.

It is, however, not in the current of political and social
change, but in the more complex world of art and literature,
that we find feelings towards suicide and types of suicide
most particular to the century. The force of romanticism,
everywhere noticeable, did not fail to modify radically the
current outlook on death. In literary circles it became, in
theory at least, infinitely desirable; on a mental plane it
represented the peace and equilibrium which physically was
offered by sex. No longer cruel and repulsive, it lifted all
burdens and solved all problems. It was the only lover that
did not disappoint, the only safe retreat for ideals and aspirations which did not wish to bear the heat and burden of the
day and which, in fact, were inclined to consider the temporal
struggle as soiling and unworthy. There could be no greater
contrast to the spirit of macabre which in the Middle Ages
had shuddered at corruption and seen in death only resurrection or the buried skull. Until late in the century it is only
here and there, in poets like Baudelaire and Beddoes, who
" lent his senses unto death ", that the worm comes into
its own and the macabre skeleton points a finger. On the
other hand, the new attitude marks the complete victory of
escapist melancholy—Hamlet's retreat from life into sadness and death which make no demands upon consistent
action.

The rise in the social status of death which made it the
poet's friend and confidant, or the idealist's faithful ally,

was directly reflected in the change of feeling towards suicide. No longer the criminal and foolhardy act that whipped a sinful covering of skin from trembling skeletons, it was a brave and gracious approach to peace, a proof of sincerity and of unwillingness to temporize with the world. If death was desirable, voluntary death was doubly so, and in a pantheistic atmosphere it represented the most direct reunion with Nature and God. Thus suicide was ennobled and romanticized. Even if the poets were often unwilling to come out into the open intellectually, or support it with argument against Church and *bourgeoisie*, emotionally they were favourable. In the fantasy of their writings, where opinions were not penalized, they showed this favour without hesitation. On paper, if not in life, suicide acquired heroic qualities, and often became *par excellence* the fine ending and the worthy exit.

Innumerable poems, novels, and letters of the time testify to this change in the literary attitude towards death and suicide, and prove its currency among romantic writers of almost every type. Keats, half in love with easeful death, had longed to cease upon the midnight with no pain. In Byron death is "a quiet of the heart", and the impulse to suicide flies in *Don Juan* its true romantic colours as "the lurking bias . . . to the unknown." Beddoes, for whom hemlock brewed "murder for cups within her cavernous root", says, with extraordinary simplicity and beauty, referring to an attempted suicide in *Death's Jest Book* :

> It was his choice; and why should he be breathing
> Against his will?

He could have written no more moving apology for his own lonely suicide that was to occur in Basle some years later.

The strain runs right on to Hardy at the end of the century. Death beckons to the artist, and his creations take

the nearest, quickest road. At last in Housman, a " lover
of the grave ", as is the ever-recurring country figure he
writes about, suicide becomes a permanent rule of conduct,
the proper behaviour if you go astray :

> Play the man, stand up and end you
> When your sickness is your soul.

In France the more pronounced character of romanticism
brings literature and suicide even closer together. Examples
come to hand on every side. As a young man, translating
the *saddest* passages of Job and Lucretius, finding his
autumn pleasure only in " leaves which fall like time, these
flowers which fade like our hours, these clouds which pass
like our illusions, this light which grows dim like our intelligence, the sun turning cold as our loves ", Chateaubriand
almost inevitably walks out into the woods to kill himself.
In all the *élan* of their idealism the thoughts of Lamartine's
Raphael will swing round suddenly to death, and in the
happiness of her love a mutual suicide seems to Julie the
finest way out of life. She says to Raphael : " O, let us die
in this exaltation of soul and body which will allow us to
taste only death's joy. Later we shall wish to die, and perhaps we shall die less happy." Elsewhere we have seen
Villier de l'Isle Adam's glorification of a suicide pact under
very similar circumstances. For these French Romantics
self-destruction has something mysterious, sacrificial, and
ennobling about it. Even Balzac's precise and practical eye
looks for a moment on this aspect of the subject. In the
Peau de Chagrin he says : " *Il existe je ne sais quoi de grand
et d'épouvantable dans le suicide. Les chutes d'une multi-
tude de gens sont sans danger, comme celles des enfants qui
tombent de trop bas pour se blesser; mais quand un grand
homme se brise, il doit venir de bien haut . . .*" In Baudelaire the love of death and complaisance towards suicide is
still obvious, but it has recaptured an old, and taken a new,

flavour—it is both macabre, and already *fin-de-siècle*. It has a different note :

> *J'ai prié la glaive rapide*
> *De conquérir ma liberté,*
> *Et j'ai dit au poison perfide*
> *De secourir ma lâcheté.*
>
> *Hélas ! le poison et la glaive*
> *M'ont pris en dédain et m'ont dit:*
> *" Tu n'es pas digne qu'on t'enlève*
> *A ton esclavage maudit . . ."*

To sum up the whole attitude of romanticism to suicide, as it existed in an extreme but characteristic case, one cannot do better than turn to George Sand. With the exception of the drowning of the servant-girl, Noun, the part played by suicide in *Indiana* is altogether artificial, and in fact the last chapter, which is devoted to the subject, comes close to ruining a moving novel. These last pages, however, in their leisurely and considered treatment of the subject, reveal clearly the romantic feelings about suicide, which here are not introduced by any necessity of the plot. On the contrary, the plot is used as a stalking horse for the presentation of the literary attitude to suicide. Indiana, penniless and alone, ruined and abandoned by the man for whom she has sacrificed everything, in a half-crazy state comes near to drowning herself. Rescued by her devoted cousin, Ralph, silent and lonely as herself, she reproaches him for having saved her, and he answers, " *j'ai pensé qu'il valait mieux se donné la mort avec réflexion* ". His reply is typical of the romantic attitude which, probably rightly for artistic purposes, made a distinction between the frantic suicide of the desperate soul, and the action of the intellectual or the idealist in his collected abnegation of life.

Time passes for these two unhappy people, and reflection leads Ralph at last to propose the suicide which Indiana has already attempted. Materially they now lack nothing, but

Indiana is heartbroken, and Ralph, who throughout a solitary life has hidden a love for Indiana which he believes can never be returned, is unwilling to live out to the end his meaningless existence.

> *Partons ensemble* [he says] *retournons à Dieu, qui nous avait exilés sur cette terre d'épreuves, dans cette vallée de larmes, mais qui sans doute ne refusera pas de nous ouvrir son sein quand, fatigués et meutris, nous irons lui demander sa clemence et sa pitié . . . Le baptême du malheur a bien assez purifié nos âmes: rendons-les à celui qui nous les a données.*

Their action is not to be the result of a momentary blindness, but the goal of a reasoned determination, taken in a spirit of calmness and piety: " *il importe que nous y apportions le receuillement d'un catholique devant les sacrements de son Eglise.*" Here appears very clearly the mystical, sacrificial element in romantic suicide, to which we have already referred.

Resolved that they will commit suicide together, they decide that they are not yet fit to die. Time is needed to prepare their minds for the sacrifice, and to attain the necessary objectivity and peace. They must go through a probation and then in some more worthy spot fulfil their destiny. Thus it is that they decide to take a ship for that East Indian island where they both grew up; where Ralph first came to love Indiana, and where, " in the virgin bosom of nature, far from the profanities of human life, they will recapture the feeling of God's omnipresence ".

It is striking to notice how, in the smallest details, the attitude to suicide fits exactly into the larger romantic background and how, in the passage we have just quoted, Rousseauistic conceptions of nature influence the suicides in their choice of time and place.

When, several months later, Indiana and Ralph reach the Ile de Bourbon they still act within the framework of European romanticism. Setting out on a still and brilliant moonlit night they climb into the solitude of the tropical woods and emerge on a natural platform beside which a waterfall plunges into dark and invisible depths. This, one of the favourite haunts of their childhood, is to be the scene of their suicide pact; they are to be carried down the cascade into the deep pool far below. Death seems infinitely sweet to them, and it is at this point that Ralph can honourably avow his long-hidden love, and thus emphasize to the unobservant reader the close connection between sex and the romantic urge towards death and self-annihilation : a connection which George Sand further unconsciously accentuates by the obvious sexual symbolism of the scene, the moon, the plunging volume of the cascade, and the pool of oblivion which is its goal.

Indiana listens with sudden enlightenment to the long tale of Ralph's life and devotion. She realizes at last whom she should have loved.

" *Sois mon époux dans le ciel et sur la terre, lui dit-elle, et que ce baiser me fiance à toi pour l'éternité.*"

" *Leurs lèvres s'unirent; et . . . sur le seuil d'une autre vie, résuma pour eux toutes les joies de celle-ci.*" Ralph then takes her in his arms and turns to plunge with her into the gorge, intending to end their lives in the way that George Sand evidently thought worthiest of her heroine. It was an end long planned by reason and in which death and love turned out to be almost one, an end by which the force of gravity would literally hurl these voluntary sacrifices back into the primeval bosom of nature and reunite them with a universal deity who, by a typical paradox of thought, was to be found on an Indian island and not in the streets of Paris.

Leopardi would have believed that this intimacy which we have discovered between romanticism and suicide had important repercussions outside the written page. He claimed in his time to find a certain change among the actual suicides of daily life—a type of change only attributable, as we should now see, to romantic influences. People, he said, no longer committed suicide as in classical times on account of concrete misfortunes, but from a vague *malaise* and weariness of life. Suicide was no longer imperative and passionate; no longer the escape of the old, but the resort of bored youth. It seems, however, that Leopardi was wrong, and on the last point at any rate statistics do not bear him out. His error arose in imagining that the suicides of literature had a correspondingly important counterpart in life: in practice suicides from *taedium vitae* were probably no more common than they had been since the Renaissance. Concrete ills, shame, disease, desertion, poverty, were still the determining cause of most suicides.

Indiana and Ralph, on the brink of death, did not finally take their leap into the gulf, and the writers who could create such characters, though they often longed to die, rarely took the practical step. Self-preservation was as much an instinct among the romantics as anywhere else, and it usually took some pretty tangible misfortune to overcome it. Thus Keats who wrote to Bailey, " I am never alone without rejoicing that there is such a thing as death," clung to life with his last breath; and Goethe, though he confessed that he had " considered at length the various means which a man may best employ to kill himself ", lived to a ripe age. Chateaubriand resorted with his shotgun to a lonely wood on his father's estate, but the opportune arrival of a gamekeeper saved his life. His reflection on the event is characteristic of the time: had I killed myself, he says, no one would have known of my unfortunate history; I should have died unknown and my sorrows with me. More dramatic and even less determined was Musset, who owns up to having twice laid the point of a dagger against his heart. No blood was drawn. Indeed, these young despairs translate themselves better into literature, where, heaven knows, they can be moving enough, than into practical suicide.

When these nineteenth-century writers and artists do take their lives the old specific troubles, the concrete causes, have usually nagged at their elbow with greater insistence than any ideal weariness. Though Maupassant had always emotionally flirted with death, it took disease to lead him to the altar, and Beddoes, familiar as he was with the idea of his own skeleton, only put off flesh when nearing fifty, poor, and disregarded. Poverty, illness, and a woman finished off Gérard de Nerval. Much the same did for Kleist; while embittered and neglected, Haydon and Gros laid their deaths at the door of the public. Yet these literary and artistic suicides of the nineteenth century, who gathered corpse by corpse would make a fairly impressive total, probably gained some consolation in their last moments by the romantic conception of suicide which many of them shared. One hopes so. It is easier to suffer when life ends on a fine note. A dagger, driven home because the earth in no way tallied with the mind's ideal conception, would slip in more gently than if thrust from a twisted heart and empty purse.

III. THE FUTURE

The inhabitants of Dublin in 1901, the contemporaries of Bloom, had, as we have seen, no clear idea upon what their anti-suicide prejudices were based. Had they attempted to account reasonably for these prejudices they would have found it very hard to do so. We to-day should find it no less difficult.

Four arguments, which are familiar in these pages, have always been used to condemn suicide: of these three are illogical or founded upon false premises, while the fourth rests upon faith. It will be well to recapitulate them and to show finally that, for the average man, they are not strong enough to prove suicide either a crime or an evil.

The first argument, current from Aquinas to Leopardi, and adequately disposed of by Hume, attempts to prove that suicide is unnatural, because it runs contrary to the instinct of self-preservation. So, however, do motor-racing, tightrope-walking, and soldiering, professions of the greatest respectability. Again, we are told that sex is the fundamental instinct complementary to self-preservation. The monk denies sex, the suicide disregards self-preservation : both should be equally guilty, yet one is a saint and the other a sinner. Further, the term *unnatural* itself represents no real or constant value. In practice it is impossible to define logically unless one accepts Thomas Huxley's definition of the natural, which will include suicide. He says : " Nature means neither more nor less than that which is; the sum of phenomena presented to our experience; the totality of events past, present, and to come." Usually, however, the term *unnatural* as used in argument does not even attempt to approach logicality. On inspection it often turns out to mean " unusual ", or merely " something I don't like ". It has been applied at different times to smoking, the steam-engine, vaccination, and anaesthetics. As a criticism of suicide it carries no weight, and one could as justly apply the term to the arbitrary interference with " nature " which we call cooking.

Secondly, Aristotle stated, and it has been repeated ever since, that suicide is cowardly. Sir Thomas Browne said : " When life is more terrible than death, it is the truest valour to live." However, for most of us suicide demands more bravery than we can muster. The number of those who have wished to die is incomputable; only the isolated individual has the courage to put his wish into execution. Colton wrote with truth in his *Lacon* : " As many live because they are afraid to die, as die, because they are afraid to live." The courage or cowardice of suicide will always be disputed; yet supposing it did invariably take more bravery to live than to

die, this constitutes no proof of the wrongness of suicide.
The more unpleasant of two alternatives is not necessarily
the right one, and to adopt so illogical a principle as a basis
for action would lead to fantastic results. Thus, though
suicide may be cowardly, it is not for that reason necessarily
wrong. The easier action may often be the wiser one.

Again it has been immemorially argued that suicide constitutes a danger to society and is therefore anti-social. This
idea is only valid if one takes a purely artificial view of
society. In practice the abstract entity " society " is nothing
but the striving individuals which compose it. When such
of these individuals as are misfits voluntarily remove themselves and their misery by suicide, society directly benefits
by their actions. Suicide thus appears as a process by which
society rids itself of elements of misery and dissatisfaction.
Though society is the poorer for the loss of people like
Romilly, Kleist, Chatterton, and Gérard de Nerval, such
examples are exceptions. More often the end of a suicide is
the gain of the living. Finally, in all those cases where suicide
merely forestalls the processes of disease and old age, to
speak of society's loss or gain is beside the point. A man has
done his work, and reason simply anticipates death.

That suicide may be harmful to a certain section of
society, the friends and relatives of the dead man, is sometimes true. As often as not, however, the suicide of the
business man saves his family, and that of the melancholy
neurotic comes as a secret relief to those around him. Moreover, those who have others dependent on them do not often
kill themselves. Responsibility interposes. Suicide is the
act of the solitary.

We cannot, in fact, say that suicide is a danger to society,
we can only say that sometimes (like marriage, or anything
else) it may be irresponsible, ill-timed, and thus anti-social.
Usually suicide will turn out to be a natural prophylaxis
beneficial to society, but each case must be examined on its

own merits. Mill said that " actions are right in proportion as they tend to promote happiness, wrong as they tend to produce the reverse of happiness ". This is the only legitimate criterion that we can apply to suicide. We shall discover that it separates fairly clearly the social from the anti-social suicides: those that reduce the misery in the world from those that reduce its happiness.

Lastly, there come the religious arguments against suicide, and these, for the orthodox Christian, are incontrovertible. The Church has time and again denounced suicide as a major sin, and faith must accept the rulings of the Church. Given the Christian premises the Church's attitude is logical enough. A Christian can find no holes to pick in arguments that have been handed down from the time of Saint Augustine. Lamartine could feel the special force of the Christian argument, and he was thinking quite straight when he said, " Had I been of Cato's religion, I should have died a thousand times the death of Cato." If this world is merely the prelude to another, if agony and misery are the purging fires of God's providence that, well borne, prepare the sufferer for paradise, if the brevity of pain here contrasts with the eternity of punishment beyond, suicide is not only sinful, but extremely foolish and short-sighted. Many people, however, are unable to accept the starting-point of the Christian argument. For them faith and passion, whether religious or secular, do not seem practical or appropriate means for conducting complicated human affairs. Belief without reason is distasteful to them, and thus they find that the whole Christian attack on suicide is without foundation.

To people with a tendency towards mysticism the Quietist attitude, which in relation to suicide we have seen put forward by Plotinus and Schopenhauer, is probably more sympathetic to-day than that of the Church. All desire is a perturbation of the mind, and to wish inordinately for death is as bad as to long overmuch for life. This attitude has certain affinities with Christianity, and for many people will possess similar disadvantages, in that it estimates states of mind without regard to their context, and gives them value not in relation to this world, which we know, but in relation to some mystical abstract (the equivalent of "another world"), to which most of us cannot attain.

Though to-day all the important arguments that try and prove suicide wrong, with the special exception of the Christian one, can be put out of court by reason, it is not easy to forecast the future status of suicide. In England the attitude of the public certainly is, and has been for some time, growing more tolerant. Yet since reason is so little a predominating factor in behaviour, and man is so capricious and so constantly allows his emotions to act against his best interests, one is unable to tell whether opinion may not swing back to the old antagonisms and primitive fears. Historically we have seen that the tolerance of suicide goes hand in hand with development of personal values and personal culture. Thus it should not be difficult to predict the status of suicide in Marxist or corporate Fascist states as they are developing to-day. Not only a disregard of personal values, but the magical and primitive element in Fascism (particularly strong in Germany), should lead to a revulsion of feeling. There is therefore every reason to expect the absolute condemnation of suicide in such states. Already German and Italian newspapers, acting on orders, but surely in sympathy with general sentiment, repress all accounts of suicide. As far as the public are concerned people do not kill themselves in authoritarian states. One must not, of course, overlook the simple propaganda behind the repression of suicide-news: the impression to be conveyed is that no one under a benevolent Fascist government could possibly wish to kill himself. It is interesting to look back and find a similar tendency at work in France during the imperial expansion of Napoleon. An anonymous petition protested against the publication of suicides. Napoleon handed on the petition to the chief of police with the observation that journalists should be told to replace suicides by events "which would excite the courage and humanity of the French and honour the national character". Apart from the use of the term *humanity*, his orders have a perfect twentieth-century ring.

There remains to discuss, not the future attitude of society, but the future of suicide itself. Owing to the breakup of ancient cadres and the naked exposure of man to life, suicide increased considerably, alarmingly, throughout the nineteenth century. For the first time in two thousand years man peeped out from behind the shelters of faith, realized his own responsibility, and was thoroughly frightened. Without retreats and bolt-holes the problem of coping with life drove people more and more frequently to suicide. The point at which life becomes unbearable depends upon the meaning which life assumes and the degree of protection available. Thus it alters from generation to generation. Comedy at one place and time is death at another. The new meaning that life began to present to the average educated man in the later nineteenth century, and the new effort that it demanded, were most disturbing. The sharp upward curve of suicide statistics made people wonder whether the whole of civilized society, like those long-persecuted communities of Jews in the Middle Ages, might not kill itself in desperate distaste at existence.

This seemed not altogether fantastic, since it was found that as national, geographic, and religious protections were broken down by internationalism and the exchange of ideas, those countries which previously had enjoyed a certain immunity from suicide began to increase their rate. Throughout Europe, as culture became more general and less national, all suicide figures tended to converge at a high level, and the suicide rate in places like Italy, was seen to be rapidly overhauling the rate in the classic countries of suicide. It seemed that soon all Europe would be headed for suicide at the same break-neck speed.

As statistics piled up over a length of years, however, and time carried investigation well into the twentieth century, a reassuring fact was observed. In districts where the greatest number of suicides occurred (for instance, Denmark) the rate of increase had slowed down and finally stopped. The numbers of suicides annually were either stabilized at a high figure or even began to decrease slightly. The era of steadily increasing suicide seemed to be drawing to a close.

For two reasons common sense leads one to suppose that this is actually the case. First, and least important, new cadres are growing up in certain sections of the population to replace the religious, and supplement the family, frameworks. The ideas of socialism, its practical unions and purely recreative associations, not to mention a feeling of solidarity among many workmen, are all antidotes to isolation, shelters from reality, and combatants against silence and fear. They are the new sodalities in which many people can lose the sense of their loneliness and inevitable ending.

Such groupings, in so far as they replace the consolation of churches and guilds, are merely palliative however. They may be said to delay effectively, until in the process of time they themselves break up, the number of suicides which are demanded from men by the evolution of individuality and the final acquisition of the power to stand alone. Such associations—one is, of course, not speaking of their practical and political programme, but of their emotional aspect —in a long view put the clock back. They retard the comparative emotional independence—*Unabhängigkeit* seems to be the precise word—which civilization may at last achieve for the individual. Suicide is indeed a sort of tragic growing pain, a proof of the stress and strain of the weaning, testimony to the difficulty which we yet find of standing

on our feet with the old supports gone and the leading
strings snapped.

The second explanation which common sense puts forward
to account for the fact that suicide seems in certain places to
have reached a saturation point, is that the individual has
survived the shock of finding himself alone. Though no
longer hedged round with its old defences, personality has
come through safely. Man is going to preserve his equilibrium; he will walk without leading strings. This is a
conclusion full of hopeful promise, and if true it means that
suicide, once the present period of transition is over, will
tend to grow rarer. An inverse motion will set in.
Statistics seem to show that we are successfully turning a
difficult corner in the development of the individual. We
turn it, however, in spite of ourselves. Perhaps the strongest
motive in world reaction to-day, which so absolutely masks
itself behind political and economic events, is the fear of
facing the new landscape which lies beyond, rare and extensive but undoubtedly lonely. People naturally are afraid of
leaving even the wreckage of old ideological shelters for,
what is at yet, no-man's-land. Marx is the official bogey; but
the secret enemy is the horror of a world without God and
the old confraternities, the horror of a landscape where
people will find themselves standing in an unaccustomed
space and silence, where nothing but the individual throws
a shadow down the perspective from birth to the grave. The
inevitability of death then becomes only less unescapable
than the personal responsibility of living.

Meanwhile, suicide is the price paid by many to view the
unfamiliar new landscape. The transition to self-sufficiency
has often lain for the weak, the unfortunate, and the mis-
placed, via self-destruction. Such deaths, which have been
multiplying for a hundred years, are one of the oddly distributed taxes that are levied against gigantic change. Yet this
tax falls on us coincidently with an alleviating consolation.

The past centuries had no such need of suicide, and, fearing hades, they had no such trust in it. For this century, without the hope of paradise, there always remains free access to the reliable panacea of death. It is one of the gentle compensations created by, and for, the complex difficulty of the time. Such a compensation, however, should grow more and more unnecessary as individuals accustom themselves to the new lie of the land. When the number of those who are giddy standing alone grows less, then time will reduce the number of suicides also. As certainly as those beliefs are passing whose dying agonies cause the numberless self-destructions on which we look, the crisis in suicide will itself die away.

CHAPTER IX

EPIDEMICS AND ECCENTRICS*

I

A SUCCESSFUL man looking back on his life believes that the plans he followed, the happy trains of thought and action that he elaborated, were his own. It is only the failure, wishing to be excused, who foists on to others the burden of his life. He discovers that no moment of his existence was his own, that at every turning, every crisis, the idea and the instrument that came to hand were public property, forced upon him by his age, his education, the fortuitous circumstances in which he found himself. So he stumbles on a half-truth. But probably he will not follow it so far as to realize that even if he commits suicide his very death will be no more his own than his life. Even in the disposal of our bodies, and our exits, we are without free will; the bullet that quietens the brain, or the rope that jerks us into safety, comes to hand and is chosen from a variety of other salves, because of some precedent, some other man's action, seen, heard of, read in the midday issue of a paper, and stored away in a corner of our brain. From there it darts out and, on a last and momentous occasion when at least we thought ourselves free, issues dictatorial orders and prescribes the method by which we die. Thus, modish even in death, the suicide is the slave of the same fashion that dictates to the dandy. Voltaire fires at the suicide this couplet:

* This chapter and the one that follows serve as an elaborate, but necessary, appendix to the history of suicide.

Coûtume, opinion, reines de notre sort,
Vous reglez des mortels et la vie et la mort.

The contagion of example, the imitative instinct operative
everywhere, are particularly marked when we come to look
at suicide. Time and again, a house, a town or a country,
have been swept by an epidemic. These crises, usually as
brief and transitory as they are marked and violent, have
always been the subject of fear and comment. Strange interpretation and conjecture have been put upon them, as
though in their coming and going they were arbitrary or
embodied unknown and occult laws. In practice, however,
all of them can be assigned to decent and rational causes, and
a large proportion of them reveal the same fury of fashion as
compels a certain style of hairdressing to rule throughout a
season, or creates overnight the intense and fleeting success
of a *boîte de nuit*.

Among these epidemics we can distinguish two sorts, one
of which really owes nothing to imitation, or contagion in
the usual sense of the word. To this, which might be called
the Collective Type, belong those large group suicides,
where the impulse is not handed on from individual to individual but seems to be created spontaneously in every
member of the group at the same time. It is, in fact, a
uniform mass-reaction created in a social body by a particular
combination of events. Such epidemics of suicide show
that " vehemence of societie, ravishing particular judge-
ments " to which Montaigne refers when speaking of the
classic example provided by the city of Xanthus. Before the
armies of Harpagus and Alexander this town had already
twice immolated itself and revived like the phoenix, when in
the first century B.C. Brutus brought up his forces against it.
The inhabitants, expecting the fall of their city, seem once
more to have thought that suicide was the only possible
response to the situation. Though the Roman general
promised clemency and offered a reward for every Xanthian

who was saved, a helpless army watched the majority of the population kill themselves. Apparently only about 150 women survived. The story of Abydos is rather similar. Philip of Macedon in vain withdrew his besieging army for three days, in order to stem a frenzy of suicide. When the troops returned the epidemic had played itself out and they found a city without a people.

Such non-imitative mass-epidemics seem to have been brought about by disease as often as by anything else. A plague, by disorganizing and tormenting society, sometimes demands from it efforts which it is unable or unwilling to make. Suicide is the alternative. Thus a pestilence in the seventh century, and the Black Death in the fourteenth, both produced minor epidemics in England. Similarly the first ravages of smallpox among the Indians were followed by waves of suicide. A traveller in the eighteen-thirties wrote of the Mandans and the neighbouring tribes:

> When they saw all their relations buried, and the pestilence still raging with unabated fury among the remainder of their countrymen, life became a burden to them, and they put an end to their wretched existence, either with their knives and muskets, or by precipitating themselves from the summit of the rock near their settlement.[1]

Political, religious, and racial oppression or maladjustment seem equally able to produce this mass-suicide psychology. We have seen in the cases of Peru, Hispaniola, the Jews, and the heretic sect of the Circumcelliones, how effective and determined this self-destruction can be. Further examples are provided by the brave towns of Sidon and Tyre: the Sidonians burned their city and themselves when besieged by Artaxerxes Ochus, and numbers of the Tyrians, when conquered by Alexander preferred self-destruction to sur-

[1] Cavan, *Suicide*. Quoted from *Early Western Travels*; Ed. Thwaites.

render. However, it is not necessary to turn back to the past. The nineteen-twenties saw minor epidemics in Budapest and among the Jews in Warsaw, and to-day a mass-suicide is being carried out with unparalleled coolness and decision by a dwindling Indian tribe.

The Seris were once a powerful nomad people, wandering over what are now the south-western states of the American Union and North-western Mexico. To-day they hardly number eight hundred and are confined to the small island of Tiburon in the gulf of California. Contact with the white man has been too much for them; robbed of their hunting-grounds, and reduced by disease, they are broken in spirit. Degenerate and poverty-stricken, some native dignity still remains to them : rather than live on sufferance and eke out the last generations of a dwindling tribe, they have decided to stop breeding. Their past glories can only be recalled, not imitated; life holds no possible opening for them. Death is the only honourable alternative.

Juan Tomas, the chieftain, and a handful of the elders have long realized the hopelessness of their situation, and appear to have presented the policy of extinction to the body of the tribe. They prophesy that within fifty years there will be no Seri Indian alive. It is probable that this suicide pact will be facilitated by the infertility of the tribe. Though a few recalcitrants should insist on the right to breed, it is improbable that their enthusiasm would be more than a slight and temporary palliative against extinction.

The Seris, having lost interest in life, have themselves meditated their end. The process is conscious. It is significant that a similar *lack of interest in life* is apparently the first cause for the disturbing disappearance of those Oceanic peoples whose populations have involuntarily vanished sometimes within a lifetime. Such depopulations Pitt-Rivers categorically asserts are not due to the usual reasons given by superficial observers. " No native races," he says, " have been extinguished by violence, starvation, and civilized drink and diseases, whatever the extent to which their numbers may have been reduced by these means."[1] It seems that under normal circumstances a continuous decrease in fertility—and thus in population—only occurs where a people are no longer interested in living. Such a lack of interest has in our time only achieved intensity among the primitive peoples whose social, religious, and ideological framework has been smashed by the white man. Events seem to have driven these Oceanic peoples to achieve unconsciously what the Seris have premeditated. The impulse in each case is the same : lack of interest or hope in life as it presents itself to them.

From these premises it would be possible and interesting to work up an argument to the following effect : that no people continuously decline in numbers unless they are tired of life and subconsciously want to cease living. If this is true, a steadily declining population is, in a more exact sense than is usually meant, a racial suicide.

Distinguished from the resolution of the Seris, and those suicide epidemics, where the will-to-die of the community expresses itself collectively, are those crises of imitative suicide where the contagion spreads from person to person. Such suicides usually have a genealogical tree, often inescapably clear, and it is possible to trace back each death, via others, to the original cause which first set the epidemic in motion.

The force of personal example is especially notorious in the matter of fear and courage, and it seems to be hardly less active where suicide is concerned. Thus the death of Castlereagh is said to have precipitated an epidemic of the purely personal sort to which we are referring. The importance of the man and the publicity given to his death drew the attention of various people with latent suicidal

[1] Pitt-Rivers : *The Clash of Culture.*

tendencies to a particular form of self-destruction. A small crop of suicides appears to have resulted.

It is not even necessary that a striking suicide should occur in real life; it is enough that it should be written of. In this way Goethe's *Werther*, Byron's *Manfred*, Chateaubriand's *René*, Lamartine's *Raphael*, and particularly the drama of *Chatterton* by Vigny which was performed in Paris, are all said to have led to suicide by imitation. The contagion, however, of individual suicide seems never to be very strong or violent unless it can be attached to some particular thing or place, which acts as a stimulus and irritant to the imagination. At the *Invalides* there had been no suicide for two years when a soldier in 1792 suddenly took it into his head to hang himself from a beam in one of the corridors. Within a short space of time twelve other invalided soldiers (five within a fortnight) had followed his example, stringing themselves up to the same beam. When eventually the governor tardily but wisely closed the passage the suicides ceased. It was this particular beam that was the irresistible attraction. Similarly in 1813 in the quiet village of Saint Pierre Monjau, a woman hanged herself from a large tree. It was not long before several other women had repaired to the same branch. Certain churches, cliffs, and tall buildings, which are unfortunately irremovable, have exercised a similar fascination; once chosen by a suicide, they have established their train of votaries. In America, selected skyscrapers have played a part, and in Japan the Kegon Waterfall, north of Tokyo, for nearly forty years claimed a toll of from fifteen to fifty suicides a year among the tourists who came to Nikko. St. Peter's at Rome, the Cathedral of Milan, Giotto's Campanile, and the column in the Place Vendôme (closed to the public in 1881 on account of suicides) have also been favoured spots. In England, the Clifton suspension bridge, the Archway at Highgate, and the London Monument popularized by the disgruntled Miss

Moyes in 1839, have had their minor vogues. In this century they seem to have been displaced by Beachy Head and the white cliffs whose possibilities Shakespeare realized. In speaking of heights and suicides, however, one must always be rather careful. A certain number of those who appear to have " thrown " themselves from heights probably did so quite involuntarily and were simply drawn over the edge by that purely physical dizziness and fascination to which many people are subject. This fascination is usually accompanied by a feeling of pleasure and has been shown to have Freudian origins. A sharp razor often exercises an analogous fascination, which made Byron say that he believed no one had ever handled an open razor without at the same time thinking how easily it would sever his throat. There have been altogether sane and happy men who never dared to shave themselves.

Strangest of all these favoured spots or popular heights, and exercising a far greater fascination than any other, is the volcano of Mihara-Yama in Japan. The story of the suicide vogue of this mountain is hardly credible. Situated on the barren island of Oshima, which was served only by a coasting vessel from Tokyo, Mihara-Yama managed to exist for centuries without attracting the attention of the Japanese public; its wisp of smoke, its intermittent grumblings and eruptions, gained it neither notice nor notoriety. Then in February 1933 Miss Kiyoko Matsumoto, an idealistic schoolgirl of nineteen, decided that it would be the best place for her to commit suicide. Having taken a single ticket and accompanied by her friend Miss Masako Tomita, who took a return ticket, she set out for the island. Her friend, on reaching Tokyo again, reported how they had climbed the mountain and how at dawn Miss Kiyoko Matsumoto had bowed to her and jumped into the smoking crater. The affair made a great stir. It was an ideal and idealistic news story for the press; Japan lapped it up, and

Mihara-Yama, catching the public imagination, emerged from its immemorial obscurity with astounding results. In the remaining ten months of 1933, 143 people followed Miss Matsumoto into the crater, and on one day alone there were six suicides and twenty-five unsuccessful attempts. In the succeeding year the volcano lost none of its tragic attraction and claimed another 167 people. Among the individual suicides which made a great impression, one is of especial interest to us as a perfect example of the anger-revenge motive which, as we have seen,[1] used to be typical of Oriental suicide. A soldier in the Imperial army who found some difficulty in efficiently carrying out his arms-exercises attracted the curses of his drill-sergeant. One day the latter, in despair, told him that he was too stupid to live and ought to do something about it. The soldier, bitterly insulted, made the trip to Mihara-Yama and on the crater's edge he left his hat and bayonet with a note, on which appeared the words: "I always obey the commands of my superior officer." No revenge could be nicer or more complete.

Not the least astonishing feature of this epidemic, and certainly the least savoury, is the part played by business in promoting and extending the whole thing. A steady press propaganda aroused nation-wide interest, tourists began to flock to the crater, both to see the historic spot and to witness a death or two if they were lucky. The coastal steamship company ran excursions to satisfy both suicides and sightseers and "opened up" the island of Oshima on a large scale. Camels, never before seen in Japan, were imported to negotiate the desert slopes of Mihara-Yama, and a sort of "chute-the-chutes" brought the sated gazers from the mountain-top back to the harbour. Along the shore mushroom restaurants arose overnight and catered for ever-increasing crowds. By the end of 1933 the company's

[1] See page 46.

shareholders, who had got nothing on their money for three and a half years, were suddenly rewarded with a six per cent dividend.

Public excitement reached its high-water mark when the assistant editor of a large "daily" was lowered into the crater in a steel gondola. It was said that cries for help had been heard issuing from the smoking abyss, and he went down to investigate. Lowered to a distance of twelve hundred feet, half suffocated by sulphur fumes, and tossed about in his steel egg, he saw on the crater ledges a few lacerated remains and was then hauled back to the mountain-top, a half exhausted national hero. Eventually, and tardily, the government intervened. A policeman was perpetually stationed on the crater's edge, who, with the gaping crowds, must have been responsible for stopping some of the 1,208 attempted suicides that occurred in two years. Police also began to scrutinize carefully the passengers disembarking on the island, and it seems that psychological perspicacity soon enabled them to pick out from a harmless audience the prospective performers. Finally, a barrier was placed round the cone of the crater and it was made a criminal offence to purchase a one-way passage to Oshima. By the middle of 1935 the epidemic was under control and Mihara-Yama was beginning to relapse into its old neglect after what must surely have been the most lurid popularity that any "natural feature" has ever enjoyed.[1]

Though the Mihara-Yama contagion seems to have touched people pretty generally, epidemics are most apt to break out among certain classes or types, and often do not spread any farther. Soldiers and prison criminals have both been particularly liable to imitative suicide; thus in France in the sixties epidemics broke out at different times, both in the 15th and 41st line regiments. This is explicable enough as these groups constitute small, closely knit organisms whose

[1] For the whole story see *Fortune*, May 1935.

members tend to feel in the same way and whose imitative instinct is well developed. Rather more curious are the epidemics of suicide among women which appear to have occurred from time to time and are recorded from Marseilles and Lyons prior to the seventeenth century. Plutarch tells of the outbreak and cure of such an epidemic at Miletos.

> A strange and terrible affliction [he says] once came upon the maidens of Miletos from some obscure cause—mostly it was conjectured that some poisonous and ecstatic temperament of the atmosphere produced in them a mental upset and frenzy. For there fell suddenly upon all of them a desire for death and a mad impulse towards hanging. Many hung themselves before they could be prevented. The words and tears of their parents and the persuasions of their friends had no effect. In spite of all the ingenuity and cleverness of those who watched them, they succeeded in making away with themselves. The plague seemed to be of an unearthly character and beyond human remedy, until on the motion of a wise man a resolution was proposed that women who hanged themselves should be carried to burial through the market place. The ratification of this resolution not only checked the evil, but altogether put an end to the passion for death. It was a great evidence of the virtue of the women that they thus shrunk from dishonour and that those who were fearless in the face of the two most awful things in the world—death and pain—could not support the appearance of disgrace . . .

In a spiritually-knit religious group emotions are often shared to the same extent as they are in a regiment or prison, and we have seen how, among the early Christians, a suicidal fervour handed on from martyr to martyr could spread right across the Roman Empire. It is, however, among the Old Believers in seventeenth-century Russia that one meets the most impressive religious epidemic suicide in Europe. The coming of the antichrist was believed to be close, and to escape the clutches of the Great Beast the peasants began to commit suicide. The movement spread quickly by imitation, and the fervour was fanned by ardent and wandering missionaries. Soon the same business instinct that we have seen at work in Japan intervened; it was realized that the larger the crop of suicides the more advantageous for the survivors. Suicide drives were organized on a large scale, so that places might be vacated for the ambitious, and property fall to the greedy. Dull-witted peasants allowed themselves to be immured or even jockeyed towards the flames by rascals who played on their fears and credulity.

> Priests, monks, and laymen scoured the villages and hamlets preaching salvation by the flames. .... They did not spare even the children, but seduced them by promises of the gay clothes, the apples, the nuts, the honey, they would enjoy in heaven. Sometimes when the people hesitated, these infamous wretches decided the wavering minds of their dupes by a false report that the troops were coming to deliver them up to Antichrist, and so to rob them of a blissful eternity. Then men, women, and children rushed into the flames. Sometimes hundreds, and even thousands thus perished together. An area was enclosed by barricades, fuel was heaped up in it, the victims huddled together, fire set to the whole, and the sacrifice consummated.[1]

An alternative and much favoured mode of death was by starvation. To accommodate such religious suicides an old man had a building without doors or windows put up in the forest of Vetlouga. Ardent believers were lowered into it through a hole in the roof, over which a hatch was subsequently battened down. Outside, men armed with clubs acted as a patrol and watched for any fanatic who might try to escape. A day or two of starvation damped their enthusiasm, but it was too late for a change of mind; their suicide once undertaken was compulsory, and many hundreds died in this unpleasant way. Subsequent outbreaks of religious epidemic suicide occurred in Russia in the eighteenth and

---

[1] Frazer; *The Dying God*, quoting Ivan Stchoukine *Le Suicide collectif dans le Raskol russe.*

nineteenth centuries. As late as 1896 twenty-four people buried themselves alive in the Crimea.

Among those furious plagues of the Middle Ages which, as we have seen, sometimes caused collective suicide, there was one disease of a rather different nature which did not produce fear and depression, but on the contrary an exaltation and a disregard for death so complete that it was suicidal. The dancing mania which swept across Europe in the fourteenth century was transmitted by imitation from one individual to another. The patients were seized with an uncontrollable impulse to dance, and working themselves up into a frenzy, continued until they fell to the ground exhausted; whereupon others, affected merely by the sight, would feel the same impulse and take up the wild tarantella. Death often resulted from these dancings, and Lecky says that many of the tarantellas (the dancers were so called because it was believed that the disease was first caused by the bite of a tarantula spider) in their ecstasies rushed into the sea and were drowned. What is of interest from our point of view is that the dancers in the sober moments that preceded a frenzy were fully aware that by their exertions they might kill themselves, yet hardly seemed to mind. The reaction, the ague and the pains that followed their dancing, they did indeed try to alleviate in advance by binding and swathing themselves in cloths before the dance began.

One might think, considering the contagious nature of suicide and the epidemics which have occurred at various times and in various places, that whole continents might be depopulated and nations swept away. Such disasters, however, are not possible owing to certain laws which govern imitative suicide. It seems that generally one individual can influence another only where there was already a predisposition to suicide. Imitation itself seems practically never to be the original or determining factor in any given " imitational " suicide; it merely influences potential suicides (who would probably have destroyed themselves in some other way at some other time) to take their lives at a particular place or moment—Mihara-Yama, the *Invalides*, or Beachy Head. Thus we find that if the figures for suicide for a given population are taken over a number of years, say a decade, the presence or absence of abnormal bouts of self-destruction apparently due to imitation, have little or no influence on the general percentage of suicides. It is always the state of society, the ideals prevalent, the closeness of its organization, and its relative stability, which determine the suicide figures. The influence which imitation seems to play is deceptive; in practice it carries off only the man who is destined to suicide anyway. The force of a suicide epidemic is powerless to affect a social group in which there are ordinarily no tendencies to suicide. An interesting proof of this is the immunity of non-suicidal groups to influence by direct and indirect (press, photographs, literature, etc.) contact with the suicidal groups which may surround them. Thus, non-suicidal Catholic Bavaria, for as long as suicide statistics have existed, has remained uninfluenced by its neighbour Protestant Saxony, where the percentage of suicides was for a very long time higher than anywhere else in Europe. Imitation, therefore, is an incidental, not a prime factor in bringing about suicide.

II

Completely opposed to epidemic suicide of every sort is the self-destruction of the eccentric. His queer death, which seems to show a certain fantasy of mind, is at the farthest remove from the conformity of imitative suicide and is worth notice. Achieved as the curtain rings down, eccentric deaths are last-minute illustrations of the persisting oddity of the human mind and of its anomalous habits. There is even something refreshing about the nobleman who, in pretended imitation of Christ's fast, took strawberries and water for

three weeks and so died, or in the drastic but wholly understandable action of an English gentleman who committed
suicide to avoid the bother of dressing in the morning. This,
though misapplied, is originality in the grand manner. Not
so personal, but with a definite touch of eccentric humour is
a double suicide in Paris of which Winslow writes at length.

Two young men, mere youths, entered a restaurant, bespoke a
dinner of unusual luxury and expense, and afterwards arrived
punctually at the appointed hour to eat it. They did so, apparently with all the zest of youthful appetite and glee. They called
for champagne, and quaffed it hand in hand. No symptom of
sadness, thought, or reflection of any kind was observed to mix
with their mirth, which was loud, long, and unremitting. At
last came the *café noir*, the cognac, and the bill; one of them was
seen to point out the amount to the other, and then burst out
afresh into violent laughter. Having swallowed each a cup of
coffee to the dregs, the *garçon* was ordered to request the company
of the *restaurateur* for a few minutes. He came immediately;
expecting, perhaps, to receive the payment of his bill, minus some
extra charge which the jocund but economical youths might deem
exorbitant.

Instead of this, however, the elder of the two informed him
that the dinner had been excellent, which was the more fortunate,
as it was decidedly the last that either of them should ever eat;
that for his bill he must of necessity excuse the payment of
it, as, in fact, they neither of them possessed a single sou; that
upon no other occasion would they have thus violated the customary etiquette between guest and landlord; but that finding this
world with its toils and its troubles, unworthy of them, they had
determined once more to enjoy a repast of which their poverty
must for ever prevent the repetition, and then take leave of
existence! For the first part of this resolution, he declared that
it had, thanks to the cook and his cellar, been achieved nobly;
that for the last, it would soon follow, for the *café noir*, besides
the little glass of his admirable cognac, had been medicated with
that which would speedily settle all their accounts for them.

It was true enough. The enraged patron took their names
and address, but in the morning when he sent round to

demand a settlement of his bill the youthful gourmets were dead.

A suicide at once eccentric and admirable, since it sprang from artistic pride and an infinitely delicate sense of honour, was that of Vatel in the seventeenth century. Known then, as now, by the title of *le grand Vatel*, he ran the establishment and supervised the hospitality of the Prince de Condé, showing in the execution of his office all the taste and care that one would expect in a great gourmet. In April 1761, Louis XIV came to visit the Prince at Chantilly, and a magnificent three-day gala was intended. On the first evening, the king having hunted " *un cerf au clair de la lune* ", returned to a sumptuous supper, with which he was enchanted. Vatel, however, critic and gastronome, was not satisfied. There had been a slight hitch in the service which plunged him into a melancholy fit, and from this even the Prince's commendation could hardly free him : " *Vatel tout va bien, rien n'etoit si beau que le souper du Roi* ". That night Vatel was unable to sleep and in his anxiety about the banquet of the following noon he rose early. To his horror he discovered at eight o'clock that only one small basket of fish had arrived, and by a sad error he was given to understand that no more were coming. In despair he returned to his room. He imagined that the dinner was ruined and that he, the great Vatel, had failed. For a gourmet and a man of honour only one course remained open. While special couriers were actually hurrying from every port on the French coast with the pick of the catch, the rarest and richest of sea foods, Vatel fell on his sword. An hour's deliberation would not only have saved his life, but spared the embarrassment of the court, for, as Madame de Sevigné said at the time, a suicide is " *une chose fâcheuse à une fête de cinquante mille écus* ". However, if Vatel had possessed less eccentricity and artistic pride, and the stolid coolness necessary for an hour's deliberation, it is improbable that he

THE SELF-CRUCIFIXION OF MATTHEW LOVAT

(*From Anatomy of Suicide,* 1840)

would have been in any sense *le grand Vatel*, or that he could have become for revering generations the canonized marytr of cuisine.

Most eccentric suicides, however, are not in this vein. They are too painful for the fantasy to be pleasing. Even the young Polish lady, who was unhappily in love, and over a period of five months swallowed four spoons, three knives, nineteen coins, twenty nails, seven window-bolts, a brass cross, one hundred and one pins, a stone, three pieces of glass and two beads from her rosary, only appals by her perseverance. The tragedy comes uppermost.

Often what appeared to be a touch of the bizarre, an original streak, turns out, on second inspection, to be one of the perversions with which we have become so familiar through the writings of the psychologists. Even the eccentrics thus fit into stipulated categories and will soon be visible only as figures in their own class of statistic. Thus the man who tried to commit suicide by tying himself to the clapper of the church bell at Fressonville in Picardy, which roused the village by its sombre tolling at an unusual hour, becomes a mere exhibitionist. Yet, even in this category, too common in life and death, there is room for the emergence of genius, as is shown by a man who sent out advertisements to a large public announcing that he would commit suicide in Covent Garden on a certain day for the benefit of his wife and children. Tickets of admission were to be sold at the door for a guinea each. This, which would have had to rank as the *chef d'oeuvre* among suicides, never came off as the authorities intervened.

As a desire to hurt somebody else seems to be at the back of most oriental and primitive suicides, so western eccentricity seems most often to be connected with a wish to hurt oneself. This explains such curious suicides as that of a man for whom bears had a strange attraction. Having got into the bear-pit at the *Jardin du Roi* in Paris, he was hugged

U

and badly mauled. Before dying he told his rescuers that
he was very pleased to have accomplished his purpose.
Similarly, the people who not uncommonly bind their limbs
and tie themselves up in knots, like the young man at
Cambridge who committed suicide in this way a few years
ago, experience the greatest pleasure in their tortures. What
pleasure, however, a Parisian lady hoped to find who applied
a hundred leeches to her body, or what fantastic perversion
spurred her on, escapes all conjecture.

Perversions, though they belong to a set type, do
not exclude the possibility of true eccentricity. The
attempted self-destruction of Matthew Lovat provides a
locus classicus. Though conforming to a perverted psychological type, masochistic, exhibitionist, and religiously
melancholic, his mind was that of a genuine eccentric. For
this reason, it will be worth while to give an account of his
case. Born at Casale in Italy, Matthew Lovat showed an
early aversion to his parents' peasant life. Their poverty,
however, made it impossible for him to satisfy his strong
wish to go into the Church. Forced to adopt as an alternative
the trade of shoemaker, he grew silent and melancholy. For
some time his life went on normally enough and then suddenly he castrated himself. The ridicule that this aroused in
his village was so strong that he could not even attend
mass and he soon moved off to Venice. There he plied his
trade of shoemaker and then in the following year he made a
first attempt to crucify himself. Having constructed a cross
from the wood of his bedstead, he took it out into the street.
He was proceeding to drive a nail through his left foot to
attach himself to the cross, when passers-by intervened and
stopped him. He would give no explanation of his attempt
and a few days later he left Venice, returning to his native
village. There for three years he led the life of an ordinary
shoemaker, apparently normal enough except for his gloom
and religion. Actually, his original suicidal instinct was still

at work. In his little third-story room he began making in his spare time the machine on which he intended to carry out his plan, providing himself with the nails, bands, and crown of thorns, necessary for the part that he was to play. Having finished the cross, he saw that in spite of the bracket he had prepared for his feet it would be impossible to nail himself to it firmly, so he made a net which would, if necessary, take some of his weight and slung it over the cross. Having attached the latter by a rope to a beam in the ceiling, he laid it out on his bedroom floor pointing towards the window, and with the bottom end resting on the sill which was very low and almost on a level with the floor itself.

The scene was now set. Early in the morning he put on the crown of thorns, some of which entered his forehead, and, stripping himself, girded his loins with a white handkerchief. He next crawled into the net and, sitting on the cross, put his feet into the bracket that he had prepared. Then with a mallet he drove a nail through them and into a hole that he had already made in the wood. His next move was to tie himself securely to the cross with a cord, and last of all he wounded himself in the side with one of his shoemaker's knives, which represented, as he said, the spear of Christ's passion.

All this had taken place inside his bedroom. Now, with his two hands which were still free, he began to edge himself forward through the window, until the foot of the cross protruded so far that it overbalanced the head and the whole affair toppled out and hung above the street by the rope which held it to his bedroom ceiling. Suspended there, he nailed his right arm to the cross; the left arm, however, proved too much for him in spite of the fact that, foreseeing difficulty, he had previously transfixed his palm with a nail. The latter would not enter the wood.

In this position the passers-by in the street below discovered him. In due course he was rescued and taken off his cross. To the doctors who, on his recovery, questioned him as to his motives, he would say nothing but that " The pride of man must be mortified; it must expire on the cross ". He was never given the opportunity to attempt for the third time this grim and eccentric suicide, though, it appears, that he found an imitator at Königsberg in the late nineties. Lovat died in an asylum, largely as a result of self-starvation.

CHAPTER X

THEORIES AND CIPHERS

THEORIES

THE attitude of the public towards suicide is inevitably affected by the prevalent theories as to its cause and origin. It was natural that the suicide should have been persecuted when he was believed to be *instigatus a diabolo*; similarly it may be hoped that since much modern theory lays the responsibility at society's door, the latter will grow kinder. Theories, therefore, are of importance to us indirectly, for they modify the attitude of the living to the dead. The critical examination of suicide really begins with the nineteenth century, but ideas have moved far in a hundred years, and it will be wise to consider only those which seem relevant to-day.

I

Two schools, physiological and sociological, independently claim to account for suicide. The physiologists say, in the words of Esquirol, who may be considered to have first explored this line of approach in the eighteen fifties, that every suicide is " the result either of some mental disease or of extreme mental excitement ". Chavigny, an important modern exponent, puts the position even more simply: " *tout suicide*," he says, " *doit être interprété au point de vue psychiatrique* ". Certain aspects of suicide, which will have inevitably presented themselves to the reader in the preceding chapters, lead one to doubt the validity of such extreme claims. This doubt can only be increased by the statistics which form the second section of this chapter.

A great gulf divides the doctor and the layman. To the former, no one appears quite normal. To the latter, the abnormal man is an exception. Yet even the physiologists find it difficult to agree as to which are the madmen and the neurasthenics. It is no irresponsible task to swell these categories which may well come to include all living. About twenty-six per cent of suicides appeared mad or drunk to a modest nineteenth-century investigator, fifty per cent seemed a fairer estimate to a twentieth-century expert, and finally Dr. Achille-Delmas, who maintains an extreme position, finds physiological factors predominate in all cases. Ninety per cent of suicides are cyclomythic, and ten per cent are hyperemotivated.

The interpretation of statistics probably has a lot to do with the totally different aspect that suicide presents to the sociologist and the physiologist. Figures can be twisted to suit any conclusion, and probably (as Dr. Blondel has tried to point out) the truth lies somewhere between the two warring factions. In reply to Achille-Delmas's categorical statements, based on his statistics, the sociologist has confidently answered, " Statistics do not allow us to believe that the greater part, or even a large number, of those who commit suicide are madmen or drunkards." Yet granted even the prevalence of insanity or neurasthenia among suicides, the sociological position is unshaken. The neurasthenic, says the sociologist, is simply a man who by his delicate mental constitution is more sensible to the social causes which determine suicide. Even frankly pathological suicides raise sociological questions. As the most prominent sociological spokesman says : " *Les maladies mentales ont un double aspect. Ce sont des troubles organiques qui relèvent de la psychiatrie. Mais, en même temps, tout malade mental est un homme qui n'est plus adapté à son milieu* ".

The sociological approach to suicide is comparatively recent. The essence of modern sociological theory may be stated in the following proposition : the degree of integration in any given social unit is inverse to the number of suicides in that unit. The work of Cavan in America and of Halbwachs and Durkheim in France has been chiefly influential in drawing attention to the supreme importance of the social background. Figures seem to prove that it has an exact and determinable influence on the suicide rate.

Broadly speaking : " *Le suicide varie en raison inverse du degré d'integration de la société religieuse, de la société domestique ou de la famille, et de la société politique ou de la nation.*" (Durkheim.) Where a society is closely organized, whether on a religious, family, or national basis, suicide is correspondingly rare. Conversely, where society is loosely organized and where the individual is developed as a separate self-conscious unit, suicide is correspondingly common. The reasons for this are more or less obvious. In a closely knit society the community shoulders half the individual's problems; tradition and the customary outlook of the crowd provide an answer pat to all the most vexing questions posed by life and death. In a fixed cadre no difficulties of procedure confront the single man : a certain situation calls for a certain known and approved response. No torturing uncertainty harasses troubled minds and pushes them to the precipice edge; by contrast, there is always a hand to take and an arm to lean on. The authority of the family, the comfort of the Church, are always reserves of strength which can be called upon if need be.

But there are other reasons likely to lead to a partial decrease of suicide in a closely integrated society. These reasons link up with the attitudes of moral condemnation which we have spoken of in previous chapters. A closely integrated society is nearly always a young society, a non-intellectual, a non-complex society; in other words, it is a society where the *morale simple* will prevail and, hence, where suicide will be frowned upon and most probably legislated against and hedged round with penalties. Further, a tightly knit society will demand control over its units in everything, even in the matter of dying. Suicide, the most individual of actions, will always in such a society appear as a direct affront to its authority and prestige. Among termites, suicide from the point of view of the community would appear an abominably treasonable and treacherous action; in a totalitarian state, or even in the bosom of the universal Catholic Church, it is bound to appear in rather a similar light.

At every point history bears out this close relationship between suicide and types of social organization. In the great epochs of individual achievement, when the spur is not the glory of God, the nation, or the tribe, but a consciousness of the dignity, complexity, and possibilities of each human life, when, in fact, people stand on their own feet and act for principles and things which they feel to be inherent in themselves, suicide increases, and the attitude to suicide grows more lenient. The Renaissance is a typical period of this sort. Where creeds of individualism and individual self-reliance are consciously developed and set up as standards in such an epoch, the suicide increase becomes even more rapid. Stoicism gave this sort of artificial impulse to suicide, accentuating and directing individualistic tendencies in imperial Rome. Again in times of social flux, when systems break down and a period of disorganization intervenes, people have to face new questions and problems to which there are no apparent answers. Suicide is often a solution, and statistical figures go up at such times. Post-war Europe is the classic example of such a period.

On the contrary, when society has been stable and closely

organized history shows a decrease in suicide. As a result the closely knit medieval world gives few cases of ordinary suicide. Similarly the Jews, thanks to their interdependence and integration, used to show remarkably few cases of suicide (when left to themselves and not persecuted). It is the same within the close framework of other religious bodies and among any people or section of society dominated by a strong corporate instinct. Strangely enough, war, by tightening national links and sentiments, and by subordinating the individual to the struggling community, comes thus to rank among the forces which decrease and inhibit suicide.

By defining the relationship of the suicide to his social background, and determining the sort of framework within which suicide increases or grows less, it is possible to throw new light on statistics and on the various immediate causes —such as love, poverty, humiliation, madness and so on— which push an individual directly into suicide. So far so good. A moment's reflection, however, makes one realize that this does not touch the root of the question. Why, when faced with certain difficulties in a certain social framework, will a man make the extraordinary gesture of taking his own life, rather than evolve some other defence? Why does he take this particular line which runs so decidedly counter to (what appears to be) the fundamental life instinct and the desire for self-preservation? The extreme constancy of suicide figures which in a stable environment vary even less than the figures for death and marriage, and the exceedingly trivial causes which are so often made the excuse for suicide (in fact, the uniform *desire* in many thousands of people to escape from the business of life), make one pause. Does it not look as if there were a universal and natural desire for death working itself out? If this is so the suicide is not pushed reluctantly towards the knife and the poison; on the contrary, circumstances clearing the ground of certain inhibitions and ties to life, allow a death instinct to break through and achieve a desired end. Such a death instinct would, of course, be something distinct from melancholy or depression and would exist in its own right apart from any feelings induced in a man by pain, sorrow, disappointment in love and so on. Time and again the facts lead writers on suicide towards such an instinct, but either they do not see it or sheer nervously away. In spite of its constant recurrence, suicide has been regarded always as a strange, unnatural and anomalous event, imposed on the human being by circumstances from without. Never is it envisaged as the release of a certain natural and inherent instinct. Donne once writes of suicide as " this *naturall* desire of ease ". But this is only in passing, an intuitive phrase, rather than a definite statement. A death instinct is nowhere discovered or directly postulated.

There are, of course, definite reasons for this silence and the unwillingness to take such a step. The idea of a death instinct runs sharply counter to the main lines of nineteenth-century thought with its rather easy ideas of progress, and its belief that movement could only be in a straight line. The fundamentalism of life preservation is deeply ingrained, and a death instinct seems at first sight directly opposed both to this and to the usual ideas of evolution and the propagative urge. Also, as far as I know, there was until recently no theory of the death instinct with a psychological and reasoned basis. The writer on suicide would have had no authority for suggesting that such an instinct existed, much less that it might lie behind the phenomena he was investigating. To-day, on the contrary, such an authority does exist: Freud believes that beyond the search for pleasure he has found a death instinct which is even more fundamental.

II .

Tentatively, and with the scientist's reservations, Freud has enunciated his theory of the death instinct in *Beyond the Pleasure Principle*. It is not possible here to go into his ideas in detail, but some sort of summary is necessary. Freud's observations first brought to his notice certain psychological phenomena which neither fitted in with the ideas of the human make-up that psycho-analysis generally reveals nor conformed to the basic theory that people's actions are, broadly speaking, motivated by a desire to avoid pain and obtain pleasure. A careful examination of these phenomena, which occur chiefly among children, led Freud with certainty to the idea that a compulsion to repetition was the most fundamental of all instincts. By this repetition compulsion he meant " a tendency innate in living organic matter impelling it towards the reinstatement of an earlier condition ".

The acceptance of such a fundamental repetition compulsion will lead us to the most revolutionary conclusions. Let us see its implications with reference to the development of life and evolution.

> If all organic instincts are conservative [repetitive] and are directed towards regression, towards reinstatement of something earlier, we are obliged to place all the results of organic development to the credit of external, disturbing and distracting influences. The rudimentary creature would from its very beginning not have wanted to change, would, if circumstances had remained the same, have always merely repeated the same course of existence.

The idea of development here put forward obviously runs directly counter to the usual notions of evolution. Evolution was just what the organism did *not* want. When at some point and in some way that altogether escapes conjecture, the element of life developed in lifeless matter, the primitive organism did not rejoice, did not thrust eagerly forward on its long career. On the contrary its instinctive desire was to return to a former state of complete peace and equilibrium. Forces acting on it from without compelled change, and its own efforts to counteract these forces, to regain equilibrium, not only automatically complicated the organism and laid it open to further and ever greater stimuli which in their turn had to be offset. These stimuli gave to the instincts of the organism " the delusive appearance of forces striving after change and progress, while they are merely endeavouring to reach an old goal ". The development of organic matter can, in fact, be compared to the life of a man who is run into debt through no fault of his own and whose frantic efforts to get quit of his burden and pay off his indebtedness entail ever greater borrowing and ever increasing obligations.

The repetition compulsion shows us everywhere in life (for even among the protozoa this regressive inner tendency exists) a desire to get back to an earlier condition, to " that state from whence we came ".[1] But what is this goal of life, this " ancient starting point, which the living being left long ago, and to which it harks back again by all the circuitous paths of development "? It is, as Freud says, the equilibrium of death. " If we may assume as an experience admitting of no exception that everything living dies from causes within itself, and returns to the inorganic, we can only say ' *The goal of all life is death* ', and, casting back, ' *The inanimate was there before the animate* '." Freud, emphasizing the subconscious nature of this repressive death

[1] An interesting point is raised by protective-colouring. Apparently it exists in many animals whose enemies hunt by smell and not by sight. Thus the idea that it is adopted to avoid danger may well be an unjustified anthropomorphic interpretation of the facts. The alternative explanation would be that protective colouring in these living things is an unconscious attempt to reassimilate themselves into inanimate matter.

instinct, next explains how it fits in with instincts of self-preservation. The living organism, he says, is determined to die only in its own way and thus the paradox comes about that it resists with all its energy dangers which could help it to reach its life-goal by a short circuit. Such behaviour, he points out, is just what characterizes a pure instinct, such as the repetition compulsion, as contrasted with intelligent striving.

There remain, however, two things which to the ordinary man will appear to run directly counter to a regressive death instinct—the desire for perfection, and the sex mechanism. The restless striving towards further perfection which may be observed in a minority of human beings is accounted for, Freud says, by the excess of satisfaction demanded over that found in all attempts to recapture a *primary* experience of satisfaction. The perfection urge represents, in other words, the desire to regain an unattainable equilibrium which in the final event is always the first perfect equilibrium of death and inorganic life.

At first sight Freud admits that sex appears in opposition to a death instinct. While " one group of instincts presses forward to reach the final goal of life as quickly as possible, the other—sex—flies back at a certain point on the way only to traverse the same stretch once more from a given spot and thus to prolong the duration of the journey ". A further examination, however, seems to prove that there is no real antinomy between sex and the repetition compulsion. Sex may, in fact, be based upon a desire to reinstate an earlier condition. It may be the desire of two bodies to return to a unity which *pre-existed*. The break up of this original unity, the differentiation of the sexes, we can still watch to-day in the most primitive forms of life where it is typified in the splitting up of single cells in the protozoa. To illustrate his arguments, which are too complex to develop here, Freud quotes the idea—half myth, half theory—which Plato in his *Symposium* puts into the mouth of Aristophanes. It summarizes the situation beautifully and shows just how living substance comes to strive for reunion by means of the sexual instincts, which thus appear also to be regulated by the repetition compulsion.

> Human nature was once quite other than now. Originally there were three sexes, three and not as to-day two; besides the male and the female there existed a third sex which had an equal share in the first two. . . . In these beings everything was double, thus they had four hands and four feet, two faces, two genital parts, and so on. Then Zeus allowed himself to be persuaded to cut these beings in two, as one divides pears to stew them. . . . When all nature was divided in this way, to each human being came the longing for his own other half, and the two halves embraced and entwined their bodies *and desired to grow together again.*

If you agree that there is truth in this Platonic myth and concede to Freud that the most universal instinct of all living matter—universal because it presses into its service even sex, aspiration, and the self-preservative instinct—is the desire to return to the peace of the inorganic world, then it will be possible to draw certain conclusions relevant to our theme.

The acceptance of a universal death instinct convicts us all of a sort of suicide, and one of the best contemporary poets seriously puts forward the idea that no one would die if they did not want to—an old argument that we intuitively feel has always a certain accusatory force and rightness. But how, in actual fact, can we apply this death instinct to suicide? Have we any right to believe that it ever emerges from the instinctive, that it ever becomes conscious and inhibits the self-preservative instincts from seeing that our bodies reach their long-desired equilibrium in their own normal way? Let us look at religion for a moment. The fundamental preoccupation of religions, as opposed to their social, dogmatic, and superficial preoccupations, seems to be death, or (if the words are preferable) complete equilibrium and nirvana. Even under the aggressiveness of Islam and the practical façade of Christianity this primary element appears. The words of the Buddha are echoed by the Christian who says " there is no more time in heaven ", thus reducing heaven to nirvana as soon as he takes it seriously. All big religions seem to be based on this praise of being dead.

Now, in view of Freud's theory of the death instinct, the intuitive wisdom of this preoccupation becomes clear. Let us take the isolated instance of a single successful mystic. He is the man for whom the repetition compulsion has come through into consciousness. Instead of trying to create an equilibrium between the ever-varying and the evermore complex stimuli which attack his organism, instead of trying to cope with the debts that have been foisted on him, by a perfect stroke of wisdom he cuts right back to a first equilibrium. He refuses to " play "; the game was not chosen by him. Unlike the humble infusoria, he knows better than to try and offset the first stimulus that comes to provoke him. It passes over him, and by virtue of his very passivity is unable to complicate his life against his wishes. At every moment the simplest organisms, provoked by similar stimuli, start unwillingly on an endless career of development; the first parry involves a second, and so on to eternity.

The mystic who has somehow had an intuition of things, and for whom the nature of his fundamental wish for staticism has been revealed, having had a taste of this career, prefers not to walk the endless tight-rope.

If on one plane this knowledge of his essential desire for a primitive equilibrium can leak through to the mystic, there is no reason why, on another plane, it should not reach the suicide. A feeling of the inevitable " rightness " of his actions often characterizes the suicide, and in place of the torn soul, which does, of course, exist, and which popular horror represents, an extraordinary calmness, elevation, and lack of struggle is not an unusual feature in suicides. It is as though an intuition—less pure than the mystic's, but still definite—an intuition of the fictitious nature of their struggles, and of their true desire for stillness, had come home to them.

However, it is not necessary to believe in this rather hypothetical emergence of the primary death instinct into consciousness. Given its existence at all, it satisfactorily accounts for this most curious thing that we call suicide. The occurrences of unfavourable stimuli—unfortunate facts, unhappy situations — may make it impossible for the organism to maintain its precarious equilibrium; the mechanism of the self-preservative instincts (which, as Freud says, exist specifically to see that an organism reaches the death for which it longs only in its own proper way and at a proper time) is upset; the protection which these instincts offer against outer danger and the barrier which they present to a direct discharge of the death instinct, are both broken down. The death instinct, even if subconscious, is left with a clear field and directly *vis-à-vis* its desired goal. The suicidal outcome is inevitable.

With reference to the death instinct, it is interesting to discover how common death-wishes and the suicidal impulse can be among normal people. Recently, in reply to a questionnaire answered by 201 American students under thirty years of age (i.e. before the really suicidal period of life had set in), four-fifths said that they had wished for death. In one case after another it appeared that the writer had envisaged suicide as a response to different problems. In practice, of course, various deterrents, such as consideration for one's family, one's reputation, and a fear of pain and the future, usually stop the wish from being translated into action.

To recapitulate. Freud suggests that the death instinct, based on the repetition-compulsion, is always present, and precedes the other instincts, but its discharge is circuitous and via the subconscious. When, however, the self-preservative instincts which condition this circuitous route are, for some reason, suspended or dulled, the death instinct finds a natural and direct outlet which is suicide. (It would be possible to argue that an alternative form of this direct outlet is to be found in mysticism and that the attainment of nirvana is the most elevated suicide.[1])

III

Freud's death instinct is still a theory rather than an accepted principle. The modern psychologist, basing his arguments on analysis, puts forward a variety of other reasons to account for suicide. Some will apply to one type of suicide, some to another, and psychologists themselves differ in opinion as to the truth of certain of the explanations advocated by their colleagues. A very brief survey will give some idea of the lines along which the more interesting modern ideas on the subject seem to be running. For the normal man[2] situations do from time to time arise, so intolerable that suicide is a natural, wise, and practical move. The suicide of such a man will be reasonable, and brought about by an examination of his situation. Circumstances will offer him two or more courses of action; if, of

[1] Possibly the mystic is always occupied with *some* sort of consciousness (' cosmic ', or whatever he may call it), and if one really wants to bring his activity into line with the death instinct, it raises the point whether the latter really harks back to inanimate matter or to some very primitive, first and general, consciousness.

[2] A definition : " *Un homme normal est un homme qui se conduit comme s'il avait été psychanalysé.* J. Frois-Wittmann.

X

these, he chooses suicide, it is because this course appears least repugnant to him. Or, to look at it from another angle, his suicide will result from his inability to reconcile his personal interests with the objective and external world. He finds himself in an *impasse* from which death provides the only practical outlet. Such a man is of no particular interest to the psychologist. On the other hand the abnormal, the man whose suicide seems to be without sufficient justification, and in whom appear to be traceable subconscious forces pushing him towards death, he is the mark for the psychologist. It is around him that theories centre.

The perennial idea that suicide is the result of a superego, the act of the supreme egotist, is familiar and needs no development. Writers, as far back as the eighteenth century, touched on this, noting the presumption of suicide and the idea of one's own exclusive importance that is bound up with so many instances of self-destruction. Almost equally familiar to-day are three or four ideas, deriving from Freud's discoveries; they cover most of the important ground.

First of all there is the straightforward idea that if one concentrates all one's libido on one object and that object fails, with it will fail the libido and the desire to live. This has been said before in a different way and simply means that if you put *all* your eggs in one basket and are unfortunate enough to break them, life will have no further interest for you. Thus the lover who concentrates all his ideals, hopes, pleasures, his very life, in one woman, may very well end by suicide. Secondly, there is the call of stillness, which is connected with primary narcissism and tne desire, which everyone has in some degree, to regain the quiet of the womb. Since this is an infantile wish that can never be satisfied in the grown man, he loses faith in life and love and develops a melancholy, frustrated and embittered outlook, that may lead to self-destruction. Suicide in such a case may represent a release from an inner tension set up by infantile repressions. (This regressive desire for the quiet experienced in the womb will link up with the repetition-compulsion.) Thirdly, there are the suicides that are caused by an inverted sadism. It has been said that the desire of the ego for extinction can only arise from its inversion of sadism against itself. Apparently this inversion usually occurs as the result of a subconscious moral impulse. This moral impulse will make people feel the necessity of self-punishment for the death which, as infant boys or girls, they wished either on their father or mother. Suicide comes as a just retribution; thus it has been said: "No one kills himself who has not wished for the death of another." Lastly, one meets the revenge motive, so common in primitives, and which in its subconscious form is concerned with inflicting punishment on the unpopular parent.

STATISTICS [1]

With columns of statistics we leave the individual for the cipher, the particular for the general. We also move away from the kernel of our subject. To discover that in 1882 seventeen "females" in England ended their lives with vermin-killer while only one was wise enough to take chloroform, helps us little to gauge the attitude of society. There are, however, several characteristics of suicide which only statistics can explain and which must be understood if the general picture is to be filled out.

Though there are statistics dating back to 1783, it was not until about 1816 that there was a general move, led by Switzerland, to collect and keep authentic figures. These are harder to obtain on suicide than on almost any other subject

[1] Figures from Brierre de Boismont, Morselli, Westcott, Durkheim, Norwood East, Halbwachs, Cavan, Mortimer, London Statistics, Criminal Statistics 1934, and the *Encyclopædia Britannica*.

of equal importance, as families and friends, urged by shame
or prudence, try to hide the cause of death and are able often
enough to pass it off as the result of illness or accident. In
spite of this, fairly full figures are often available. In the
course of over a hundred years' study the main fact that
emerges is a steady increase in suicide, as the following table
shows. The causes of this increase and the prospects for the
future have been indicated in a chapter on the nineteenth
century.

SUICIDES PER MILLION

	1836–45	1922–25	Per cent. of increase
Saxony	167	344	106
Austria	45	201 (1911–13)	347
France	80	229	186
Prussia	104	221	112
Bavaria	65	152	134
Sweden	66	148	124
Denmark	222	147	− 34
Belgium	50	137	174
England	62	110	77
Italy	29	86	187
Norway	107	60	− 44

It will be noted that in Denmark and Norway alone have
the rates decreased. More recent figures show that these
countries are again on the increase.

Upon other points statisticians have been less unanimous.
Not that there has been dispute about figures, but about the
interpretation that should be put on them. There are so
many different forces to be taken into account and so many
ways of reading the final results. Broadly speaking, the last
twenty years have produced an important shift of emphasis.
Factors such as race and climate which were once considered
decisive now appear to be of secondary interest and the first
place in importance under all circumstances is claimed for
types of social organization. It is this which determines

whether the suicide figure in any given group of people shall be high or low.

I. AGE, SEX AND MARRIAGE

The romantic suicides of youth, owing to their popularization in literature, have received an undeserved prominence. The romantic period of life is not the chosen age of suicide. Broadly speaking, suicide increases with years. In childhood and up to the age of fifteen suicide is exceedingly rare; in exceptional districts one might find five cases per million; in others, fewer. Between fifteen and twenty-five, the rate starts going up, and suicides then continue to increase steadily. There are, in fact, twice as many suicides at fifty as at twenty-five. Once middle age has been reached there is a tendency for the speed of increase to slack off and the rate of progress is slower. Only for upwards of seventy-five do suicide figures show much variation, indicating in one place a sharp rise and in another an equally pronounced fall. This is probably due to the fact that the percentage of the population who reach extreme old age is very small and that statistical figures are therefore rather unreliable. The following table gives suicides per 100,000 by Age Groups for the County of London in 1922 :

Age	No. of Suicides	Rate
5—15	1	0
15—25	29	4.00
25—45	159	12.00
45—65	229	26.00
Over 65	87	34.00
Total	505	11.00

It seems almost unnecessary to give reasons for the increase of suicide with age. Hope is replaced by experience, and health by physical weakness. Specifically we find that suicides from love and domestic causes decrease, while suicide from illness increases. Melancholia also does not usually develop until middle age.

Firmly established as is the relationship between increasing age and suicide, it is not as regular as that which links the two sexes to suicide. As long ago as 1777 it was stated that in Geneva two out of every three suicides were men. Statistics have shown this preponderance of male suicides to be true everywhere in Europe and America. Whatever the general intensity of suicide in a given population, there will be almost invariably about three times as many men as women suicides.[1] The following figures taken in two places as far removed as London and Chicago at an interval of exactly fifty years illustrate the relationship between male and female suicide. The almost exact correspondence in the figures is an amusing exaggeration of the comparative constancy between the sexes.

SEX OF SUICIDES PER 100

	London 1874	Chicago 1924
Male	73.6	73.8
Female	26.4	26.2

The cause of this difference between men and women is not, as might at first be thought, a sexual propensity for suicide on the part of the male. It is simply that the wife is more completely absorbed into the family unit with its ties of affection and anti-suicide influences than is the husband. Secondly, and perhaps even more important, education has not yet spread so far among women; the unsettling influence of independence of thought, the weight of abstract problems of life and death do not disturb them. The difference is thus simply due to environment, and, for various reasons, in parts of the East the suicide figures are reversed.

[1] Parts of Spain seem to be an exception.

In the Indian Empire (in 1907) there were 171.4 female per 100 male suicides.

¶ Though an examination of figures has shown that men and women in the West commit suicide from more or less the same causes, women, due to their environment, allow these causes to push them to suicide far more rarely than men. We may expect, however, that as the family breaks up, and women become more generally educated and take a larger and wider part in intellectual, professional and business life, the figures for female suicides will begin to approach more closely to those of male suicides. Already statisticians have noted that the gap is not so wide in urban populations where the family unit is less compact, and the woman, therefore, is less sheltered. The following figures are indicative of a slight increase in the female rate relative to the male :'

SUICIDES PER MILLION IN ENGLAND

	Men	Women
1911–14	152	49
1921–25	154	54

Another factor which may help to account for the difference in the number of male and female suicides is that women fail to kill themselves more often than men. Thus in Italy every other man who attempts suicide is successful, while only one woman in five achieves her object. Since so many things smash one like an egg, or in some way finish one off decisively, such failures are one of the most curious features of suicide. Though death pulls one way, life pulls in the other, subconsciously limiting a dose of poison or deflecting a revolver's aim. In 1836 there were 192 successful suicides in London and 155 failures; to-day the failures actually outweigh the successes.

The question of marriage and suicide is not quite so simple. It is said that celibates commit suicide more often.

than married people, but this is a generalization which does not always hold good. To arrive at the truth it is necessary to deal with the sexes separately. We find that married women with children commit suicide less than any other class of either sex. But from the age of twenty-five upward married women *without* children commit suicide more often than spinsters, and more often even than widows who are left with children.

Among men the lowest figure is again provided by the husband with children, but on the other hand the husband without children, though nearly twice as prone to suicide as the father, never has as high a rate as the bachelor or the widower.[1] Some French figures from Durkheim illustrate these points.

INFLUENCE OF THE FAMILY ON SUICIDE

MEN	Numbers	Coefficient of preservation in relation to the unmarried	WOMEN	Numbers	Coefficient of preservation in relation to the unmarried
Bachelors of 45	975	—	Spinsters of 42	150	—
Married with children ...	336	2.9	Wives with children	79	1.89
Married without children...	644	1.5	Wives without children ...	221	0.67
Bachelors of 60	1504	—	Spinsters of 60	196	—
Widowers with children ...	937	1.6	Widows with children......	186	1.06
Widowers without children	1258	1.2	Widows without children...	322	0.60

From these facts and figures it appears that marriage itself is not of prime importance; it gives the man only a slight immunity against suicide, and even *increases* a woman's chances of killing herself. Children emerge, on the other hand, as the deciding factor. It is not as husband and wife

[1] These statements do not apply to men under 25. Before this age children are usually impossible for economic reasons, and marriage seems to lead to suicide. Among young people there are often as many as 10 married suicides to a single celibate suicide in a given area.

that people gain immunity from suicide, but as father and mother. It is the family, not the conjugal relationship, which is decisive. The family group, like the religious group, by giving a feeling of unity and solidarity, becomes a strong anti-suicide factor. It allows for the expression of possessive and power instincts which cannot be easily satisfied elsewhere, and it protects its constituents from loneliness. It is the lifebelt of which other forms are God, the nation, and innumerable sodalities. Thus a family makes suicide rarer, and where families are large and well co-ordinated the danger is even further removed. The increase of suicide which has brought the French rate to the front in the last fifty years (from 5.4 suicides per 100,000 in 1826 to 23 per 100,000 in 1913) characteristically enough corresponds with the sudden decrease in the French birth-rate. Celibacy thus encourages suicide only indirectly, in that the celibate has usually no children, and cannot situate himself in the safety of a family group.

II. RACE, PLACE, AND RELIGION

We have seen that the family, the smallest of social groups, acts as a bias against suicide. What of the large groups into which people are divided: race, nationality, and so on? What effects do they have on suicides?

Racial theories of suicide were once very much to the fore. It was said that the fair-haired Nordic type was in itself particularly prone to suicide, while the Latin races were relatively immune. Biologically, there is no reason why such a theory should not be true, and why a *penchant* for suicide should not be a trait inherited in certain breeds. Statistics, however, show the falsity of such an idea. If suicide were a racially inherited tendency it would not affect one sex more than the other, neither would it develop progressively with age as the force and impression of environment grow stronger. Though suicide is higher among the Northern peoples than among the Latins, the rates are demonstrably due to differing environments and degrees of group organization, and not to race. Two simple proofs of this may be advanced. In Norway and Sweden, both Nordic countries, the suicide rates over a hundred years have been respectively halved and doubled. In Australia, mainly populated by the English, the suicide rate is regularly one-third higher than at home. Obviously race can play no part in these changes.

With the *idea* of race, however, it is different. When this, the widest of human groups, is regarded by its members (real or imaginary) as a rallying point, a refuge from personal loneliness, and an effective association from which the individual can gain strength (like the family or any other association), it naturally exerts a pull against suicide. This has been so among the Jews for centuries, and it is probably true of Nazi Germany to-day. Such a race influence has obviously nothing hereditary about it or racial in the proper sense of the word.

When one comes to nationality the same distinction must be made. A *sense* of nationality, a sense of belonging to a national group, is a prophylactic against suicide. It destroys a man's isolation, and it provides solutions and answers to problems and questions. It relieves him in part from the necessity of thinking. Oppression and difficulty will increase this sense of national coherence; prosperity and power will dissipate it. Thus modern wars, by giving the individual a strong sense of participation in the national group, and by substituting the slogans of propaganda for the arduous necessity of personal thought, always bring about a decrease in suicide rates. Apart from this, there is no more a national than a racial charm against suicide. The suicide figures at a given time in a given country depend not on the name and people of that country (whether France,

Russia, or Siam), but on various social factors such as the closeness of economic groups and the vigour of the family and the Church. Figures for suicide in contemporary Europe have therefore only a secondary value; they indicate chiefly the strength and distribution of certain group forces which are usually non-national.

A man can associate himself not only with his race, nation, and family, but, often more effectively, with his God and his religion. In so far, then, as a religion provides a group in which the individual can sink his identity it limits and discourages suicide. This limitation depends very little on ideas of immortality, or on suicide prohibitions in particular religions. It does, however, depend directly on the degree of integration of a given church and on the extent to which it regulates the lives and supplies the wants of its members.

Facts and figures illustrate this. Catholicism, which is essentially the church of positive teaching, organized on a group rather than an individual basis, and dictating on matters as secular as marriage, contraception, schools, and stockings, has the greatest influence on the limitation of suicide. Among Catholics 58 per million was the rate given by Morselli in the second half of the nineteenth century. Among Protestants on the other hand the rate was above 100, and Morselli puts it as high as 190 per million. The reason is not difficult to find. Protestantism does not offer the same shelter and complete " way of life " as Catholicism. By encouraging reflection and individual research after truth, by allowing a man to go his own way to salvation, and to exercise some reason and choice in the ruling of his actions, it fails to provide that sort of set framework for a life which suicidal instincts are unable to penetrate. The Protestant is more lonely than the Catholic; he has to cope with his own conscience and his own salvation. Catholicism thus produces low rates as in Spain, Portugal, and Southern Ireland; and Protestantism the reverse as in the Swiss Protestant Cantons,

Denmark and Saxony. Most exceptions to this rule are only apparent. England, for instance, though Protestant, has a medium-low rate of suicide; closer inspection shows, however, that the Anglican Church—established, hierarchical, and dogmatic—dictates a " way of life " very nearly as complete as her Catholic rival. The parson-squire combination persists in many districts as the nucleus of a highly organized group. Similarly, France, throughout large sections of the country, is Catholic only in name; religious organization does not touch a large section of the people, and thus it is not surprising to find her suicide figures are high. Another sect, the Mormons, exemplify perhaps as well as any the protection which is afforded by a close religious group. These people, whose religion is inquisitive and ubiquitous, and whose fathers lay down a comprehensive law, have in the Mormon states of Utah and Idaho a suicide rate half as big as that found in the states which surround them.

Since the nineteenth century when Legoyt, Morselli, and Durkheim, collected their statistics, the gradual weakening of dogmatic faith and established religion, has decreased the influence of religious groups in preventing suicide and has much lessened the gap between the numbers of Catholic and Protestant suicides. Among many educated people these religious categories are no longer very real. As the integration of a religious group breaks up so suicide among its members increases. The supreme example of such a disintegration is offered by the Jews. In the middle of the nineteenth century the suicide rate among the European Jews, in spite of a relatively high level of education and an urban life, was definitely lower than that prevailing in any other large religious group. For this immunity their compact ghetto life was responsible; centering round the synagogue, it was highly organized and communal in flavour. Concerning the coherence of the old religious communities of the Jews, Cavan writes as follows:

The mere establishing of a synagogue calls for a neighbourhood group of ten families as a minimum. The rabbi in the Jewish community is a learned man who is regarded with respect, to whom troublesome questions of conduct are brought. By assimilating into their personal codes of conduct the teachings of the rabbi, a homogeneous community of one moral standard and one system of customs is built up and people find their lives organized through their religion. Under such conditions they have little opportunity for personal disorganization so long as the Jewish community remains culturally isolated from non-Jewish contacts. Moreover, the Jewish religion and the Jewish religious community recognize many of the major needs of life and provide for them. Rules of health, dress, food, recreation, occupation, philanthropy, the rituals of funerals, of food preparation, of obtaining a wife, are all prescribed.

With the break-up of the ghettoes and the penetration of alien ideas and influences into Jewry, these social ties have been loosened. Simultaneously, the purely religious hold of Judaism, like that of other faiths, has weakened. As a result in the last sixty or seventy years the Jewish suicide figures have gone up by leaps and bounds, in some places registering a 600 per cent increase. With the loss of their old religious organization their immunity from suicide has gone too. To-day Jewish suicides lead those of the other religious groups.

It is not only the more important types of group organization that keep down suicide figures. Though statistics are obviously impractical to collect, one must suppose that many humble sorts of social organization—clubs, societies, and so on—with which the individual can identify himself, perform a similarly useful function. Freemasonry and school ties must both be life preservers in their own way. Even occupation provides a lot of men with some sort of prophylactic group-feeling. Generally the simple manual crafts and employments produce a low rate of suicide; the " higher " one climbs the larger grows the relative number of suicides. Of course it is not as simple as this really, and religion, education, etc., play the predominating part in determining these figures. However, there is a certain poetic justice in the fact that capitalists, hotel-keepers, police, and journalists, head the suicide list, whereas farmers, foresters, shepherds, monks, and fishers bring up the rear.

Family, associations, religion, nation, race—such are the chief group-redoubts to which the individual flies to immure himself. From such vantage points he more effectively combats the desires for death that may attack him. The proportionate importance of each of these redoubts depends not only on the individual, but on the time and place. The savage knew only the tribal association or the family group, the twelfth century felt chiefly the value of a religious unity, and we, in our time, have unfortunately seen how modern wars bring to the fore the sense of nationality and of participation in a national whole.

III. TIMES AND SEASONS

Latitude.

Ideas about the effects of climate and season on suicide have also changed in the last fifty years. Once they were considered to be of the first importance in affecting the numbers of suicides. Now it is recognized that they are only very secondary, and that the changes in suicide rates which they appear to bring about are really due to social causes. This error was easy to make. Statistics show that in Europe extremes of heat and cold tend to produce a low rate, and that the highest number of suicides are found in a temperate belt, that comprises such high suicide areas as London, the North of France, Belgium, the Rhineland, and Saxony. By contrast, Calabria, Sicily, Portugal in the south, and Ireland, Scotland, Finland in the north, have very low figures. In mountains and in fen and marshland suicides are also relatively sparse. The variations in these suicide figures, however, are due neither to climate nor geography. The temperate suicide belt corresponds with areas of intense activity and industrial progress, where the old social, religious and ideological cadres have largely broken down, developing the individual and increasing that sense of personal isolation and responsibility which makes for suicide. The suicide belt is also the belt of heavy industry and coal deposits. Conversely in Ireland and Portugal, in inaccessible mountain regions and in fen districts, social cadres have remained fairly intact. They have not been broken down by economic changes or new trends of thought. The individual is still conscious of being a unit in social and religious groups to which he owes his allegiance and to which his individuality is, to some extent, subordinated. It is exactly in such closely knit groups that we should expect to find suicide rare.

Italy is an example which bears out conclusively that climate is not responsible for the level of suicide. In Imperial times suicide in Italy was common, but with the first nineteenth-century statistics it is seen to lag far behind the other great European powers. Morselli said the warm climate was the reason for this. Only when industrialization reached Italy and Italian figures[1] rose suddenly to a level not far below that of England, France and Germany, was his idea disproved. In Italy, as elsewhere, not the climate, but the organization of society was the deciding factor. In Norway a large decrease in the suicide figures, owing possibly to social legislation, demonstrates the same thing.

Season.

Though Montesquieu said that fogs accounted for the English suicides, it was long ago discovered that November, far from being the " Suicides' Month ", probably yields less

[1] In 1875 there were 922 recorded suicides for Italy; in 1913 there were 3107. An increase of nearly 337 per cent.

suicides than any other month in the year. On the contrary spring is the season of suicides. The rate increases constantly from January to June, and then as constantly drops away until December. Various facts, such as the decline in the torrid months of July and August, prove that increase in heat cannot account for this. Figures do, however, correspond almost exactly with the length of the days, as is shown by the following table which Durkheim worked out for France :

	Hours of Daylight	No. of suicides per month per 1000 suicides
January	9 hrs. 19 mins.	68
February	10 ,, 56 ,,	80
March	12 ,, 47 ,,	86
April	14 ,, 29 ,,	102
May	15 ,, 48 ,,	105
June	16 ,, 3 ,,	107
July	15 ,, 4 ,,	100
August	13 ,, 25 ,,	82
September	11 ,, 39 ,,	74
October	9 ,, 51 ,,	70
November	8 ,, 31 ,,	66
December	8 ,, 11 ,,	61

Here it will be seen that the greatest number of suicides occur about midsummer eve and decline proportionately until December is reached. Now it has been discovered that four-fifths of most suicides occur in the daytime or early evening; and this is because most human activity occurs in the light and thus most setbacks, *contretemps*, quarrels and despairs. The increase of daylight will therefore account for an increase of suicide.

The monthly increase of suicide thus corresponds with the natural increase in human activity, moving from the atrophy of winter into the frenzy of spring and early summer, and then on into the decline of autumn. In agricultural districts where the pace of life is conditioned strictly by the yearly cycle, the spring increase, keeping pace with the rising sap of anxiety, is even more marked, and more marked too is the autumn respite, when the young fruit is out of danger and harrows can proceed to their leisurely business.

Urban life, speculation, and business conditions in the twentieth century, introduce certain new factors which modify this immemorial rhythm. December, for instance, becomes anomalous, a bad month situated between good ones, simply because payments fall due before the New Year and there is then a sudden increase in the volume of human activity and apprehension. Similarly, in the period preceding " Quarter day " the number of suicides rises. Also business crises, and the " slumps " of capitalism, from time to time distort the figures in the same way that, in the past, "acts of God", storms, floods, and famines, produced temporary changes.[1]

The Day and the Time.

If we keep in mind this idea that periods of maximum individual activity and tension are also the periods of greatest suicide frequency, we shall expect the middle of the morning and the middle of the afternoon to be the times preferred for suicide. This is, in fact, the case, and statistics bear us out. In various countries, and between rural and urban populations, the exact hours differ, depending on the time people get up in the morning, and more particularly when they take their midday meal, and whether they take a long or short siesta. Broadly speaking, suicides are rare, but increase slowly in numbers between one a.m. and breakfast; there is then a sudden jump which about doubles

---

[1] It has been claimed that there is a correspondence not only between suicide and seasons, but between suicide and the moon. Inconclusive statistics from Prussia for 1869 show that, particularly among men, it was much commoner in the first and last quarters of the moon.

Y

the figures, and they continue to increase until the midday break, when there is a sharp drop. Suicides speed up again with the resumption of work, and finally fall off as the afternoon closes. Evening, with its reduction of human activity, further cuts down the figures until they reach their minimum once more in the early hours.

When we come to see how suicides are divided among the days of the week the law " Maximum activity—maximum suicide " does not altogether hold good, for a week, unlike a day or a season, is a very artificial unit. None the less, among men, suicides are distributed rather as we should expect to find them. Monday, with a return to labour or office, sets an average high rate which is maintained up to, and including, Thursday. On Friday there is a perceptible drop. The respite of the week-end is within view; hope sets in. (Also, in countries where there is a strong religious feeling, not only is Friday a day of semi-fast for which many people are far better off, but public activity slows up considerably.) With Saturday, wages and the week-end have arrived, and with them comes a further and considerable reduction in suicide. With Sunday the labours of the new week are again in view; there may be an alcoholic head to combat, and a good slice of the last week's wages will have disappeared; thus there is an increase up to about Friday's figure.

And so a new week begins again.

Women, on the other hand, seem to show no marked preference for any day but Sunday. This is possibly because on every other day of the week a woman subordinates herself to, and is absorbed in, " the home ", the closest and most exacting of social units. Only on Sunday does she come out of her shell and altogether assume a personal individuality that is more sensitive and vulnerable.

IV. SUICIDE AND HOMICIDE

Suicide appears to vary inversely to homicide. As the one increases, the other decreases. Statistics show this to be true, not only for nations, but usually for the distribution of homicide and suicide in counties, departments, and so on.[1] The opposition of the two phenomena is exact on a great many points. Take the following:

1. Homicide is commonest in *rural* districts, whereas the suicide rate per 100,000 for *urban* districts is twice the country figure.

2. Protestantism, we have seen, provides the least religious immunity against suicide, but it also produces very few murders. On the other hand, the Catholic countries with low suicide rates, are rich in homicides. Those Catholic strongholds, Spain and Ireland, are, it seems, the only countries where the number of murderers is greater than the number of suicides.

3. The age curves for homicide and suicide are altogether different; the former reaches its maximum between thirty and thirty-five, and the latter somewhere above sixty.

4. War, which immediately cuts down suicide figures, stimulates homicide in a community.

5. Last, but not least, a high level of education decreases homicide but increases suicide.

The reasons for this apparent opposition between homicide and suicide are straightforward enough. Education, urban life, and a general refinement of manners, produce a horror of bloodshed; among the educated homicide rapidly decreases. Simultaneously urban life and education break down the old protective cadres, and by making people perceive their isolation and think out their own problems, indirectly stimulate suicide. Science can only step in when

[1] The large towns of the United States constitute an important exception. Various unusual factors play a part in the American crime wave.

dogma breaks down, and it is significant that the level of education in Protestant countries has been steadily higher than in Catholic ones. Education and science call for reason, but the old social groups rest on passion and emotion. Passion is the energy that causes homicide, and it is therefore not strange to find vendettas in families, and a long tradition of religious murder in the history of the Church.

The following Italian figures, which cover the period in which modern civilization reached Italy, illustrate beautifully how, as old group organizations are broken up by science, education and economic change, and as the isolated units gain a sense of the importance of individuality, a sense of the problems of the person rather than the group, murder decreases and suicide increases:

		Charges of Murder	Suicides
1875	....	3280	922
1913	....	1389	3107

Both the suicide and the homicide are people for whom life is unsatisfactory. To remedy this the over-passionate man will turn to crime and homicide, *unless* he has been educated and sensitivized to a point where he submits his own passions to reason and taste. Conversely the incipient suicide in a closely integrated social *milieu* does not bring his suicidal tendencies to fruition; the latter can only happen when he stands alone and when education has neutralized group attractions. It should be noticed that, though suicide and homicide are apt to vary inversely, there is no absolute ratio between the two. Suicide is very rarely a sort of sublimation of homicide. The suicide is not the homicide, educated and sensitivized. Each type is evoked by a different social *milieu*, and its frequency depends, in each case, on the value that society places on the individual and on individual personality. Where that value is low, homicide is common; where it is high, a degree of homicide is replaced by suicide.[1]

V. SOLDIERS

Suicide in the army was, for a long time, a very baffling problem, and seemed to offer some strange paradoxes. The following table gives comparative figures for army and civil suicides in various countries during the late nineteenth century :

SUICIDES PER MILLION INHABITANTS, 1876–90

	Soldiers	Civilians of the same age	Coefficient of increase in military suicide
Austria	1253	122	10
U.S.A. (1870–84)	680	80	8.5
Italy	407	77	5.2
England	209	79	2.6
Prussia	607	394	1.5
France	333	265	1.25

It can be seen from the above that army rates are considerably higher than civil rates. Even ten times greater in the old Austrian Empire. It is impossible to attribute these

[1] Though suicide is sometimes connected with the state of mind and absence of fear caused by drink, regions where alcoholic consumption is large are by no means those with the highest suicide rate. All efforts to connect suicide with immorality have failed notably. Contrary to the popular idea, suicide among harlots is not excessive; while in countries like Denmark and Sweden, the home of domestic virtues, the rate is very high. People with clinical experience have noticed that a tendency to suicide is usually found among kind and gentle patients. Out of 3400 suicides examined by a nineteenth-century investigator, only 43 per cent were ambiguously labelled as having " bad characters ".

suicides to the natural explanations which spring to mind, such as the hardship of the life, or a distaste, particularly among conscripts, for military service. The following facts demand a quite different explanation :

1. Suicide becomes much more frequent with length of service, when habit has made the life tolerable and smoothed out initial difficulties.

2. It is commoner among volunteers, and especially among veterans who have re-engaged for a second or third period, than among conscripts.

3. It is commoner among officers, and above all among N.C.O.s, whose lot is pleasanter and easier, than among the rank and file.

4. Lastly, it is commonest in the cavalry and those crack regiments whose keenness and pride in their *métier* is unquestioned.

Since it bears no relation to a distaste for military life, another reason must be found for the frequency of military suicide. Let us look at a very interesting statistical table for the seventies, which presents us with the fact that military suicide is commonest in those countries where civil suicide is rarest, and *vice-versa*.

	Coefficient of the increase of military over civil suicide between the ages of 20 and 30	Civil suicides per million
France	1.3	150
Prussia	1.8	133
England	2.2	73
Italy	3 to 4	37
Austria	8.0	72

This table shows us that the cause of military suicide must be altogether different from that of civil suicide (e.g. in Austria, where military suicide was high before 1914, civil suicide was low; in France, where the civil figure was high, military suicide was correspondingly rare). Now a high suicide rate develops among the civil population where social organization is loose and where consciousness of personal individuality is *well-developed*. We have, however, seen in our study of institutional suicide that there is a second type of self-destruction which prevails where the sense of personal identity is *underdeveloped*, usually owing to the bands of a close social organization.[1] It is to the latter type that we must assimilate the majority of military suicides. The profession, in the first place, attracts a type in whom the sense of personal individuality is not so highly developed as in the general population; this underdevelopment is aggravated by years of barrack life, intensive training, abnegation, and the traditions of the service. The better soldier a man is, the more he has learnt to suppress his individuality and work as a unit. The soldier's centre of gravity is outside himself; it rests in the regiment, as that of the primitive rests in the tribe. Thus the soldier's suicide resembles the primitive's. Granted, the reasons are no longer the same. We neither see in the ranks *suttee* or religious sacrifice, but we do find a decrease in the sense of personality to such a point that the old soldier kills himself for the merest trifle—a hard word, an unjust punishment, a point of honour.

This conclusion enables us to explain the curious fact that military suicides are common where civil suicides are rare, and *vice-versa*. Suicide is frequent in a country where the social organization is flexible, and personalities highly developed; it is these very reasons which make citizens of such a country who join the army likely to resist the steady depersonalization of the service, which leads to military suicide. Such nationals rarely submit to a complete mental and emotional regimentation approaching the primitive's. On the other hand, in those countries where suicide is already rare among the general populace, and where individuality is already submissive to a close social organization,

[1] *See* page 18.

there is a predisposition to the suppression of personal expression. This, intensified by a long military career and a life lived in accordance with a close group ideal, achieves the complete subordination of personal values. The impersonal tribe outlook replaces them and develops in the soldier a tendency to suicide, allied to that found in primitive society.

Within the last twenty years one would expect a general decrease in military suicide.[1] The ideals of absolute submission, passive regimentation, and uniformity are disappearing. It has been found that good soldiers are even better when intelligent. Also, military life to-day is lived in a less water-tight compartment. The soldier is closer to the civilian and shares, to some extent, in the contemporary life of ideas.

VI. THE IMMEDIATE CAUSE AND MEANS

The immediate cause is often far from the real one, and to discover even the immediate cause is not always easy. Whether any given occasion will produce a suicide depends, as we have seen, not only on the individual, but on his social *milieu*. The alleged causes must usually be regarded as the last straw which made a burden too heavy. Brierre de Boismont, in the middle of the last century, lists the *supposed* causes of 4595 French suicides as:

652 Lunatics	237 Ennui
530 Alcoholism	134 Remorse and fear of the law
405 Painful or incurable disease	145 Hypochondriac and hysterical
361 Domestic troubles	121 Misconduct
311 Sorrow or disappointment	99 Indolence and want of occupation
306 Disappointed love	
282 Poverty and misery	179 Various
277 Reverses of fortune	556 Motive unknown

[1] It is doubtful whether such a decrease will continue in authoritarian states.

In England there exists one investigation of suicide causes which is as reliable as such a study can be. It is compiled from a thousand consecutive *attempted* suicides up for trial in the south eastern counties, between 1907 and 1910. The following are some of the more important motives recorded:

171 Alcoholic impulse (combined with other causes)
141 Alcoholic impulse with amnesia (combined with other causes)
123 Insanity
120 Domestic troubles
112 Out of work (combined with other causes)
 64 Destitution (combined with other causes)
 46 Weak-mindedness (combined with other causes)
 28 Neurasthenia and depression
 27 Business worries (combined with other causes)

The ways and means of death are a testimony both to the absence of physical fear and to a lack of intelligent forethought on the part of suicides. When soporific drugs are at hand, it is unreasonable to use potassium or the cliff's edge. Nationality to some extent, determines the means employed. Thus, if you are an Egyptian you will be apt to use carbolic acid, and in Italy and Belgium trains are relatively popular. The French, with characteristic intelligence, as far back as 1850 were making use of coal-gas asphyxiation four times as much as anybody else. Important features of English suicide in this century are the spread of the use of coal-gas, and the quite recent introduction of Lysol. The following figures tell their tale:

	1919	1927
Coal-gas	213	994
Lysol	7	361

It is interesting to compare the chief items of Westcott's "Table of Means" for England in 1881 with recent figures from the *Encyclopædia Britannica*:

Means	1881	1900–6	1920–6
Hanging	585 (i)	6064 (i)	5463 (ii)
Drowning	383 (ii)	5242 (ii)	6066 (i)
Knives (cut-throat, etc.)	357 (iii)	3831 (iii)	4677 (iii)
Poison	228 (iv)	3757 (iv)	3022 (iv)
Fire-arms	122		
Strangling	49	*No figures given*	
Falls from a height	40		
Suffocation by vapours and gaseous poisoning	2	0.5	2876 (v)

It will be seen that the relative popularity of the various means of committing suicide varied little from 1881 to 1906. In the last table, however, noticeable changes have taken place. Drowning has replaced hanging as the first means, and gaseous poisoning and suffocation by vapour have gained considerable importance.

BIBLIOGRAPHICAL NOTE

THE following bibliography contains most of the material from which this book was written. In the text I have only acknowledged sources when quoting authors verbatim. I am especially indebted to Bayet's exhaustive work, *Le Suicide et la Morale*, and I have also made much use of Durkheim, Cavan, and Moore (whose *Full Enquiry into Suicide, 1789* is the most complete work in English from an historical point of view). In certain sections I have drawn a good deal on Frazer, Beard, and Tawney. In addition to the works listed, I am particularly grateful to Mr. Raymond Mortimer for access to his unfinished manuscript on suicide, which proved very helpful. I also wish to thank Mr. Anthony Ayscough for finding my frontispiece, the best of all Cranach's Lucreces, and Mr. Bryn Davies for suggestions and help with proofs.

As the connection between insanity and suicide lies rather outside my field, the following bibliography hardly touches on the physiological aspect of suicide.

I. WORKS ON SUICIDE

Achille-Delmas : *La Psychologie Pathologique du Suicide.* Paris 1932.
Adams : *An Essay concerning Self-Murder.* 1700.
Alpy : *De la Repression du Suicide.* 1910.
Anonymous : *Suicide.* A poem. London 1773.
—— *Le Suicide.* A poem. Paris 1845.
Bayet : *Le Suicide et la Morale.* Paris 1922.
Bell : *Suicide and Legislation.* 1888.

347

Blondel: *Le Suicide.* Strasbourg 1933.

Bonser: *The Right to Die.* 1885.

Brierre de Boismont: *Du Suicide.* 1865.

Camp, Maxim du: *Memoires d'un Suicidé.* 1855.

Cavan: *Suicide.* Chicago 1928.

Denny, Sir William: *Pelecanicidium.* A poem. 1653.

De Quincey: *On Suicide.*

Donne: *Biathanatos.* 1648.

Dumas: *Traité du Suicide.* 1773.

Durkheim: *Le Suicide.* Paris 1897.

Des Etangs: *Du Suicide politique en France.* Paris 1860.

Encyclopaedia of Religion and Ethics. The sections on Suicide, Sati, etc.

Garrisson: *Le suicide dans l'antiquité et dans les temps modernes.* 1885.

Geiger: *Der Selbstmord im Klassischen Altertum.* 1888.

Ghansamdas Malkani: *Essay on Suicide.* Calcutta 1924.

Halbwachs: *Le Suicide.* Paris 1929.

Hey: *A Dissertation on Suicide.* 1785.

Holmes: *Is Suicide Justifiable?* New York 1934.

Hume: *On Suicide.* Collected Essays.

Moore: *A Full Enquiry into the Subject of Suicide.* London 1790.

Morselli: *Suicide.* English translation. London 1883.

Stael, Madame de: *Réflexions sur le suicide.* 1814.

Steinmetz: *Suicide among Primitive People. American Anthropologist.* 1894.

Sym: *Life's Preservative against Self-Killing.* 1637.

Szittya: *Selbstmörder.* Leipzig 1928.

Tours, Moreau de: *De la contagion du suicide.* Paris 1875.

Westcott: *Suicide.* London 1885.

Winslow: *The Anatomy of Suicide.* London 1840.

Wisse: *Selbstmord und Todesfurcht bei den Naturvölkern.* Zutphen 1933.

The following works in English I have not been able to trace: Pierce, *A Discourse on Self-Murder*, 1692; Blackett, *Suicide*, a poem, 1789; *The Suicide Prostitute*, an anonymous poem, 1805; and *To Be or Not to Be*, a recent American book now out of print.

II. OTHER WORKS CONSULTED

Aristotle: *Nicomachean Ethics*. Book V.
Athenaeus: *Deipnosophists*.
Augustine: *Civitatis Dei*. Book I.
Ball: *Things Chinese*. London 1904.
Beard: *The Reformation*. Hibbert Lectures. London 1927.
Blair: *The Grave*. A poem. London 1756.
Burton: *The Anatomy of Melancholy*.
Chateaubriand: *Memoires d'outre-tombe*.
Cicero: *Opera*.
Cunninghame Graham: *A Brazilian Mystic*.
Delisle de Sales: *Philosophie de la Nature*. 1769.
De Quincey: *The Caesars. On Casuistry*.
Diderot: *Encyclopaedie*.
Dill: *Roman Society from Nero to Marcus Aurelius*. London 1925.
Diogenes Laertes: *Lives of the Philosophers*.
Dio Cassius: *Roman History*.
Eliot: *Selected Essays*. London 1932.
Erasmus: *Eloge de la folie*.
Eusebius: *History of the Christian Church*.
Fowler: *Social Life in Rome*. London 1929.
Fortune Magazine. February 1935.
Frazer: *The Golden Bough*. London 1911.
Freud: *Beyond the Pleasure Principle*.
Froude: *England's Forgotten Worthies*.
Gibbon: *Decline and Fall of the Roman Empire*.

Green : *The Spleen*. A poem. Cayme Press reprint, 1925.
Guerard : *Dictionnaire encyclopédique d'anecdotes*. Paris.
Hecker : *Epidemics of the Middle Ages*. London 1859.
Herodotus : *History*. Book I.
Hervey : *Meditations among the Tombs*. 1796.
Huizinga : *Declin du moyen âge*. Paris 1932.
Huxley : *On the Margin*. London, 1926.
Joinville : *Histoire de Saint Louis*.
Lecky : *History of European Morals from Augustus to Charlemagne*.
Leonard : *The Lower Niger and its Tribes*. London 1906.
Leopardi : *Dialogues; Bruto Minore*.
Lucan : *Pharsalia*.
Montaigne : *Essais*.
Montesquieu : *L'Esprit des lois; Lettres Persanes*.
More : *Utopia*.
Pepys : *Diary*. 1667.
Pitt-Rivers : *The Clash of Culture*. London 1927.
Plato : *Laws; Phaedo; Republic*.
Plotinus : *Dialogues*.
Plutarch : *Lives; Contra Stoicos; Five Tragical Histories of Love*.
Prescott : *History of the Conquest of Peru*.
Revolution Surréaliste. Nos. 2 and 12. 1925 and 1929.
Robertson : *Charles V*. London 1782.
Rivers : *The Todas*.
Rousseau : *Nouvelle Heloise*.
Saito : *A History of Japan*. London 1912.
Sand : *Indiana*.
Schopenhauer : *Studies in Pessimism*. London 1890.
Seneca : *Opera*.
Sevigné : *Lettres*. [1671.]
Sozomen : *Ecclesiastical History*.
Strabo : *Geography*. Book XV.
Symonds : *Renaissance in Italy*. London 1875.

Tacitus: *The Histories.*

Tawney: *Religion and the Rise of Capitalism.* London 1929.

Tylor: *Primitive Culture.* London 1929.

Villiers de l'Isle-Adam: *Axel.*

Voltaire: *Dictionnaire Philosophique; Lettres.*

Wide World Magazine. February 1937.

Wilson: *What Happens in Hamlet.* Cambridge 1935.

Woolf: *The Common Reader.* London 1929.

Wyndham Lewis: *The Lion and the Fox.* London 1927.

Young: *Night Thoughts.*